DISCOVERIES IN THE JUDAEAN DESERT · VIII

# THE GREEK MINOR PROPHETS SCROLL FROM NAḤAL ḤEVER

(8ḤevXIIgr)

(THE SEIYÂL COLLECTION I)

DISCOVERIES IN THE JUDAEAN DESERT · VIII

# THE GREEK MINOR PROPHETS SCROLL FROM NAḤAL ḤEVER (8ḤevXIIgr)

( THE SEIYÂL COLLECTION I )

BY

EMANUEL TOV

HEBREW UNIVERSITY, JERUSALEM

WITH THE COLLABORATION OF

R. A. KRAFT

AND A CONTRIBUTION BY

P. J. PARSONS

CLARENDON PRESS · OXFORD

1990

*Oxford University Press, Walton Street, Oxford* OX2 6DP
*Oxford New York Toronto*
*Delhi Bombay Calcutta Madras Karachi*
*Petaling Jaya Singapore Hong Kong Tokyo*
*Nairobi Dar es Salaam Cape Town*
*Melbourne Auckland*
*and associated companies in*
*Berlin Ibadan*

*Oxford is a trade mark of Oxford University Press*

*Published in the United States*
*by Oxford University Press, New York*



*British Library Cataloguing in Publication Data*
*Tov, Emanuel*
*The 'Seiyâl' collection.*
*Vol. 1: The Greek Minor Prophets scroll*
*from Naḥal Ḥever.*
*1. Greek Septuagint. Bible. O.T. Critical*
*studies*
*I. Title II. Kraft, R.A. III. Parsons,*
*P.J. IV. Series*
*221.4'8*
*ISBN 0-19-826327-9*

*Library of Congress Cataloging in Publication Data*
*Data available*

*Typeset by Stephen Cope*
*at Oxford University*
*Computing Service*

*Printed in Great Britain by*
*St. Edmundsbury Press,*
*Bury St. Edmunds,*
*Suffolk*

# CONTENTS

# PREFACE

On 8 September 1986, R. P. Pierre Benoit, OP, submitted to the competent authorities his desire, on grounds of age and health, to resign from the post of editor-in-chief of the series *Discoveries in the Judaean Desert*. He had taken up that post in 1971, as successor to R. P. Roland de Vaux, OP, at an age when most men would be preparing for retirement, and has led the project both through the substantial difficulties which followed the changes in the political status of Jerusalem, and also through the publication of two volumes of *DJD*, together with several assorted books *hors série*. He was not long to enjoy a well-earned retirement; seven and a half months after resigning the editorship, on 23 April 1987, he died in Jerusalem, and now rests among his teachers and colleagues in the cemetery of St Stephen's Priory. As his successor, the body of editors nominated the under-signed; this nomination was subsequently confirmed by the governmental authorities, who at that time expressed a pressing hope for seeing a quicker rate of publication of the series in the future, a hope which the new editor-in-chief shares, and will do his best to realize.

The present volume is the first to present the 'Seiyâl' collection, which was also entrusted to our editorial group; one more Seiyâl volume will follow, to be edited by J.-T. Milik, E. Puech and J. Schwarz. This collection was acquired in 1952–4 by the Rockefeller (or, as it was then called, Palestine) Archaeological Museum, from clandestine excavators who had shown little respect for political frontiers. They told us that the provenance of these documents was 'the Wâdi Seiyâl' and the collection was named accordingly. Later, in 1960–1, excavations in the same general region by the Expedition to the Judaean Desert (directed by Professor Y. Yadin) found, in certain of the caves which they had recorded and excavated, traces of previous excavations, and sometimes even fragments of written material of which larger parts had earlier been brought to us as coming from 'Seiyâl'. Another group of scholars, under the auspices of the Shrine of the Book, are currently preparing for publication the written material found by the Expedition to the Judaean Desert, and the two editorial groups try to work in co-ordination. For most of the collection in our second Seiyâl volume the cave of provenance cannot be identified any more precisely than 'Seiyâl', and we must use that name and abbreviation (Se) for manuscripts in that collection, not intending provenance from a specific wâdi or cave. Sometimes, however, later discoveries have made more precise localizations possible. Thus the present scroll of the Minor Prophets in Greek, No. 2 in the 'Seiyâl' collection (as it were, Se2grXII), has been reunited with some other fragments of it which came from cave 8 in Naḥal Ḥever (8ḤevXIIgr), excavated by Y. Aharoni in 1961, and published preliminarily by B. Lifshitz. Since for this manuscript the true provenance of all the fragments is known, we suggest using a common siglum for all the fragments: 8ḤevXIIgr.

The scroll published here, containing large parts of the Minor Prophets in an early revision of the Septuagint version, was published in part in a preliminary fashion, and discussed at length, by R. P. Dominique Barthélemy, OP, of Fribourg. It had been expected that the same author would produce the full edition too; but as he became more and more pressed by other obligations, he turned to another Septuagint specialist, Professor Emanuel

Tov of the Hebrew University in Jerusalem, inviting him to take over his own place as editor. The resultant edition will be, I hope, as welcome to Septuagint scholars as it is to the editor-in-chief.

The reader may notice slight typographical differences from the conventions of earlier volumes; these are due to the fact that this is the first volume in *DJD* to be typeset on a phototypesetter at the Oxford University Computing Service, from an electronic copy of the text prepared by Professor Tov.

JOHN STRUGNELL
*editor-in-chief*

*Jerusalem, June 1987*

# FOREWORD

SCHOLARS will always associate the name of R. P. Dominique Barthélemy, OP, of Fribourg with the Minor Prophets scroll because of his masterly treatment of its contents in *Devanciers* (see below), a book which in many ways has revolutionized scholarship. That monograph also presented the preliminary transcription of the scroll (R), though not in the form of an edition in the usual sense of the word. Barthélemy had, however, done a substantial amount of work towards such an edition, mainly a first attempt to reconstruct the incomplete lines. This work was discontinued because of other obligations, and when Barthélemy asked me in 1982 to prepare the present edition, he kindly placed these notes at my disposal.

Realizing that the reconstruction of the complete text, or at least of the partially preserved lines, required a full study of the translation technique, orthography and textual status of the preserved sections, I made this my first assignment after the decipherment of the fragments. In this matter I was ably assisted by P. Lippi and G. Marquis. For this purpose each individual word of MT (Masoretic Text) was aligned in a computer file with the corresponding equivalents of the LXX ('Old Greek') and R (Revision), accompanied by sigla designating categories relevant for the analysis. The complete reconstruction of the partially preserved lines (section C of this book) was facilitated by this analysis (section F) and is documented by the notes in section E.

Study of the other important aspects of the scroll was commenced at the University of Pennsylvania in Philadelphia in cooperation with R. A. Kraft during a joint seminar on R in 1985–6. It is he who initiated a computer-assisted analysis of the column structure and of the exact location of the fragments such as presented in sections B and C. For this purpose the text of the Minor Prophets was roughly restructured according to the expected translation technique and vocabulary of R so as to facilitate the correct representation of these fragments within the column structure. This was linked with calculations, also provided by the computer, of the line length and column size of various columns (see section G). A mockup of the whole scroll prepared by R. A. Kraft formed the basis for the plates presented here. The computer could not prevent mistakes since incorrectly encoded data produce faulty results, but the very use of computer-assisted research enabled calculations and an analysis of the contents which otherwise would have been very difficult. Furthermore, other computer programs facilitated the identification of several small fragments (see sections A1, D). As a result, the contributions by R. A. Kraft are much felt in sections B, C and G. He also wrote section A6 and his remarks on A1–5 are gratefully acknowledged.

The following participants in the University of Pennsylvania seminar helped with the reconstruction of the sections between the preserved fragments (not represented here, but facilitating the placing of these fragments) and with the analysis of several characteristics of the scroll: Dr. J. R. Abercrombie, D. Brueggemann, L. Cohick, D. McCartney, J. Z. Pastis, F. Watson, B. Wright III. At the Hebrew University, Miss Henson and Mrs. S. Ory assisted me in verifying details and Dr. W. Fields in the research leading to Tables 3–8 in section A1. Prof. A. Shisha-Halevi kindly read section F12. Dr. P. Parsons of Christ Church, Oxford, kindly agreed to add a much needed section on palaeography.

Much help was received from the Israel Department of Antiquities and Museums (IDAM) enabling me to locate and study the fragments in the Rockefeller Museum. I gratefully acknowledge the help provided by Mrs. A. Sussmann, head of publications, and Mr. M. Broshi, director of the Shrine of the Book. Most of the photographs presented in the plate section at the end of this book were made in the 1950s when the main portion of the scroll was found, but several new ones were made by Mrs. Z. Sagiv of the IDAM. She also managed to prepare for the plates good prints from the old (glass) negatives.

Thanks are also extended for the efforts of the editors at Oxford University Press, first Mr J. Cordy and then A. Ashby, and of the designer, Ms J. Tydeman, in producing this complicated work.

Since the contents of the various sections of this work existed in electronic form, it seemed logical that they should be typeset directly from the electronic files. It was soon realized that this process required more preparation than expected, and it is due to the able assistance of Mrs C. Griffin and Mrs J. Burnell-Higgs of the Oxford University Computing Service, and Mr S. Cope, that the present book has been successfully produced from those computer files.

It has been a great pleasure to work with the general editor of the series, J. Strugnell, who has done much more than is required from an editor. He was a source of constant encouragement and guidance during the final stages of this enterprise, and knowledgeable in so many areas, he added many a remark and found many an inconsistency and incorrect notation.

I dedicate this book to my dear wife Lika who designed the form of the tetragrammaton used in this volume, although she would have preferred to offer a more artistic contribution.

EMANUEL TOV

*Jerusalem, September 1987*

# ABBREVIATIONS AND SIGLA

THE following abbreviations are used for the biblical books:

| | |
|---|---|
| Ho | Hosea |
| Jl | Joel |
| Am | Amos |
| Ob | Obadiah |
| Jo | Jonah |
| Mi | Micah |
| Na | Nahum |
| Ha | Habakkuk |
| Zp | Zephaniah |
| Hg | Haggai |
| Za | Zechariah |
| Ma | Malachi |

Further abbreviations:

| | |
|---|---|
| LXX | Septuagint ('Old Greek') |
| MT | Masoretic Text |
| R | R(evision)—the text contained in the present scroll |

The following sigla are used in the text:

| | |
|---|---|
| ` ` | the margin as preserved (upper, lower, right or left) |
| α_β | uninscribed space as preserved between letters |
| ' ' | indicates (part of) word which has not been reconstructed |
| .. | indicates parts of letters visible on the leather, where no reconstruction is attempted |
| ? | indicates room for either a single letter or a space |
| ạ | unidentified letter |
| α̰α̰ | difference between R and the LXX (edition of Ziegler) |

# A. INTRODUCTION

## 1. Archaeological Data and Identification

THE archaeological facts about the discovery of the scroll (Se2grXII, now identified with 8ḤevXIIgr [Rahlfs: 943]) in 1952 and 1961 have been described in detail by D. Barthélemy in the preliminary publication, *Les devanciers d'Aquila*, SVT 10 (1963) [henceforth = Barth.] and Y. Aharoni, 'Expedition B—The Cave of Horror', *IEJ* 12 (1962) 186–99 and id., 'The Caves of Naḥal Ḥever', *Atiqot* 3 (1961) 158 (map) [henceforth: Aharoni]. At first the exact location of the find was unknown, but subsequent excavations in the 'Cave of Horror' in Naḥal Ḥever (Wâdi Ḥabra) brought to light a few scraps of the same scroll, together with other documents and artifacts, so that the place of origin of the scroll is now known. In the catalogue of the Rockefeller Museum the bulk of our manuscript is designated as coming from Wâdi Seiyâl on plates 528–32, 535, 537–9A (photographs PAM 40.239–40, 40.559–74, 41.690, 41.690A and IDAM 200.296–7, 204.601–3). For exact details see plates I–XX, presented here through the courtesy of the Israel Dept. of Antiquities and Museums.

We suggest that for all fragments scholars use the siglum 8ḤevXIIgr.

The preliminary publication by Barth. contains a running text of the main section of the scroll, with several fragments unidentified, and without the usual apparatus for critical editions. This preliminary publication includes only two plates, representing fragments from different columns (mainly cols 18 and B1–2). Barth.'s earlier article ('Redécouverte d'un chaînon manquant de l'histoire de la Septante', *RB* 60 [1953] 18–29) contained another plate (col 17), also reproduced in J. Allegro, *The Dead Sea Scrolls* (Harmondsworth 1956 [Penguin]) opp. p. 105.

The small fragments found in Naḥal Ḥever were published (with accompanying photographs), prior to the appearance of *Devanciers*, by B. Lifshitz, 'The Greek Documents from the Cave of Horror', *IEJ* 12 (1962) 201–7 = *Yediot* 26 (1962) 183–90 (published separately as *The Judean Desert Caves, Archaeological Survey 1961* [Jerusalem 1962] 183–90 [Hebrew]). The plate published with the Hebrew article (and its reprint) is of better quality than the one accompanying the *IEJ* article.

The major lot discussed by Barth. contains large and small sections of the following books: Jo, Mi, Na, Ha, Zp and Za. Nine small fragments were ascribed by Lifshitz to these books: Ho, Am, Jl, Jo, Na, and Za. If these identifications are correct, they would be rather important since we would then have proof that the scroll contained also the books of Ho, Am and Jl, all occurring at the beginning of the Minor Prophets. However, some of Lifshitz's identifications are problematic. For example, fragm. 6 was ascribed by him to a section also contained in Barth.'s large lot (Na 2:8–9 [see note in D on col 3 ll. 10–11]). Since the same passage in Na would then be represented twice, we would in fact have two different scrolls written in the same hand responsible for the bulk of the material—a very unlikely situation. By the same token it is not very likely that the only remains of what originally would have constituted 27½ columns of Ho, Am and Jl would be one small fragment for each book. Barth. 168, n. 9 expressed doubts on these identifications and suggested some alternatives. All of these are acceptable and two new ones are added (see Table 1).

For some of these fragments see the notes in D. Fragments 3 and 5 contain small segments of col 13 otherwise not preserved. All other fragments can easily be attributed to the fringes of the large fragments brought to Barth. in the École Biblique (note that fragments 2, 4 and 6 belong to the same col). This situation can be supported by what is known about the discovery. In all likelihood small pieces could easily have broken off from the main segments of the scroll when they were found in the cave. Cf. the observation of Barth. 163 that parts of col 18 (his col 13) had been kept by a bedouin under the lining of his keffiyeh, a situation which, in his words, did nothing to increase the legibility of the fragments!

## 2. Columns and Measurements

The size, shape and number of the columns can be reconstructed with some degree of confidence from the preserved data.

The lower part of the scroll has been preserved more fully than the top. For col 8 parts of all four margins are visible, while for most other columns portions of only the right or left margins have been preserved together with the lower margin. Preserved margins are indicated by `` in the transcription (see Table 2).

These data together with the full reconstruction of the text enable us to determine the size of the individual columns of the scroll.

The number of *lines* in each column written in hand A seems to have been relatively stable, with 42 lines probable for most columns (thus tract. *Sopherim* 2:5). Although for no column have portions of all the lines been preserved, the combined evidence suggests that 42 lines per column is well supported for those columns that can be reconstructed with confidence, with the exception of cols 3 (44) and 4 (45). Col 18 originally contained 42 lines as well, but the last line has been erased, probably in order to start the new section (Ha 3:1) at the beginning of a new column. The column that can be reconstructed with confidence from hand B (B1) contains only 33 lines. For hand B, however, the letters themselves are larger and wider spaced, so that fewer letters and lines occupy the same physical space as used by hand A. The result is that the dimensions of the blocks of writing are the same for hands A and B (see Table 3).

The absolute figures—based on the extant and reconstructed portions—are shown in Table 3 (since the measurements of the reconstructed portions are based on the extant ones

TABLE 1: *Identification of the small fragments*

| Lifshitz No | Lifshitz | Barthélemy | Our identification |
|---|---|---|---|
| Fragm. 1 | Ho 2:8 | Na 3:13 | = |
| Fragm. 2 | Am 1.5 | ? | Jo 3:4–5 |
| Fragm. 3 | Jl 1:14 | Na 1:14 | = |
| Fragm. 4 | Jo 3:2–5 | = | = |
| Fragm. 5 | Na 1:9 | Na 1:13–14 | = |
| Fragm. 6 | Na 2:8–9 | ? | Jo 3:3 |
| Fragm. 7 | Za 3:1–2 | = | = |
| Fragm. 8 | Za 4:8–9 | Na 3:3 | = |
| Fragm. 9 | Za 8:21 | Za 2:11–12 | = |

and since these are unequal due to shrinkage of the leather, there are slight differences between the various columns).

In the calculation of the number of lines per column, spaces between the individual books of the Minor Prophets are taken into consideration. Before the beginning of Mi six such blank lines have been preserved (for the practice, see B.T. *Baba Batra* 13b [referring to three lines]) and Mur XII (three lines) and similar breaks (three–four lines) are reconstructed before the beginning of all other books. It is not known whether a short title was written in these spaces.

In describing the *width* of the columns, two factors are taken into consideration; first of all the internal consistency of the scribe with regard to the evenness of the right and left margins of each column, and secondly the consistency (or lack of it) concerning the relative widths of the various columns of writing.

Each scribe was more or less consistent regarding the length of the lines in each column. The fragments by hand B show the use of a ruling device for the side margins as well as for

TABLE 2: *Preservation of Margins*

| | left margin | right margin | upper margin | lower margin |
|---|---|---|---|---|
| Jo [1](not preserved) | | | | |
| 2 | | x | | x |
| 3 | x | x | | x |
| Mi 4 | x | | | x |
| 5 | | | x | |
| 6 | | x | | x |
| 7 | x | x | | x |
| 8 | x | x | x | x |
| 9 | x | | x | |
| [10] | | | | |
| [11] | | | | |
| Na [12] | | | | |
| 13 | | | (x) | |
| 14 | | x | x | |
| 15 | x | | | |
| Ha 16 | x | x | | x |
| 17 | x | x | | x |
| 18 | x | x | | x |
| 19 | x | x | | x |
| Zp 20 | x | x | | x |
| 21 | x | x | | x |
| 22 | x | x | | x |
| 23 | x | | | x |
| [24] | | | | |
| [Hg] [25] | | | | |
| [26] | | | | |
| [27] | | | | |
| Za 28 | | x | | x |
| 29 | x | | | x |
| 30 | | x | | x |
| 31 | x | | | x |
| B1 | | x | | |
| B2 | x | | x | |

TABLE 3: *Height of relatively well-preserved columns (in cm)*

| col | extant | reconstr. | total |
|---|---|---|---|
| 2 | 12.0 | 14.4 | 26.4 |
| 3 | 15.7 | 12.0 | 27.7 (44 lines) |
| 4 | 15.5 | 12.4 | 27.9 (45 lines) |
| 8 | 15.5 | 11.6 | 27.1 |
| 14 | 14.1 | 13.4 | 27.5 |
| 15 | 19.7 | 7.6 | 27.3 |
| 16 | 13.5 | 13.5 | 27.0 |
| 17 | 21.6 | 5.2 | 26.8 |
| 18 | 19.5 | 7.5 | 27.0 (last line erased, see pl. XVIII) |
| 19 | 11.8 | 15.0 | 26.8 |
| 20 | 11.5 | 15.4 | 26.9 |
| 30 | 12.6 | 13.4 | 26.0 |
| 31 | 14.8 | 11.7 | 26.5 |
| B1 | 13.4 | 13.3 | 26.7 |
| B2 | 13.2 | 13.0 | 26.2 |

the top (and bottom?) margin. Hand B thus has very even right margins (based on 11 preserved lines in col B1), and there is no evidence that hand B used letters extending into the left margin. Hand A does not seem to have used ruled margins, but the left margin is more or less straight except for some lines in which a capital letter indicating the beginning of a new section protrudes into the left margin. The right margin of hand A consists of a relatively straight line, with a deviation of up to two letters on either side, and rarely a few more.

There is less consistency, however, regarding the relative width of the writing in the various columns for hand A, with some columns considerably wider or narrower than the average. The measurements assume the average location for the right-hand margin, relative to the actual line ends preserved (see Table 4).

Another system of measuring is based on counting the letters and spaces on each line, which is the usual practice in the study of ancient documents. In spite of the differences in width between the letters, the average number of letters per line in each column gives a good

TABLE 4: *Width of relatively well-preserved columns (in cm)*

| Col | extant | reconstr. | total | Col | extant | reconstr. | total |
|---|---|---|---|---|---|---|---|
| 2 | 9.5 | 2.0 | 11.5 | 18 | 7.5–8 | --- | 7.5–8 |
| 3 | 9.7 | 0.2 | 9.9 | 19 | 8.5 | --- | 8.5 |
| 4 | 6.2 | 3.5 | 9.7 | 20 | 8.1 | 0.4 | 8.5 |
| 5 | 8.1 | 0.2 | 8.3 | 22 | 8.0 | --- | 8.0 |
| 7 | 8.3 | 0.5 | 8.8 | 23 | 5.6 | 3.1 | 8.7 |
| 8 | 8.3 | 0.2 | 8.5 | 28 | 6.5 | 1.4 | 7.9 |
| 9 | 6.2 | 2.6 | 8.8 | 31 | 5.6 | 2.9 | 8.5 |
| 14 | 8.8 | 0.1 | 8.9 | B1 | 3.9 | 5.0 | 8.9 |
| 16 | 9.2 | --- | 9.2 | B2 | 6.6 | 2.5 | 9.1 |
| 17 | 9.1 | --- | 9.1 | | | | |

indication of the relative widths. These data are provided under the published text in section B. The average number refers only to lines of which at least one letter (or part of the margin) has been preserved (see Table 5).

These data show that there are considerable differences in width between the various columns of hand A, even within the material relating to a single book. Thus, Jo is written in wide columns, with an average of respectively 43 and 41 letters. At the same time, the next book, Mi, is written in narrower columns, with respectively 38, 34, 35, 33, 33, 31, [33], [33] letters. The other books vary likewise: Na [33], 35, 32, 33; Ha 34, 35, 28, 29; Zp 30, 31, 29, 29, [30], and Za 29, 30, 32, 33.

Most columns written by hand A thus have an average of 30 to 35 letters, with wider columns in the early books Jo and Mi and narrower ones in the later books Ha, Zp and Za. In principle these differences could be attributed to the physical limitations of the individual sheets of leather composing the scroll, but we have no firm evidence on this matter. For example, when space would begin to run out on one of the sheets of which the scroll is composed, the scribe might decide to use the remaining space either for two narrow columns or one wide one. However, this hypothesis cannot be tested since with one exception it is not known where the sheets were joined. Joining by sewing is well attested in antiquity, as in most Qumran scrolls and in our hand B (see additional fragment 6 [plate XX]); but the columns written by hand A seem to have been joined with some kind of adhesive (see the margin between cols 17 and 18). Apparently this system is not known from Qumran, and is otherwise rejected by the first of the quoted authorities in the tract. *Sopherim* 2:11.

TABLE 5: *Average number of letters for the preserved lines in each column and reconstructed number of lines*

| Col | no. of letters (preserved ll.) | | reconstructed no. of ll. | Col | no. of letters (preserved ll.) | | reconstructed no. of ll. |
|---|---|---|---|---|---|---|---|
| 1. | [no evid] | Jo | [[42]] | 21. | 31.38 | | 42 |
| 2. | 42.88 | | 42 | 22. | 29.25 | | 42 |
| 3. | 41.00 | | 44 | 23. | 28.71 | | 42 |
| 4. | 38.00 | Mi | 45 | 24. | [30.12] | | [[42]] |
| 5. | 34.00 | | [42] | 25. | [no evid] | [Hg] | [[42]] |
| 6. | 34.83 | | 42 | 26. | [no evid] | | [[42]] |
| 7. | 33.41 | | 42 | 27. | [no evid] | | [[42]] |
| 8. | 32.84 | | 42 | 28. | 29.10 | Za | 42 |
| 9. | 31.36 | | [42] | 29. | 30.25 | | 42 |
| 10. | [33.49] | | [[42]] | 30. | 32.50 | | 42 |
| 11. | [32.90] | | [[42]] | 31. | 33.32 | | 42 |
| 12. | [33.12] | Na | [[42]] | 32. | [no evid] | | [[42]] |
| 13. | 35.00 | | [42] | 33. | [no evid] | | [[42]] |
| 14. | 32.25 | | [42] | 34. | [no evid] | | [[42]] |
| 15. | 33.16 | | [42] | 35. | [no evid] | | [[42]] |
| 16. | 33.71 | Ha | 42 | 36. | [no evid] | | [[42]] |
| 17. | 34.87 | | 42 | 37. | [no evid] | | [[42]] |
| 18. | 27.53 | | 42 | B1. | 21.88 | | [33] |
| 19. | 29.00 | | 42 | B2. | 24.05 | | [[33]] |
| 20. | 30.33 | Zp | 42 | | | | |

With hand A, the last two columns leading up to the join between columns 17 and 18 do not differ from the other columns that immediately preceded, but the next two columns, constituting the first columns of the next sheet (18, 19) are distinctly narrower than the other cols, having an average respectively of 27.53 and 29.00 letters. The margins between 17 columns have been preserved, and in one place several continuous columns with margins are present (columns 16 to 22). However, these margins do not provide any clue to understanding the differing widths of the columns. Such a clue may come from the one place where we know with certainty that two sheets were joined, that is, between cols 17 and 18. Note that cols 13 to 17, which certainly were written on the same sheet, have an average of 32–35 letters, while columns 18 to 22, written on a different sheet, were narrower, with an average of 28–31 letters. At the same time the presumably different sheet containing Jo and the beginning of Mi has an average of 38–43 letters (cols 2–4), while what may have been the next sheet, containing the remainder of Mi (cols 5–9), averaged 31–35 letters. While a more thorough study of the relevant material in the Qumran scrolls is in order, a study of some large scrolls shows that the columns often differ much from each other, though within each sheet a certain consistency is visible (see especially 1QS, 1QIs[a] and 11QTemple), presumably because each individual sheet was ruled at the start into roughly equal-width columns.

The measurements of the margins between the columns, and of top and bottom margins, when preserved, are as follows.

TABLE 6: *Margins between columns*

| | | | |
|---|---|---|---|
| col 2–3 | 1.5 | col 18–19 | 1.1 |
| col 3–4 | 1.7 | col 19–20 | 1.6–1.8 |
| col 6–7 | 1.9 | col 20–21 | 1.4 |
| col 7–8 | 2.2 | col 21–22 | 1.4 |
| col 8–9 | 2.1 | col 22–23 | 1.4 |
| col 14–15 | 1.5 | col 28–29 | 2.3 |
| col 16–17 | 1.4 | col 30–31 | 1.2 |
| col 17–18 | 1.8 | col B1–B2 | 1.7–1.9 |

TABLE 7: *Top margins*

| | | | |
|---|---|---|---|
| col 5 | 3.4 (slightly ragged) | col 14 | 4.5 (complete) |
| col 8 | 4.0 | col B2 | 4.2 (complete) |
| col 13 | 4.5 (complete) | | |

TABLE 8: *Bottom margins*

| | | | |
|---|---|---|---|
| col 2 | 3.5 (ragged) | col 19 | 3.8 (complete) |
| col 3 | 3.4 (ragged) | col 20 | 3.8 (complete) |
| col 4 | 3.0 | col 22 | 3.9 (ragged) |
| col 6 | 3.1 (ragged) | col 23 | 3.9 (ragged) |
| col 7 | 3.1 (ragged) | col 28 | 3.7 (ragged) |
| col 17 | 3.5 (ragged) | col 31 | 3.5 |
| col 18 | 3.5 | | |

These partial data allow us to reconstruct the height of the leather as 35.2 cm for hand A (4.4 cm for the top margin, 27 cm for the average col [see Table 3] and 3.8 cm for the bottom margin). Similar data cannot be reconstructed with complete confidence for hand B, although the top margin of col B2 is 4.2 cm and col B1 is about 26.7 cm high (no bottom margin is preserved).

## 3. Content and Scope

For the sake of simplicity, the following discussion assumes that we are dealing with a single manuscript written in two different hands. The evidence for and problems with such a hypothesis are discussed in A5.

Major and minor portions of 25 (or 26—see additional fragment 6 [plate XX]) columns have been preserved from Jo, Mi, Na, Ha, Zp and Za. Together with the reconstructed sections these books comprised 55 columns according to the reconstruction shown in Table 9 (double square brackets denote columns for which no data have been preserved, while data within single brackets refer to columns which have been partially preserved, lacking at least the top or bottom line) (see Table 10).

Adding the numbers for the individual books (see Table 10) we reconstruct 33½ columns for hand A covering the following books: Jo, Mi, Na, Ha, Zp and Za. To these we add 3 columns for Hg between Zp and Za, even though no fragment of that book has been preserved. Altogether, for hand A 37 columns are calculated, to which 18 columns are added for hand B. This brings the tentative calculation of the scroll to at least 55 columns. This calculation is based on the assumption that scribe B started to write exactly in the first column preserved in his handwriting, that is in Za 8. This assumption is made for the sake of convenience only, for if we assume that scribe B started with the first column after the last preserved fragment of hand A, we would have to add to the calculation another 3½ cols

TABLE 9: *Reconstructed content of the scroll (Jo–Za)*

| | | | |
|---|---|---|---|
| col [1] | [[ ? ]]–Jo [[1.5]] | col 21 | Zp [1.6b]–1.18a |
| col 2 | Jo [1.5]–[2.7a] | col 22 | Zp [1.18b]–2.10 |
| col 3 | Jo [2.7b]–4.5a | col 23 | Zp [2.11]–3.7 |
| col 4 | Jo [4.5b]–Mi [1.7a] | col [24] | Zp [[3.8–3.19]] |
| col 5 | Mi 1.7b–[2.7] | col [25] | Zp [[3.19]]–[[Hg (start)]] |
| col 6 | Mi [2.7]–3.6a | col [26] | [[Hg]] |
| col 7 | Mi [3.6b]–4.5 | col [27] | [[Hg]] |
| col 8 | Mi 4.6–5.4(5)a | col 28 | [Hag (end)]–Za 1.4a |
| col 9 | Mi 5.4(5)b–[6.4] | col 29 | Za [1.4b]–[1.15a] |
| col [10] | Mi [[6.5–7.2]] | col 30 | Za [1.15b]–2.12(8)a |
| col [11] | Mi [[7.2–7.14]] | col 31 | Za [2.12(8)b]–3.7a |
| col [12] | Mi [[7.14]]–Na [[1.5]] | col [32] | [[Za 3.7b–4.10]] |
| col 13 | Na [1.5]–[2.5a] | col [33] | [[Za 4.10–5.9]] |
| col 14 | Na 2.5b–[3.4] | col [34] | [[Za 5.9–6.12]] |
| col 15 | Na [3.4]–[3.18] | col [35] | [[Za 6.12–7.10]] |
| col 16 | Na [3.18]–Ha 1.11a | col [36] | [[Za 7.10–8.8]] |
| col 17 | Ha [1.11b]–2.8a | col [37] | [[Za 8.8–8.18]] |
| col 18 | Ha [2.8b]–2.20 | col B1 | Za [8.18]–[8.23a] |
| col 19 | Ha [3.1]–3.15a | col B2 | Za 8.23b–[9.7] |
| col 20 | Ha [3.15b]–Zp 1.6a | col [B3–18] | [[Za 9.8–end]] |

between chaps. 3 and 8 since the columns of hand B contain less text. This assumption may well be correct if the identification of additional fragment 6 (Za 4:7–8?) in the handwriting of scribe B is stable.

[In the reconstruction the sequence Jo–Mi is sound since the fragments containing col 3 (end of Jo) and 4 (beginning of Mi) make a convincing join (see plates I, III, IV). The fragment containing col 4 also contains two letters of the ends of lines of col 3 (epsilon on l. 25 and eta on l. 33).]

The sequence of the books follows that of MT and not of the LXX.

[In the case of Hg we are relatively confident that the book was contained between Zp and Za in the original scroll, since without it the structure of the scroll becomes more

TABLE 10: *Calculation of the columns by book*

| | | |
|---|---|---|
| *Hand A* | | |
| Jo | ½ | first col reconstructed (beginning) |
| | remains of 2 | cols preserved |
| | ½ | last col reconstructed (end) |
| Mi | remains of 5½ | cols preserved |
| | next 2½ | cols reconstructed |
| Na | ½ | col reconstructed (beginning) |
| | remains of 3 | cols preserved |
| | ⅛ | col reconstructed (end) |
| Ha | remains of 4 | cols preserved |
| | ½ | col reconstructed (end) |
| Zp | remains of 3½ | cols preserved (beginning) |
| | 1½ | cols reconstructed (end) |
| Za | remains of 3½ | cols preserved |
| | 6 | cols reconstructed |
| *Hand B* | | |
| | remains of 2 | cols preserved |
| | 16 | cols reconstructed (?) |
| | 1 | unidentified fragment preserved (additional fragment 6) |

TABLE 11: *Order of books in the Hebrew and Greek (MSS ABS; MS V resembles MT) tradition compared with the contents of the scroll*

| Hebrew | preserved books of scroll | | Greek |
|---|---|---|---|
| Ho | | | Ho |
| Jl | | | Am |
| Am | | XX | Mi |
| Ob | | | Jl |
| Jo | XX | | Ob |
| Mi | XX | XX | Jo |
| Na | XX | XX | Na |
| Ha | XX | XX | Ha |
| Zp | XX | XX | Zp |
| Hg | [XX] | [XX] | Hg |
| Za | XX | XX | Za |
| Ma | | | Ma |

problematic. If Hg did not follow Zp in the scroll, Zp would be followed immediately by Za; in that case the join between the end of Zp and the start of Za would be unusually cramped.]

*Size*—The material written by hand A probably did not begin with Jo because in that event Jo would start half way down the 'first' reconstructed column, which suggests that it must have been preceded by at least one other book. If, as seems possible, the scroll contained all the Minor Prophets, it would have required another 7 columns for Jl and Ob and another 22 for Ho and Am, that is, altogether 66 columns for hand A to the point where hand B is preserved.

The material from where hand B begins would cover 18 columns for Za and 7 for Ma, totalling 25 columns. Thus a complete scroll of the Minor Prophets in this format (hand A plus hand B) would have contained at least 91 columns. Furthermore, if the section between the last column of hand A and the first one of hand B was all written by hand B, and not by hand A, another 3½ columns must be added to this calculation, that is, 94½ columns altogether. Alternatively, if hand B wrote *only* 3 columns, that is, if these were a mere 'patch'—like in the Hebrew 4QDeut$^{n}$ ['All Souls']—the reconstructed total length could be 80 columns. Note that if hand B was a patch, additional fragment 6 must have come at the end of the patch, to be sewn on to whatever followed.

Returning now to the width of the preserved columns, the length of the scroll can be calculated on the basis of the assumption that it contained all the books of the Minor Prophets. The data provided in Tables 4 and 6 point to an average of 8.9 cm for each column (based on 17 columns totalling 151 cm) and to an average of 1.7 cm for the margins between the columns. The average column with margin is thus 10.6 cm which would yield a scroll of either 9.64 meters (based on 91 columns) or 10.07 meters (based on 95 columns). Such a scroll would be longer than any published Qumran scroll. The longest preserved scrolls from Qumran (in Hebrew!) are 1QIs$^{a}$ (7.34 meters) and 11QTemple (8.148 meters, but reconstructed to a full length of at least 8.75 meters). To assume a length of 10 meters for the Minor Prophets scroll is thus unusual but perhaps not impossible.

## 4. Special Characteristics

### 4a. *Division into Sense-Units*

The text of the scroll has been subdivided into paragraphs with both minor and major breaks, as observed by Barth. 166 and J. M. Oesch, *Petucha und Setuma, Untersuchungen zu einer überlieferten Gliederung im hebräischen Text des Alten Testament*, OBO 27 (Freiburg–Göttingen 1979) 303–9. What has not been observed by these scholars is that the scroll contains also a division into 'verses' and that in all three divisions the scroll agrees to a great extent with the Masoretic tradition, not only regarding the system of subdividing the text, but also regarding the location of the divisions themselves. On the other hand, this fact had been recognized by E. J. Revell on the basis of published photographs: 'The Oldest Evidence for the Hebrew Accent System', *BJRL* 54 (1971–2) 214–22. Revell goes much further, since he identifies in the scroll a division into hemistichs and the beginning of the accent system later found in MT. This view has been further developed by Revell on the basis of photographs of the complete scroll in 'Biblical Punctuation and Chant in the Second Temple Period', *JSJ* 7 (1957) 181–98.

The Minor Prophets scroll reflects the framework and content of the Masoretic system of subdivisions which distinguishes between 'open' sections, in which the remainder of the line is left blank after the last word, and 'closed' sections, in which a given number of spaces is left between sections. Most of the open and closed sections in the scroll agree with similar indications in MT, although in some instances an open section of the scroll agrees with a closed section of MT or vice versa: see Table 12.

[In addition, the 'paragraphos' sign occurs in the following places at the beginning of a prophecy or prayer (as in certain Greek papyri in which it indicates the beginning of direct speech): Jo 4:2, Mi 1:5, Zp 1:2, Za 1:14, 2:17, 3:7. (The intention of the paragraphos in Za 1:13 is not clear.) In all these instances a closed section is reconstructed or preserved (Mi 1:5).]

TABLE 12: *Open and closed sections reflected in the scroll*

This table lists the open and closed sections found *before* the verses indicated (p = *petuḥah* [open]; s = *setumah* [closed]) in codex Leningrad B19[A] (L) of MT and the scroll (for additional—usually smaller—spaces, see Table 13). It also records the existence of a 'paragraphos' sign (third column), denoted in the scroll by a horizontal stroke between lines, and of 'capital letters' (fourth column) protruding into the left margin after the open or closed section ('cap protr' in the Table). '[?]' in the third column denotes that the fragments are not adequately preserved to permit seeing the interlinear space in which the 'paragraphos' sign would be expected. '[?]' in the fourth column indicates that the beginning of the next line (only after an 'open' section) which would have contained a capital letter has not been preserved (such capital letters have been included in the reconstruction).

| *elements found before:* | *codex L* | *scroll* | *paragraphos* | *capital letter* |
|---|---|---|---|---|
| Jo 2:1 | | p | [?] | [?] |
| Jo 2:6 | | s | | |
| Jo 3:10 | | p | para | cap protr |
| Mi 1:2 | | s | | |
| Mi 3:5 | p | p | [?] | [?] |
| Mi 4:5 | | [s] | | |
| Mi 4:6 | p | p | end of col | [?] |
| Mi 4:8 | p | p | [?] | [?] |
| Mi 4:9 | | p | [?] | [?] |
| Mi 5:1 | s | p | [?] | cap protr |
| Mi 5:6 | s | [s] | | |
| Na 2:7 | | p | [?] | [?] |
| Na 3:8 | | [p] | para | cap protr |
| Na 3:11 | | [s?] | | |
| Ha 2:1 | s | p | [?] | [?] |
| Ha 2:15 | s | [s] | | |
| Ha 2:18 | s | s | | |
| Ha 2:19 | s | p | [?] | [?] |
| Ha 2:20 | | s | | |
| Ha 3:1 | p | p | end of col | [?] |
| Ha 3:14 | p | p | para | cap protr |
| Za 1:4 | | s | | |
| Za 2:3 | s | [s] | | |
| Za 2:8 | | p | | |
| Za 2:12 | s | [s] | | |
| Za 3:1 | s | [p] | para | cap protr |
| Za 8:20 | p | p | [?] | [?] |
| Za 9:1 | s | [p] | [?] | cap protr |

In the scroll, the indication of *open* sections is consistently combined with two scribal practices. All open sections are indicated by large letters at the beginning of the next line, protruding into the margin. Furthermore, a horizontal line—'paragraphos'—between the lines indicates the same phenomenon. This mark occurs either below or above the line in which the open section occurs. (Often the beginnings of the lines where the paragraphos would have stood have not been preserved. Such instances have been noted in Table 12 as '[?]'.) Note further that the use of the paragraphos for new sections is also known from many Hebrew non-biblical scrolls from Qumran (1QS, 1QS[ab] 1QMyst (27), 1QpHab, 4Q502–504, 509, 512), from the Aramaic 4QTestLev[a] as well as from secular Greek and Aramaic documents from the hellenistic period. In 1QIs[a] the paragraphos is used 70 times (mainly for open sections, but also for closed sections and 'indentations' [see Y. Maori, *Textus* 10 (1982) א–ג, esp. ד]). For secular Greek documents and literary texts, see the material collected by E. G. Turner, *Greek Manuscripts of the Ancient World* (Oxford 1971) 10, 15 = 2nd ed. (London 1987) 8, 12f. Furthermore, the system of our scroll resembles that of PFouad 266 in which closed and open sections are indicated with the paragraphos sign—see F. Dunand, *Papyrus grecs bibliques (Papyrus F. Inv. 266)* (Cairo 1966) and id., *Études de Papyrologie* 9 (1971) 81–150; Z. Aly, *Three Rolls of the Early Septuagint: Genesis and Deuteronomy* (Bonn 1980)—as well as that of 4QLXXLev[b] (see P. W. Skehan, *SVT* 4 (1957) 159). For a detailed discussion, see Oesch, *op. cit.* 206–31.

The second convention used in connection with open sections is that of enlarged initial letters which we would call capitals, often protruding to the left of the margin. This system, otherwise known only from Greek papyri of documentary texts and Christian sources, has been described in detail by C. H. Roberts, *Manuscript, Society and Belief in Early Christian Egypt* (Oxford 1979) 16–18. The presence of these capitals is indicated in Table 12.

[In addition, other 'capital' letters are found at the beginning of some 'verses', after short spaces, and often elsewhere such as the first letter of a book (see Mi 1:1) or a line (the latter can be disregarded for our purpose): Jo 2:6 (middle of v.), 4:1 (beginning), Mi 5:1(2) (middle), 5:4(5) (middle), Na 3:16 (beginning), Ha 1:15 (middle), 1:16 (beginning), 1:17 (beginning), 2:3 (middle), 2:16 (beginning), 3:10, 15 (both beginning), Zp 1:17 (middle), 3:7 (middle).]

In addition to the open and closed sections the scroll indicates with one or two spaces the beginning of what in MT is a new verse. This practice is known from a few Hebrew sources (1QpaleoLev [limited evidence] and 4QDan[a,d] [reported by S. J. Pfann]; the situation with regard to 1QIs[a] is not clear) as well as from two early Greek biblical sources: PFouad 266 and PRyl Greek 458.

It is relatively easy to recognize these spaces in the scroll since in the section written by scribe A there are otherwise no spaces between words. At the same time, the very recognition of a space is sometimes subjective, when the space is recognized only by comparing the extant space with the surrounding text and not by any absolute measure. The second scribe left spaces between most words, and for the beginnings of new verses he left

TABLE 13: *Spaces recorded between verses (excluding open and closed sections for which see Table 12)*

*Before* Jo 2:7, 3:3,8,9; Mi 1:8; 3:6; 5:4; Na 3:16; Ha 1:6,7,8,9,10,16,17; 2:2,6,7,16,17; 3:10,15; Zp 1:[2],14,16,17; 3:7.

more than one space. Likewise, the scribe of PRyl Greek 458 often left spaces within the verse, and between verses he left more than one space.

With the exception of three places (Mi 1:6; Na 2:6,8), our scroll contains at least one blank space at the beginning of each new verse (Table 13).

In the following instances a space is left in the middle of a verse where MT has an *etnachta*:

Mi 1:5, 5:4; Ha 1:15, 2:3; Zp 3:7; Za 3:4

In addition, in the following instances a space is left between different parts of a verse, suggesting that the parts were understood as independent units:

Jo 2:6,7; [4:2]; Mi 1:1,1; 5:1,2; Na 1:14; Za [3:6].

### 4b. *Tetragrammaton*

The texts of both hand A and hand B contain the tetragrammaton in palaeo-Hebrew, though in different forms. Altogether there are 24 samples of the fully or partially preserved tetragrammaton in hand A material and four in hand B.

The question of who actually wrote the tetragrammaton into the text and at what point in the process of producing the manuscript is of interest. The evidence from other sources warns us not to assume that the Greek scribe who first produced the manuscript himself wrote the tetragrammaton. In PFouad 266, the original Greek scribe left open large spaces for the tetragrammaton indicated by a raised dot on each side of the space. Then, at a later time, the tetragrammaton was added, possibly by another scribe, in the indicated spaces. In the course of this procedure one preserved space was left empty. In all other instances there is ample space both before and after the tetragrammaton. The same sort of procedure has been employed in POxy 656 (Gen.) = 905 (Rahlfs), where *κύριος* has been added by a second hand.

In our scroll hand A probably wrote both the Greek text and the palaeo-Hebrew tetragrammaton without interruption, since in some instances there is little or no space between the tetragrammaton and the adjacent words, and occasionally the tetragrammaton is written in almost one continuous movement together with the next letter (col 28, l. 37; also col 8, l. 6). In col 28, l. 37 the tail of the *yod* of the tetragrammaton and the beginning of the first letter of the next word almost touch each other in one continuous stroke. Because of the unusual shape and large size of the Hebrew letters, the scribe wrote in col 8, l. 40 the Hebrew at the level of the bottom of the preceding Greek word and when he continued with the Greek after the Hebrew he wrote one level below the previous Greek word. This, too, suggests that the same hand wrote both the Greek and Hebrew, presumably both from left to right. Likewise, the scribe of POxy 3522 (Job) very clearly wrote the tetragrammaton from left to right, creating a ligature between the *yod* and the next Greek letter. There is not enough evidence from hand B to judge these matters.

## 5. The Two Scribes/Hands

The data in Tables 3–4 and 6–7 show that the leather on which the text of hand B was written had the same measurements for the top and side margins, and the writing block was also compatible in size with that of hand A. The materials written by scribes A and B therefore could have belonged to the same scroll, or to 'sister' scrolls, in terms of height and column format.

The question of the relation between the two hands is made all the more problematic because so little has been preserved of the work of hand B, and the presumed dividing line between the two scribes occurred at an unusual point, viz., in the middle of Za, somewhere between chapters 3 and 8. Scribe B probably wrote Ma as well. On this hypothesis, his share must have been limited, unless one ascribes to him also the non-preserved books at the beginning of the scroll. If, on the other hand, it is proposed that hands A and B represent two different complete manuscripts of the Minor Prophets, it is surprising that so little of hand B has been preserved.

The differences between the script of the two hands are described in A7. In addition, the following differences between the two hands are noteworthy:

1. Hand A wrote columns averaging 42 lines (with some exceptions), while the one column that can be tested of hand B contains only 33 lines. The average number of letters on each line is 30–35 for hand A and 20–22 for hand B. Nevertheless the column block is the same for each hand since the letters of hand B are larger and each column contains fewer lines (see Table 3).

2. Unlike hand B, hand A left no spaces between words.

3. Evidence of ruled markings at the side margins as well as the top (and bottom?) margin appears for hand B, while there is no such evidence for hand A.

4. The sheets written by hand A were glued together (see the joining of cols 17–18), while those of hand B were sewn (see additional fragment 6).

5. The shape of the palaeo-Hebrew letters of the tetragrammaton is completely different in each script. In the script of the second hand all letters point downwards. This is particularly evident with regard to the *he*. The *he* of the first hand stands upright with the cross-bars in horizontal direction, while the cross-bars of the *he* of the second hand point vertically downwards. (In fact, hand A used two different forms of the *he*, the final one almost always tilting to the left, but in comparison with the *he* used by hand B they can still be called upright; likewise, the scribe of POxy 3522 (Job) used two different forms of the *he*.) Both scribes 'drew' rather than wrote the letters from an imprecise model. (This applies also to the form of the tetragrammaton in the Aquila fragments published by F. C. Burkitt [Cambridge 1897] in which the *waw* and *yod* are identical.)

6. Probably because the lines in the columns written by hand B were rather narrow, he used all the available space so that he often divided words even after a single letter, much more than hand A.

7. The leather used by hand B was prepared less well than that used by hand A (see Barth. 164). It is coarser, thicker and less polished.

The general background of the bisection of the Minor Prophets in the scroll is not clear. Although the sections written by hands A and B probably belonged to the same scroll, the unusual length of the scroll that would result from the combined work of the two scribes raises some problems. Nevertheless, the supposition that we are dealing with one scroll gains some support from the archaeological data, since the first lot brought to the École Biblique (see Barth. 163) contained mainly the work of hand A, but also a small fragment by hand B, while the second lot (very small) brought to him a year later contained the work of hand B, but also a small scrap written by hand A. Thus there is no initial presumption in favour of the assumption that we are confronted with two different lots representing two different scrolls.

The major arguments in favour of the view that the work of hands A and B belongs to one scroll are the aforementioned data on the measurements, the identical textual character of the two segments (see F), and the fact that no overlap between the work of hands A and B has yet been identified. It is thus quite possible that hands A and B wrote segments of the same scroll, as sometimes happened with other biblical manuscripts. It is not impossible that some time elapsed between the writing of hand A and the completion of the scroll by hand B (although there is no compelling palaeographic reason for this [thus P. Parsons in A7]). In this regard we are reminded of the Temple Scroll, for Yadin (p. 10) claimed that time had elapsed between the work of the first and second scribe of that scroll. It may well be that scribe A produced an incomplete scroll finished after some time by scribe B, or that a complete scroll by scribe A became damaged and was later patched by scribe B. There is even the possibility, illustrated many centuries later by a Coptic codex of the Psalms, that two originally separate scrolls have been united into one in an effort to repair damage or complete the desired corpus (see R. A. Kraft, 'An Unpublished Coptic Sahidic Psalter Codex at the University Museum in Philadelphia: A Preliminary Report', in: M. E. Stone (ed.), *Armenian and Biblical Studies* [Jerusalem 1976] 87–8). A related possibility is that we are dealing with a copy of the Minor Prophets that was produced and preserved in multiple scrolls (perhaps three?), written by two or more scribes, and portions of (at least) two of these 'sister scrolls' have survived in hands A and B.

## 6. Description of the Materials and their State of Preservation

BY ROBERT A. KRAFT

### 6a. *General Description*

The Minor Prophets materials from the Cave of Horror consist of a plethora of leather fragments of varying sizes, written only on one side, in two different hands, with numerous gaps between the fragments, both horizontal and vertical. There seems no point in measuring all the pieces individually (see the plates). The following measurements describe the larger sections of joined or nearly joined fragments, at the widest and tallest points. Thus the triangularly shaped section containing portions of cols 20 (the ends of a few lines) to 23 is described as 32 cm wide (at its widest point) and 14 cm tall (at its tallest point). Each of the larger sections may encompass a number of smaller fragments that have been pieced together.

On the measurements of each preserved column, see A2. No column of writing is fully preserved, although contiguous portions of all but eight lines of col 17 have survived. The largest conjoined portion of material is from cols 17–19, about 25.2 cm tall by 25 cm wide; if this section is rejoined to the remaining lower portions of cols 19–20, the total width of the combined sections would be increased to about 42 cm. The immediately adjacent large fragment containing portions of cols 20–23 was about 14 cm tall by 32 cm wide before it broke into two parts. The much more brittle and now fragmented section representing cols 2–4 was at least 19 cm tall and about 30 cm wide at some point in its recent history. The material from the lower portion of cols 6–8 was about 10 cm high and 27 cm wide.

All of the aforementioned sections, plus relatively smaller portions from cols 16, 28–29 and 30–31, represent the lower portion of the roll. The largest surviving block of material that includes the top margin is cols 13–15, at perhaps 27 cm high and 19 wide (only part of the uninscribed top margin of col 13 has survived). Cols 8–9 preserve another significant chunk that includes the top margin, about 12 cm high and 15 cm wide. A smaller and more mutilated portion of top margin appears for col 5, about 5 cm high and 11 cm wide. The largest fragment of hand B also comes from the top of its roll and is 17.7 cm high by about 12 cm wide.

The main body of material (hand A) is written on a relatively thin and relatively smooth leather surface that was probably pale yellowish brown in its original state. Despite extensive damage and some discoloration, it still has an attractive appearance, with its neatly written rows of clear black letters. There is a tendency for the writing to be relatively more cramped towards the bottoms of columns. The average 'letter block' (i.e. from start of a letter to the start of its neighbour, and from base line to adjacent base line) for the letters alpha and theta is about 0.5–0.7 cm high and 0.2–0.3 cm wide. The widest letters are omega and mu, at nearly twice the width of alpha. Delta, zeta, lamda, nu, xi, pi, tau and chi are about one third to one quarter again as wide as alpha. On the narrow end of the scale, iota is about half as wide as alpha, while beta, gamma, epsilon, omicron, rho, and sigma are about three fourths the width. Upsilon varies greatly in width, but with eta, kappa, phi and psi is usually just slightly wider than alpha. The four palaeo-Hebrew letters of the tetragrammaton together take from 5 to 7 times the width of an alpha.

Hand B uses larger and heavier lettering, with slightly browner ink, on leather that is also thicker and perhaps a bit less yellow in tone. The average letter block for hand B is about 0.8 cm high by 0.4 cm wide (for alpha), in the small portion that is preserved. Both scribes have written on the usually paler 'flesh side' of the leather, but only hand B employs rulings to outline the margins at the sides and top (and bottom?) of the columns of writing. Stitching is evident on one fragment from hand B, while an adhesive apparently was used to join panels of leather in the material by hand A (cols 17–18).

### 6b. *Damage and Decay Patterns*

Thus far, the preserved materials have yielded few unambiguous clues concerning the physical form and circumstances in which they survived through the ages. The fragments are extensively damaged, both with reference to the reconstructed original scroll or scrolls from which they derive, and also in relationship to the larger sections of the originals that remain relatively intact. To help focus the discussion, the preserved fragments will be examined in relationship to the following contrasting hypothetical models: (1) The remains (at least those from hand A) represent a single scroll that had been relatively intact and rolled up neatly when it was deposited in antiquity, but suffered extensive decay and damage from the ravages of time and the carelessness of its bedouin discoverers. (2) The remains were already extensively damaged in antiquity and the effects of time and modern mistreatment have only added to the existing situation.

Important unknown factors in the discussion are the extent to which the bedouin may have contributed to the degeneration of the materials, and the exact circumstances in which the archaeologists discovered the 13 'shreds of parchment' described by Lifshitz, of which 4 scraps are contiguous and one other is blank (thus 9 fragments with writing). If the archaeologists found the fragments *in situ*, or at least adhering to the (disturbed) layers of bat dung that apparently covered the cave floor, we would have a better idea of which edges were exposed to the outside in antiquity. If the archaeologically discovered fragments were simply mixed in with the disturbed debris, as separate items, that would suggest that they could have broken off from the larger lot when the bedouin attempted to remove their new treasure.

Just how the bedouin succeeded in exiting the cave with their discoveries is also a relevant question, since the cave is described as virtually inaccessible (80 meters down from the top of an almost sheer cliff face), and they presumably did not have appropriately protective containers in which to transport the delicate manuscript materials. To what extent did they divide up the discoveries, fold the material for more convenient portability, etc.? On the other hand, the discovery apparently took place in late August, 1952, when the value of such scrolls was not unknown to their finders—indeed, the bedouin obviously were searching for such relics and thus probably were anxious to preserve as much of value as possible. Thus it seems unlikely, a priori, that large portions of the material would have been lost or destroyed by the bedouin, except by accident. It is possible that additional portions of the scroll(s) fell into private hands and will some day surface. But for now, we must work with what we have, and it is severely fragmented and damaged.

If we assume that the roll from which the bulk of the materials (hand A) derived was rolled up neatly when it began the period of dormancy from which its recent discoverers disturbed it, we might expect to find some repeating patterns of decay where moisture, vermin, or other destructive factors left their mark, over time, on adjacent layers of the roll. From such information we might also be able to make related conjectures concerning the original length of the roll, its contents, structure, etc.

With this ideal model in mind, it could be argued that the preserved portions from hand A exhibit such a pattern. The best evidence comes from cols 13 to 23, which represent a fragmented consecutive section of more than 105 cm in length, mostly from the lower half of the original roll. Similarly positioned and shaped decay holes are found near the bottom of cols 17, 20 and 22/23, approximately 25–32 cm apart. In addition, the preserved material from the upper portion of cols 14/15 and 17/18 originally would have been about 27–33 cm apart, and thus could have been adjacent. If such a pattern were accepted as probable, it would suggest that almost four turns of the roll have been preserved in this section, with the wider intervals ('panels') to the left, requiring about 29–33 cm for a full turn, and the shorter to the right, needing about 23–24 cm per turn. Each successive panel (or turn) varies from the adjacent panel by about 1.5–3.5 cm in width. It is not possible to determine whether the writing faced inward (as expected) or outward on this hypothesis, but the scroll itself would have been rolled up from right to left so that the first part of the text would be encountered first as the scroll was unrolled.

Cols 2 to 9, which originally covered about 86 cm of the roll, show some similar patterns. The top margin is preserved for cols 5 and 8/9, about 32–40 cm apart. Since the missing cols 10 to 13 would have required about 40 cm (a little more than one turn or panel at that point), it is not unreasonable to think that the top margin of cols 8/9 could have backed up to the top margin of col 5. Again, cols 28 to 31 represent a section that originally was about 38 cm wide, and lower margins are preserved for col 28 and for 30/31. The interval is about 16–25 cm. At this point in the hypothetical roll pattern, we expect the 'panel' to be about 19.0–20.5 cm wide, since the missing columns 24–27 would have required about 42 cm (almost two turns/panels of the roll).

This results in a reconstructed picture of a somewhat loosely rolled body of material in ten turns/panels for cols 1 to 32, with the following adjacent/overlapping representative points at the start of each sucessive panel (estimated widths of each panel in parentheses below):

| cols 2 | 5/6 | 9/10 | 13 | 16/17 | 19/20 | 22/23 | 25 | 27/28 | 30 |
|---|---|---|---|---|---|---|---|---|---|
| (42) | (39) | (36) | (33) | (31) | (28) | (25) | (23) | (21) | (...) |

With slight adjustment, allowing for looser rolling at the outside and tighter nearer the centre, it could be argued that there is even a certain symmetry to the larger picture: two panels preserved (cols 2–9), then one lost (10–12); 4 preserved (13–23), then 2 lost (24–27); 2 preserved (28–31), then an unknown number lost (but probably not more than 10 panels, depending on how tightly the interior is rolled, containing another 10 cols or so).

Such a reconstruction, however, encounters serious difficulties. With the possible exception of the holes in cols 17–23, the supposedly similar decay patterns only approximately coincide—there are few impressive detailed replications of shapes to support the hypothesis. Furthermore, unless a great deal of material was lost, destroyed or retained by the modern discoverers, how is it possible to account for the large gaps between the preserved 'sections' as well as within each of those sections? When all is said and done, the reconstruction does not seem to work for all of the preserved fragments, although it may be satisfactory for the middle portion (cols 13–23) as a sub-unit of the original scroll.

### 6c. *Other Evidences of Damage: Folding and Crumpling*

The fragments contain other clues of value for making conjectures about the physical state of the material at the time it was left in the cave. Many fragments attest that the leather had been crumpled and folded, whether in antiquity or by later explorers. Much of this evidence comes from the early columns: cols 2–4 show folds that run at a slight angle from the upper left to the lower right as well as a few creases running from lower left to upper right. The top of col 5 appears to be crumpled as well, as does the small fragment from near the top of col 6 (plate V, fragment a). A series of fold marks can be seen between cols 7 and 8, on a slight diagonal from upper left to lower right, and with various offshoots. The bottom of col 6 and the top of cols 8–9 also appear unusually wrinkled.

Nor are remaining sections free of such marks. The top of col 14 is badly crumpled and has various diagonal folds running almost perpendicular to each other. The lower margin at col 17 seems to show heavy fold/crumple lines (see col 16 as well). The material from cols 30–31 also reveals similar damage, with prominent, almost vertical fold lines as well as a heavy diagonal fold from lower left to upper right. Even the large fragment of hand B (plate XIX, fragment a) shows evidence of diagonal folding at the top right (see also additional fragment 6, from hand B).

These damage lines do not all seem to be recent, although some of them may very well be. Notice that the breaks between the portions of Lifshitz' reconstructed larger fragment from near the top of col 3 (plate III, fragment a) suggest a similar pattern of diagonal fold damage, which strengthens the case for such damage being ancient. Vertical lines of damage would be expected in a normally rolled scroll that had aged and/or had been crushed, especially in the innermost, more tightly rolled panels. A prominent horizontal 'fold' half way down the roll sometimes appears as well, as in 1QIs$^{a}$ cols 1–17; see also 1QS col 1)—perhaps the result of a heavy guideline for ruling, or a manufacturer's fold to help produce evenly cut upper and lower edges? Patterns of diagonal folds seem abnormal.

Thus it may well be that the material was already in a dishevelled, and possibly heavily damaged state when it was abandoned to history. Whether such damage would have been intentional or accidental can only be conjectured—e.g. perhaps the scroll was accidentally dropped and trampled upon during the confusion surrounding the last days of the cave's occupancy in antiquity? Perhaps it had been damaged at an earlier time, and had been put aside to await appropriate disposal? Perhaps the Roman soldiers sacked the cave after the inhabitants had succumbed to famine and other terminal forces, and tore the materials apart? Although the excavators discovered no evidence of Roman presence in the cave, they did find the remains of a large hot fire in the centre of the cave-corridor, and conjectured that 'the besieged occupants . . . evidently decided to make a great bonfire . . . and destroy all their belongings in it—apart from the Greek scroll of the Twelve Minor Prophets which, together perhaps with some important documents, was buried between the rocks of the end chamber' (Aharoni, 199). It may also be that the fire was the work of a Roman military 'mop up' crew after the occupants had succumbed, or of others who discovered the situation soon after the Romans had departed from their camp atop the cave area. In any event, occasions on which the scroll could have received serious damage do not seem to have been lacking in antiquity. Perhaps it is worth noting at this point that the excavators also found three scraps of unconnected papyri *in situ* under the top layer of dung not far from the mouth of the cave, and concluded that 'these documents . . . must therefore have been torn up and dropped at this spot in antiquity' (Aharoni, 195). By whom, and why? And can this tell us anything about the history of the Minor Prophets materials?

One other possibility is suggested by the details of the site report. The modern bedouin and the archaeologists were not the first to disturb the cave in its isolated slumber from the second century to the 20th. At least one other intruder left a calling card—an intact byzantine lamp from no earlier than the 5th century in the centre of the cave (Aharoni, 194). Does this have any relationship to the reports of manuscript discoveries in the Judaean caves in the late 7th century? Doubtless there were also others who made their way to this treacherously remote but not quite impenetrable spot. What such visitors may have found, and what they may have done with their finds, can only be conjectured.

### 6d. *Matching Patterns of (Ancient?) Damage*

The damage patterns on the fragments can be used in support of a hypothesis that the material was already badly damaged in antiquity. For example, for cols 13–23, it is possible to fit the rightmost panel (cols 20/21–23) atop cols 18–20 in a slightly skewed manner such that the curved shape of cols 20/21 fits nicely over the damage pattern in the middle of col 18, while the rightmost portion of col 23 overlies the lower margin of col 20. Similarly, if the section containing cols 13–15 is turned so that the top lies under the similarly shaped sections of col 16 and col 17, the fold patterns and deterioration patterns approximately (but not exactly) coincide in various places.

Again, the destruction patterns found on col 6 are very similar to those on col 30/31 and col 28/29, including a heavy diagonal fold running from lower left to upper right on an angle not prominent elsewhere. Each of these fragments also seems to have similar heavy vertical folds. Perhaps they were adjacent to each other during the trip from antiquity? Indeed, it is tempting to place this packet among the outside layers of the preserved mass, along with the panel containing cols 13–15, to help explain the relationship to the Lifshitz fragments, which come from cols 3, 13–15, and 30–31.

Other possible overlaps in the destruction patterns could be suggested, but with even less conviction. Nothing really aligns unambiguously, but, based on the presently available evidence, the model of a damaged mass of material abandoned in antiquity seems somewhat more probable than the model of a neatly rolled consecutive text.

Furthermore, there is reason to suspect that the scroll rested alongside other written companions in antiquity. According to the excavation report concerning the discovery of the fragments later published by Lifshitz, the scroll materials probably came from the back part of the cave, near the opening to the 'end chamber' where numerous burials were located. A piece of papyrus containing cursive Greek writing (from a letter?) was also found at the same location, suggesting that the (damaged?) scroll may have been part of a larger collection of written materials, deposited in a grave or buried among the rocks, or otherwise left in that relatively remote area. This may also help explain Barthélemy's vague reference to 'Hebrew-Aramaic papyri' from the same cave, apparently as reported by the bedouin (see Aharoni, 198), and perhaps also the presence of Minor Prophets Greek 'hand B' fragments, which in this context could easily be viewed as coming from a different roll.

## 7. The Scripts and Their Date

BY PETER J. PARSONS

*Abbreviations*

| | |
|---|---|
| Barth. 1953 | D. Barthélemy, 'Redécouverte d'un chaînon manquant de l'histoire de la Septante', *RB* 60 (1953) 18–29. |
| Barth. 1963 | id., *Les devanciers d'Aquila*, SVT 10 (Leiden 1963). |
| GMAW[2] | E. G. Turner, *Greek Manuscripts of the Ancient World* ed. 2 (London 1987). |
| GLH | C. H. Roberts, *Greek Literary Hands* (Oxford 1956). |
| Kahle | P.E. Kahle, *The Cairo Geniza* ed. 2 (Oxford 1959). |
| LSSE | G. Cavallo, *Libri Scribi Scritture a Ercolano* (Naples 1983). |
| Menci | G. Menci, 'Scritture greche librarie con apici ornamentali (III a.C.–II d.C.)', *Scrittura e Civiltà* 3 (1979) 23ff. |
| PGB | W. Schubart, *Papyri Graecae Berolinenses* (Bonn 1911). |

### 7a. *Description*

#### *Scribe A*

(*a*) Modulus. The script is in intention bilinear (only $\phi$ reaches well above the line; the descenders of $\rho$, $\phi$ and $\psi$ are normally curtailed), although uncertainty in execution, and the enlargement of initial letters, gives an irregular impression. For the sizes of the letters, see A6a.

(*b*) Shading. The pen is thick, and there are variations of thickness in the strokes, though not, it seems, to any consistent effect. But in several places the scribe can be seen to sharpen his pen, or take a newer and thinner one: cols 8, l.12, 20, l.35.

(*c*) Ornament. The script is profusely ornamented. The feet of verticals and descending obliques carry blobs or hooks or half-serifs (horizontal or angular or arched) or—rarely—full serifs; hooks and half-serifs normally point to the right; they may be very large. A glance at fig. 1 will show that there is no consistency; any suitable letter may carry any of these ornaments. Some verticals ($\eta$, $\iota$, $\kappa$) may be hooked to the left at the top. In some places the verticals themselves are given a sinuous shape, which enhances the mannered look.

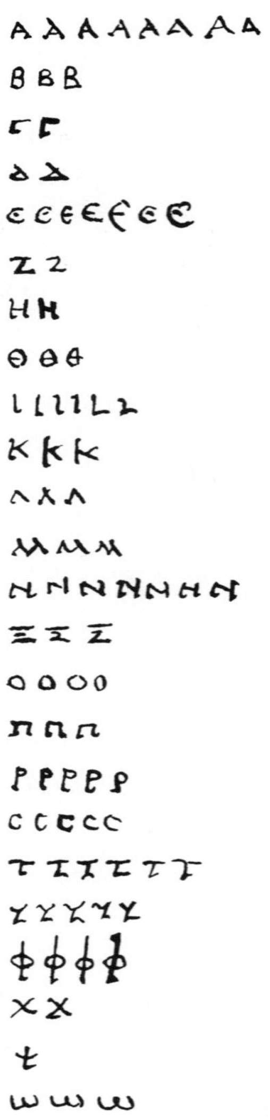

FIGURE 1 Scribe A cols 17–19

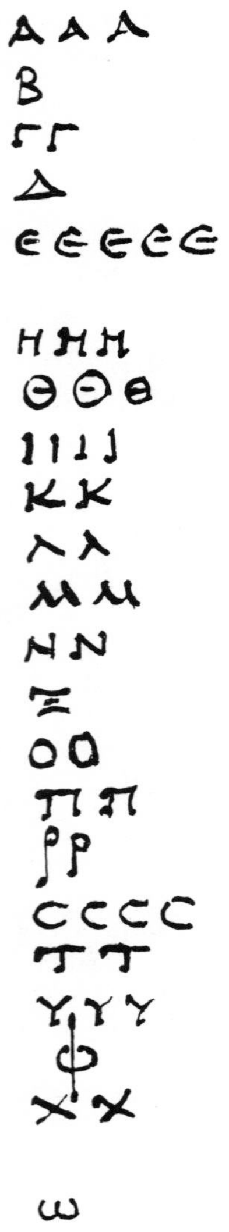

FIGURE 2 Scribe B

(*d*) Letter forms (see fig. 1)

*A* appears mostly in the capital shape (horizontal cross-bar, three movements); sometimes (especially when the letter is enlarged) the right-hand oblique projects above the apex. But there are also examples of the pointed form (the cross-bar sloping upward from the left foot).

*B* sometimes has its loops made in a single movement, sometimes the base is supplied as a separate horizontal stroke.

*Δ* The right-hand oblique projects above the apex.

*E* appears in various forms: in two movements, sometimes with the cross-bar detached (as a short oblique or an arc) or reduced to a dot, or in three movements, with its top right-hand portion added as a separate stroke.

*Λ* sometimes has the right-hand oblique projecting above the apex.

*M* with oblique sides, and the central dip touching the line; the right-hand junction well below the top of the right-hand oblique. Various forms: sometimes certainly in four movements, more often in three (sometimes perhaps strokes 1 and 2 in one movement, then 3 and 4 separate; sometimes strokes 2 and 3 in one movement, with the central dip correspondingly rounded).

*N* in three movements, the right-hand junction normally well above the foot of the right-hand upright.

*Ξ* sometimes has three separate strokes, sometimes the middle and lower joined in a single movement.

*O* in two movements, the right-hand arc often straighter than the left; the joins at head and foot are often imperfect, giving a gap or an overlap.

*Π* with the right side gently curved.

*Σ* sometimes has its cap made as a separate stroke.

*T* sometimes has its top in a single stroke, sometimes divided (the left-hand part written in a single movement with the stem).

*Ω* generally in a single movement, but some examples of the two-movement form (the right-hand arc added separately).

(*e*) General. This aspires to be a book-hand (there are only occasional ligatures). But the performance is inconsistent: individual letter forms vary (e.g. *ϵ* and *σ* are now full and rounded, now narrower and ovoid); ornamentation differs widely in application and execution; some whole passages are copied more neatly than others (contrast cols 18–19 with col 20).

*Scribe B*

(*a*) Modulus. (i) Vertical. The script is bilinear (allowing for the enlargement of some line-initials), except for *ρ* and *ϕ* (this scribe makes no attempt to curtail them). (ii) Horizontal. The general effect is round and square; rounded letters tend to a circle and even an oblate circle, but there are examples of oval forms as well. For the sizes of the letters, see A6a.

(*b*) Shading. Thick strokes (horizontals, obliques descending from left to right) and thin strokes (obliques ascending from left to right) are clearly differentiated; verticals may be either.

(*c*) Ornament. The feet of uprights, the tops of uprights in *ι*, *κ*, *ν*, *ϕ*, and the left-hand tips of *υ* and *χ*, take decoration in the form of blobs, hooks and half-serifs (horizontal or oblique), rarely full serifs; hooks and half-serifs more often (but not consistently) point to the left.

(*d*) Letter forms (see fig. 2)

*A* sometimes in the capital shape, with horizontal (or concave) cross-bar, sometimes with cross-bar sloping to lower left (in at least one place made in a single movement with the first oblique?).

*E* has its cross-bar detached; sometimes the back is made in a single movement, sometimes the cap is added as a further short curved or horizontal stroke.

*Θ* sometimes has its cross-bar detached on the left side or on both.

*Λ* has its right-hand stroke projecting above the apex.

*M* has sloping sides, and its bow touches the line; the junction well below the summit on both sides. Generally (always?) in three movements, the second and third strokes in one.

*Π* with the right side curved (and made in one movement with the top?).

*Σ* generally (always?) in two movements, the top supplied as an additional straight or curving stroke.
*T* has a strong curl down on its left-hand end; that part of the cross-bar is often thickened.
*Υ* apparently in two movements, the left-hand prong and the stem formed in one.
*Φ* has a large bowl which fills the whole normal line-space.
*Ω* sometimes (not always?) in two movements.

(*e*) General. We have only a small sample of this script; what survives suggests a much more fluent and consistent copyist than hand A.

## 7b. *Dating*

### *Principles*

The manuscript came originally from the 'Cave of Horror'; we therefore have a terminus ante quem of *c*.A.D. 135 for its writing (see A1). For a terminus post quem we have no objective evidence. No certain deductions can be made from the format of the roll (see A2) or from the orthography (see F12); the heavy soiling of upper and lower margins, and of the back, which Barth. reports, may prove heavy use, but whether intensive use over a short period, or recurrent use over a long period, who can say?

We have therefore to base our date on palaeographic evidence. The reader who surveys the bibliography will not need to be warned that such evidence is shifting sand. Barth. 1953 dated the script (that is, hand A) towards the end of i A.D. Roberts apud Kahle (p. 226) opted for 50 B.C.–A.D. 50, and Schubart ibid. for a date around the reign of Augustus; Barth. 1963 accepted Schubart's date for hand A, found parallels for hand B in dated papyri of i A.D. and assigned the whole manuscript to mid i A.D.

The scientific aspect of the process is simple enough: it consists in pointing out similarities between the script to be dated and other scripts to which an objective (non-palaeographic) date can be attached. But such dated hands are rare; and the use to be made of them must be qualified by subjective and ideological factors. I list some particular difficulties:

(i) 'Styles' and 'similarities'. Ideally, we group scripts together by their similarities; and within one group try to see a definable 'style' of script with its own dynamics of historical development; then undated hands may be placed chronologically within the schema articulated by the dated examples. The difficulties are twofold. (a) What is a 'similarity'? Two characteristics referred to above are 'ornament' (the use of decorative serifs and the like) and 'shading' (the deliberate alternation of thick and thin pen-strokes, related to the angle at which the pen meets the paper). In one 'style' definable by other criteria ornament seems to be essential (the 'Roman Uncial'); in another (the 'Biblical Uncial') heavy shading is always present. But in other possible 'styles' shading and ornament seem to be facultative. Thus Turner (GMAW$^2$ p. 21) rightly insists that Schubart's 'decorated style' (to which Schubart assigned hand A) is not really a style, but a single feature of several styles, spread over a period of at least four centuries from ii B.C. (b) What is a style? Some palaeographers speak of a 'canon', that is, a fixed and unitary prescription to which good scribes can be seen conforming, and whose development and decay can be charted. Other palaeographers emphasise that we know effectively nothing about ancient views of these matters or about the training of ancient scribes; therefore 'canon', with its suggestion of scientific precision and historical realism, is inappropriate; 'style', and 'development' within a style, are no more than modern analytic concepts.

(ii) Local Styles. There is no special reason to suppose that the same styles of script existed at the same time, and developed at the same pace, in all parts of the Mediterranean world. It is, for example, arguable that styles which contrast wide and narrow letters appear at Herculaneum in i B.C., but in Egypt not until ii A.D. (see GMAW² no. 78). Comparative material from three areas is listed below; it remains an open question how far papyri from Egypt and from Herculaneum are relevant.

(iii) Personal styles. We have to add further factors. (a) A scribe may have a working life of 50 years; in that time he may not change his script. Therefore, even if a style can be assumed to show a linear diachronic development, not all practitioners will develop with it; very precise datings are risky. (b) Occasionally we can point to certain examples of archaising writing: thus POxy L 3529, which I should have assigned on palaeographic evidence to the early Roman period, is shown by its content to date after A.D. 307. We do not know whether archaism was a matter of personal choice or the habit of certain scriptoria or the requirement of certain patrons, or whether it was more likely at certain periods or places or in the copying of certain genres of text (say, scriptural texts).

### *Comparative Material*

Hands A and B clearly differ in size and polish (hand B looks much less crabbed and inconsistent than hand A); but they are of the same type, bilinear and decorated. I list some datable comparative material:

(i) Egypt. The overwhelming bulk of our material is from here; but even here the dated examples are rare. GLH provides an essential selection; for the serifed styles with which we shall be concerned see the detailed lists in Menci.

| | | | |
|---|---|---|---|
| i B.C. | GLH 8a | document | 99 B.C. |
| | PLond III 1209 | doc. | 89 |
| | 883 | doc. | 88 |
| | PAmh II 51 | doc. | 88 |
| | GLH 8b | doc. | 30–29 |
| | PGB 12 | doc. | 13 |
| | GLH 9a | doc. | *c*.7–4 |
| | PQasrIbrim | Homer | later i B.C.? |
| | [See JEA 62 (1976) 116; all datable texts from this find have been early Augustan.] | | |
| | PMerton II 52 | Homer | before 5 B.C. |
| | [The verso carries a document of that date.] | | |
| | GMAW 56 | LXX | later i B.C.? |
| | [See GMAW² Add. 125, where Turner judges a cursive note in this papyrus to be 'unmistakably Ptolemaic'. Since dated cursive hands are relatively common, the palaeographic dating of such hands is relatively reliable.] | | |
| | [GMAW 12, a good parallel, has no objective date: see GMAW² Add. 16.] | | |
| i A.D. | POxy 2555 | horoscope | after 46 |
| | POxy 3700 | mime | before *c*.48–9 |
| | GMAW 64 | doc. | *c*.50 |
| | POxy 3332 | doc. | 53 |
| | POxy 3250 | doc. | *c*.63 |
| | GLH 10c | doc. | 66 |
| | POxy 2987 | doc. | *c*.78–9 |

Most of this material is documentary; but the comparison is rather appropriate, since the use of enlarged initials at line-beginning (hands A and B) and phrase-beginning (hand A) and (set out in the margin) to mark a new section (hand A) gives this manuscript a documentary look (see A4). The fact is itself remarkable. Early Christian books show the same characteristic; copies of the Greek classics do not. It has therefore been tempting to argue that the texts of the Early Church stood closer to the world of business than to that of literature, and to draw conclusions about the social milieu in which the texts circulated or the esteem in which they were held. Now we see the same thing in a Jewish manuscript of pre-Christian date. This may suggest that the Christians inherited the practice, rather than inventing it; the problem remains, why Greek-speaking Jews should have adopted it in the first place.

In Egyptian context, both hands give a clear immediate impression of being late Ptolemaic or early Roman; that was the meaning of Roberts's original dating '50 B.C. – A.D. 50'. The question is, whether the period can be narrowed down.

Hand A could certainly be ascribed to the earlier part of the period. It has striking similarities with GLH 8a, of 99 B.C. (not to be pressed too far, for part of the similarity—the fact that both scribes handle a thick pen clumsily—is irrelevant). The literary style to which it aspires, the bilinear serifed manner in which only the riser of phi breaks the mould, occurs in two Homer texts, assigned on objective grounds to i B.C., and (in a less insistent form) in GMAW 56 (PFouad Inv. 266), reasonably assigned to the same period, as well as in many literary papyri dated on simple palaeographic grounds to that century; in the epsilon whose cross-bar occasionally becomes a dot there is a point of contact with the 'Epsilon Theta' style, which is represented at Herculaneum (i.e. before *c.*40 B.C.?) (see Cavallo, *Cron. Erc.* 4 (1974) 33; Menci 38–40). Among letters one may note some older-looking forms, which appear alongside later (more cursive) shapes of the same letter: alpha in the capital form, mu in four movements, xi in three strokes.

All in all, I can see nothing against ascribing this hand to the later first century B.C., and nothing specifically in favour of dating it later. But POxy 2555, a horoscope for A.D. 46 (copied, therefore, some indefinite period after), warns that the later date would be perfectly possible.

Hand B has at first sight a later look; that may be merely that the execution is more regular and elegant, and the round letters wider and fuller. But the width has parallels e.g. in GLH 8b, 9b–c (later i B.C.); and, although this hand deliberately makes rho and phi break the bilinearity, there is a likeness to the two Homers cited and to PFouad Inv. 266 (note here the neckless upsilon). Among letter-forms, Mr. Skeat notes theta with the cross-bar detached; add the tau with the left extremity thickened and hooked down, which in this form seems to me a Ptolemaic inheritance (though the ductus which produces this form, i.e., ⁊, is still found in documents of the early Roman period).

(ii) Herculaneum. The Greek papyri, all literary, come from a single library. There is a certain terminus ante, A.D. 79, when the town was buried. There is a less certain one *c.*40 B.C., the presumed date of Philodemus' death: since the collection includes so many of Philodemus' own works, some (it can be argued) in draft as well as in fair copy, and includes no author demonstrably later than him, it seems reasonable to suppose that this was Philodemus' own library. Where the books were originally copied, and where the local copyists were originally trained, we have no means of saying. Bilinear serifed hands are common in this library, as a glance at LSSE will show. I should make a general comparison with PHerc 182 (LSSE pl. 18) and 1005 (pl. 22) (both assigned by Cavallo to mid-i B.C.), and of hand B with PHerc. 1471 (pl.36) (assigned to earlier i B.C.), 1186 (pl. 33) (assigned to mid-i B.C.), 1423 and 1507 (pll. 50 and 53; these often have alpha in the pointed, not the capital form, and are assigned to later i B.C.).

These parallels tend to show that the hands of our scroll could be of i B.C. (though of course they cannot exclude a later date).

(iii) Judaean Desert. These hands should be the most relevant. But it seems that no very precise archaeological dates can be given. At Qumran, the material probably antedates A.D. 68 (*DJD* VI 21), although there remains the possibility that some of the caves were occupied again at the time of the Second Revolt (*DJD* III 32); at Murabbaʿat, the terminus ante is no earlier than for the Minor Prophets scroll, i.e., *c.*A.D. 135 (or even later?: *DJD* II 47f).

*Qumran.* 7Q1LXXEx (van Haelst 38), see *DJD* III p. 142 and pl. 30. Assigned date: *c.*100 B.C. (Roberts). This small serifed bilinear hand has some similarities with hands A and B (note the pointed alpha, and wide tau hooked down at the left), so far as can be seen from the scrap which survives.

4QLXXLev[a] (van Haelst 49), see P. W. Skehan, *SVT* 4 (1957) 148ff with plate facing p. 159. Assigned date: late ii B.C. (Roberts). This is a pinched, undecorated hand of the type of GLH 6a, with a pronounced Ptolemaic look; not similar to hands A or B, and probably earlier.

4QLXXNum (van Haelst 51), see P. W. Skehan, *HTR* 70 (1977) 39ff with plate. Assigned date: i B.C. / i A.D. (Roberts). This bilinear script (the descenders of rho and phi are curtailed), heavily ornamented with half- and full serifs, has some similarities with hand A, but it is much more elegant and finely written; a distinctive feature is that the oval letters tend to lean backwards.

4QLXXDeut, see E. Ulrich in *De Septuaginta: Studies in Honour of John William Wevers on his Sixty-Fifth Birthday* (eds. A. Pietersma and C. Cox, Mississauga, Ont., 1984) 71ff with plate. The hand of this scrap shows no similarities with hand A or B; it is an informal script of Ptolemaic look with some cursive tendencies and no decoration except some terminal hooks and blobs.

4Qsn. A non-biblical text to be published by E. Ulrich, in a decorated hand of the same type as 4QLXXNum, but not so elegant.

7Q2EpistJer (van Haelst 312), see *DJD* III p. 143 and pl. 30. Assigned date: *c.*100 B.C. (Roberts). This tiny scrap shows a broad bilinear script without ornament (except for a half-serif on the foot of tau).

7Q4–9 (van Haelst 1094), ibid. Of these unprofitable scraps, no. 5 (assigned date: 50 B.C.–A.D. 50) shows some likeness to hands A and B (half-serifs; alpha in capital shape).

*Murabbaʿat.* PMur 108 ('Philosophical Text', but in fact clearly iambic trimeters, see C. Austin, *Comicorum Graecorum Fragmenta in papyris reperta* (1973) no. 360), see *DJD* II p. 234 and pl. 81. Assigned date: second half of i A.D. (Benoit). This good professional script, bilinear (the tail of phi curtailed) and ornamented with hooks and half-serifs, has alpha in the pointed form, epsilon leaning to the left, tau with a dipped top arched on the left. It may be compared with hand B, though the general impression is later.

This makes it clear that serifed hands are common enough (but not universal) in Judaean material assignable to the period i B.C.–i A.D. But the archaeological terminus ante falls too late (A.D. 68 or 135) to limit the date of our scroll more precisely.

*Conclusion*

Both hands give the impression of belonging to the late Ptolemaic or early Roman period. Some features favour an earlier rather than a later date; no feature recommends a later rather than an earlier date. I should therefore opt, tentatively (since I have seen only photographs, not the originals) and with all the provisos listed above, for a date in the later i B.C.; the objectively dated parallels show that such a dating is possible, though not of course necessary.

Dr C. H. Roberts and Mr T. C. Skeat have allowed me to cite their opinions. Dr Roberts would remain with his original estimate, '50 B.C.–A.D. 50'. Mr Skeat (to whom I am greatly indebted for comment and advice) inclines to i B.C., and sees nothing which would bring the date down into i A.D.

# B AND C. TRANSCRIPTIONS OF THE TEXT

THE text of the scroll is reproduced on *facing pages* in two different ways:

Section B

The text is printed so as to represent as closely as possible the contents of the scroll. The text is printed in uncials, and spacing (__) and margins (` `), when present, are indicated. The relative position of the fragment in its column is indicated as well. The main imprecision in the printed form derives from the fact that the size and printed form of the letters differ from those of the letters in the scroll. Nevertheless, the presentation of the printed form of B (never of C!) resembles as much as possible the shape of the fragments. For calculation of the real distance between different fragments of a column, or of the size of the lacunae, the plates should always be consulted.

Doubtful letters indicated by dots in C are *not* indicated as such in B.

Next to each line number follows in parenthesis the number of letters in the (reconstructed) line. Under each column the following data are provided: total number of letters for each column (including spaces when attested), the number of lines, length of the shortest and longest line (extant or reconstructed), average number of letters per line for the whole column, number of lines for which at least one letter or the margin has been preserved, and the average length of those lines. For these data, cf. A2, 3, 6, 8. The number of the reconstructed letters is naturally more reliable for single lines found between partially preserved lines than for complete sections which have not been preserved.

Section C

Printed form of the text with reconstructions for all lines on which at least one letter or part of the margin has been preserved. The other lines have been left empty except for the verse numbers (calculated on the basis of the full reconstruction of the text, which is not represented here). Punctuation marks, accents and breathings have been added.

The surviving columns are not numbered consecutively, but rather the numbering represents the place of each column in the reconstructed complete scroll from Jo to Za. The first extant column (Jo [1.5]–[2.7a]) is recorded as col 2 and not as col 1 since it must have been preceded by the beginning of that book. Books before Jo have not been included in this numbering.

All *differences* between R and the LXX (edition of Ziegler) are *underlined*, both in the extant and the reconstructed portions. Excluded from this notation are differences in capitalization, punctuation and the tetragrammaton. Pluses of R and differences in sequence are indicated by underlined words, and omissions by an underlining in the space between the words.

# B. TEXT (without reconstructions)

## Column 2 Jo [1.5]–[2.7a]

| Line | Letters | Text |
|---|---|---|
| 1 | (43) | |
| 2 | (46) | |
| 3 | (44) | |
| 4 | (48) | |
| 5 | (44) | |
| 6 | (42) | |
| 7 | (43) | |
| 8 | (39) | |
| 9 | (41) | |
| 10 | (41) | |
| 11 | (40) | |
| 12 | (42) | |
| 13 | (39) | |
| 14 | (42) | |
| 15 | (41) | |
| 16 | (44) | |
| 17 | (41) | |
| 18 | (43) | |
| 19 | (39) | |
| 20 | (43) | |
| 21 | (40) | |
| 22 | (40) | |
| 23 | (42) | |
| 24 | (43) | ΜΑΑΘΩ |
| 25 | (38) | |
| 26 | (47) | ΑΣ Ι |
| 27 | (43) | ΦΟΒΗ ΣΑΝ |
| 28 | (43) | ‡ΚΑΙΕΘΥΣΙΑΣΑΝΘ ΙΑΝ |
| 29 | (42) | - - - - - - - - - - - - - - - - - - - - |
| 30 | (45) | ΑΤΑΠΙΕΙΝΤΟΝΙΩΝΑΝ |
| 31 | (45) | ΣΤΡΕΙΣΗΜΕΡΑΣΚΑΙΤΡΕ |
| 32 | (43) | Υ |
| 33 | (41) | ΕΙ |
| 34 | (43) | |
| 35 | (46) | ΠΕΡΡΕΙΨΑΣΜ ΣΒΑΘ |
| 36 | (41) | ΟΣΠΕΡΙΕΚΥΚΛΩΣ ΝΜ |
| 37 | (41) | ΚΑΙΤΑΚΥΜΑΤΑΣΟ ΠΕΜΕΔΙΗΛ |
| 38 | (41) | ΩΕΙΠΑΑΠΩ ΕΞΕΝΑΝΤΙΑΣΟΦΘΑΛΜΩΝΣΟΥ |
| 39 | (42) | ΘΗΣΩΕΠΙΒΛΕΨΑ ΠΡΟ ΝΑΟΝΑ ΙΟΝΣΟΥ_ _Π |
| 40 | (40) | ΜΕΥΔΑΤΑΕΩΣΨΥΧΗΣ_ΑΒΥΣΣΟΣΕΚΥΚΛΩ |
| 41 | (41) | ΤΗΕΛΟΣΠΕΡΙΕΣΧ ΝΤΗΝΚΕΦΑΛΗΝΜΟΥ_Ε |
| 42 | (40) | ΩΝΚΑΤΕΒΗΝ_Η ΙΑΥΤΗΣΚΑΤΕΜΟΥΕΙΣ |

TOTALS: 1782 letters/column; 42 lines, 38 (short), 48 (long), 42.42 (average) all/part of 18 lines preserved from column, average length *42.88* letters

## C. TEXT (with reconstructions)

### Column 2 Jo [1.5]–[2.7a]

[ 6 ]
[ 7 ]
[ 8 ]
[ 9 ]
[ 10 ]
[ 11 ]
[ 12 ]
[13 ]
[ 14 ]
[ψυχῆς τοῦ ἀνθρώπου τούτου καὶ μὴ δῷς ἐφ᾽ ἡμᾶς αἷ]μα ἀ̣θῷ̣-``
[ο̣ν̣, ὅτι σύ, 𐤉𐤄𐤅𐤄, ὃν τρόπον ἐβούλου πεποίηκας. 15 καὶ]``
[ἔλαβον τὸν ιωναν καὶ ἐξέβαλον αὐτὸν εἰς τὴν θάλ]ασ̣[σαν, κα]ὶ``
[ἔστη ἡ θάλασσα ἐκ τοῦ '''''''' αὐτῆς. 16 καὶ ἐ]φοβή[θη]σαν``
[οἱ ἄνδρες φόβῳ μεγάλῳ τὸν 𐤉𐤄]𐤅𐤄̣ καὶ ἐθυσί̣α̣σαν θ[υσ]ίαν``
[τῷ 𐤉𐤄𐤅𐤄 καὶ ε̣ὔξαντο εὐχάς.]______________________``
[2.1 Καὶ προσέταξεν̣ 𐤉𐤄𐤅𐤄 κήτει μεγάλῳ κ]αταπιεῖν τὸν ιωναν·
[καὶ ἦν ιωνα̣ ἐν κοιλίᾳ̣ τοῦ κήτου]ς̣ τρεῖς ἡμέ̣ρας καὶ τρε[ῖς]
[νύκτας. 2 καὶ προσε̣ύξατο ιωνα̣ πρὸς 𐤉𐤄𐤅𐤄 τὸν θεὸν αὐτο]ῦ``
[ἐκ κοιλίας τοῦ κήτους 3 καὶ εἶπεν_ἐβόησα ἐν θλίψ]ει
[ ἐ̣π̣ε̣κ̣α̣λ̣ε̣-]
[σ̣ά̣μ̣η̣ν̣, ἤκουσας τ̣ῆ̣ς̣ φωνῆς μου. 4 κ̣α̣ὶ̣ ἀ]π̣έ̣ρρε̣ι̣ψάς μ[ε εἰ]ς̣ βάθ̣[ο̣ς̣]``
[ἐ̣ν̣ καρδίᾳ̣ θαλασσῶ̣ν̣, καὶ ποταμ]ὸ̣ς̣ π̣ε̣ρ̣ι̣εκύκλωσ[ε̣]ν̣ μ̣[ε̣·]
[πάντες οἱ ''''''' σου] καὶ τὰ κύματά σο[υ ἐ]π᾽ ἐμὲ διῆλ-``
[θον. 5 καὶ ἐγ]ὼ εἶπα̣ ἀ̣πῶ[σμαι] ἐ̣ξ̣ ἐ̣ν̣α̣ν̣τ̣ί̣α̣ς̣ ὀφθ̣αλμῶν σου·``
[ἆρα προσ]θ̣ήσω ἐπιβλέ̣ψα̣[ι] πρὸ[ς] ναὸν ἅ[γ]ιόν σου;__6 π[ερι-]
[εχύθησ̣ά̣ν̣] μ̣ε̣ ὕδ̣α̣τ̣α̣ ἕως̣ ψυχῆς·_Ἄβυσσος ἐκύκλῳ̣[σέ̣ν]
[με ἐσχά]τ̣η, ἕ̣λ̣ο̣ς̣ π̣ε̣ρ̣ι̣έ̣σ̣χ̣[ε̣]ν̣ τ̣ὴ̣ν̣ κεφαλήν̣ μου._7 ε[ἰς ''']
[''' ὀρέ]ων (7) κατέβην·_ἡ̣ [γῆ̣, μοχλο]ὶ αὐτῆς κ̣α̣τ̣᾽ ἐ̣μ̣ο̣ῦ̣ ε̣ἰ̣ς̣
[``````]````````````````[``````````]``````````````

## Column 3 Jo [2.7b]–4.5a

1 (42)
2 (42)
3 (44)
4 (47)
5 (41)
6 (45)
7 (49)
8 (46)
9 (37) Α Ι Κ Η Ρ Υ   Ο Ν
10 (41) Ρ   Σ Σ Ε _ Κ Α Ι   Ω
11 (40) Α Τ Ο Ρ Η Μ Α ⳨   Κ Α Ι Ν
12 (39) Π Ο Ρ Ε Ι Α Σ Τ Ρ Ι Ω
13 (41) Α Ι Ε Ι Σ Τ Η Ν Π Ο   Ρ Ε   Α
14 (43) Ε   Α Κ Ο Ν
15 (43) Α Φ Η Σ Ε   Τ Ε Υ Σ Α
16 (39) Ε Κ Η Ρ
17 (41)
18 (37)
19 (41)
20 (38)
21 (39)
22 (40)
23 (37)
24 (39) ˋ ˋ Π Ο Ι Κ Α Ι Τ Α Κ Τ
25 (34) ˋ ˋ Θ Ω Σ Α Ν Μ Η Δ   Ε ˋ ˋ
26 (41) ˋ ˋ Τ Ω Σ Α Ν _ Κ Α Ι Π Ε
27 (37) ˋ ˋ Τ Α Κ Τ Η Ν Η Κ Α   Ο Σ Τ Ο Ν Θ
28 (41) ˋ ˋ Κ Α Ι Ε Π Ε Σ Τ   Ε Ν Α   Ε Κ Τ Η Σ Ο Δ Ο   Υ   Η Σ Π Ο
29 (41) Α Π Ο Τ   Δ Ι Κ Ι Α Σ Τ Η Σ Ε Ν Χ Ε Ρ Σ Ι Ν Α Υ Τ Ω Ν _ Τ Ι Σ   Δ
30 (45) ˋ ˋ Ε Π Ι   Τ   Π Α Ρ   Ι Ο Θ Ε Ο   Ρ Ε Ψ
31 (42) ˋ ˋ Α Π Ο   Η Σ Α   Ι Ο Υ Μ Η Α Π Ο Λ   Θ Α _ _ _

32 (43) ˋ Κ Α Ι   Δ Ε   Τ Α Ε Ρ Γ Α Α Υ Τ   Τ Ι Ε Π Ε Σ Τ Ρ Ε Ψ Α Ν Α Π Ο Τ Η Σ
33 (41) Υ Α Υ Τ   Η Σ Π Ο Ν Η Ρ   Ε Κ Λ Η Θ Η Ι Θ Ε Ο Σ Ε Π Ι Τ Η ˋ ˋ
34 (44) Α Κ Ι Α Η Ε Λ   Η Σ Ε Ν Τ   Τ Ο Ι Σ Κ Α Ι Ο Υ Κ Ε Π Ο Ι Η Σ Ε Ν
35 (44) ˋ Κ   Λ   Ω Ν Α Λ Υ   Κ Α Ι Η Θ   Κ Α Ι Π
36 (44) ˋ ˋ Ε Υ Ξ Α Τ Ο Π Ρ Ο Σ ⳨ ⳨

37 (43) ˋ ˋ Ο Λ Ο Γ Ο Σ Μ Ο Υ Ε Τ Ι Ο
38 (41) ˋ ˋ Ε Φ Θ Α   Τ Ο Υ Φ Υ Γ Ε Ι
39 (41) ˋ ˋ Ε Λ Ε Η   Ω Ν Κ Α Ι
40 (39)
41 (32)
42 (36)
43 (40)
44 (41) Ι Τ Η Σ Π Ο Λ Ε Ω   ˋ ˋ

TOTALS: 1799 letters/column; 44 lines, 32 (short), 49 (long), 40.88 (average) all/part of 25 lines preserved from column, average length *41.00* letters

## Column 3 Jo [2.7b]–4.5a

[αἰῶνα ]
[8 ]
[ ]
[9 10 ]
[ ]
[ 11 ]
[ 3.1 ]
[ 2 ]
[τὴν πόλιν τὴν μεγάλην κ]αὶ κήρυ[ξ]ον [πρὸς αὐτὴν]
[τὸ κήρυγμα, ὃ ἐγὼ λαλῶ π]ρ[ὸ]ς σέ._3 καὶ [ἀνέστη ι]ω[να καὶ]
[ἐπορεύθη εἰς νινευη κατ]ὰ τὸ ῥῆμα 𐤉[𐤄𐤅𐤄·] καὶ ν[ινευη]
[ἦν πόλις μεγάλη τῷ θεῷ] πορείας τριῶ[ν ἡμερῶν. 4 καὶ]
[ἤρξατο ιωνα τοῦ πορεύεσθ]αι εἰς τὴν πό[λιν πο]ρε[ί]α[ν]
[ἡμέρας μιᾶς καὶ ἐκήρυξεν καὶ] ε[ἶπεν ἔτι τεσσερ]άκον[τα]
[ἡμέραι καὶ νινευη καταστρ]αφήσε[ται. 5 καὶ ἐπίσ]τευσα[ν]
[ἄνδρες νινευη τῷ θεῷ καὶ] ἐκήρ[υξαν νηστείαν καὶ]
[ ]
[ 6 ]
[ ]
[ ]
[ ]
[7 ]
[ ἄνθρω-]
``ποι καὶ τὰ κτ[ήνη, οἱ βόες καὶ τὰ πρόβατα μὴ γευσάσ-]
``θωσαν μηδ[έν, μὴ νεμέσθωσαν καὶ ὕδ'' μὴ πι]έ-``
``τωσαν._8 καὶ πε[ριεβάλοντο σάκκους οἱ ἄνθρωποι καὶ]
``τὰ κτήνη, κα[ὶ ἀνεβόησαν πρ]ὸς τὸν θ[εὸν ἐν ἰσχύι·]
``καὶ ἐπέστ[ρεψ]εν ἀ[νὴρ] ἐκ τῆς ὁδο[ῦ α]ὐ[τοῦ τ]ῆς πο[νηρᾶς]
[καὶ] ἀπὸ τ[ῆς ἀ]δικίας τῆς ἐν χερσὶν αὐτῶν._9 τίς [οἶ]δ[εν]
``ἐπι[σ]τ[ρέψει καὶ] παρ[ακληθήσετα]ι ὁ θεὸ[ς καὶ ἐπιστ]ρέψ[ει]
``ἀπὸ [θυμοῦ ὀργ]ῆς α[ὐτοῦ κα]ὶ οὐ μὴ ἀπολ[ώμε]θα;___[______10]
`Καὶ [εἶ]δε[ν ὁ θεὸς] τὰ ἔργα αὐτ[ῶν, ὅ]τι ἐπέστρεψαν ἀπὸ τῆς
[ὁδο]ῦ αὐτ[ῶν τ]ῆς πονηρ[ᾶς, καὶ παρ]εκλήθη <ι> θεὸς ἐπὶ τῇ``
[κ]ακίᾳ, ᾗ ἐλ[άλ]ησεν τ[οῦ ποιῆσαι αὐ]τοῖς, καὶ οὐκ ἐποίησεν. 4.1
`Κ[αὶ ἐ]λ[υπήθη ι]ωνα λύ[πην μεγάλην] καὶ ἠθ[ύμησεν.] 2 καὶ π[ροσ-]
``εύξατο πρὸς 𐤉𐤄𐤅[𐤄 καὶ εἶπεν__'''''''' 𐤉𐤄𐤅𐤄, οὐχ οὗτος]
``ὁ λόγος μου ἔτι ὄ[ντος μου ἐπὶ τῆς γῆς μου; διὰ τοῦτο προ-]
``έφθα[σα] τοῦ φυγεῖ[ν εἰς θαρσις, ὅτι ἔγνων ὅτι σὺ θεὸς]
``ἐλεή[μ]ων καὶ [οἰκτίρμων, μακρόθυμος καὶ πολυέλεος]
[ 3 ]
[ ]
[ 4 ]
[ 5 ]
[ἐκάθισεν ἀπέναντ]ι τῆς πόλεω[ς· καὶ ἐποίησεν ἑαυτῷ]``
[``````````````]`````````[`````````````````]

## Column 4 Jo [4.5b]–Mi [1.7a]

| Line | Letters | Text |
|---|---|---|
| 1 | (41) | |
| 2 | (39) | |
| 3 | (40) | |
| 4 | (41) | |
| 5 | (39) | |
| 6 | (41) | |
| 7 | (41) | |
| 8 | (40) | |
| 9 | (41) | |
| 10 | (40) | |
| 11 | (43) | |
| 12 | (41) | |
| 13 | (41) | |
| 14 | (39) | |
| 15 | (41) | |
| 16 | (39) | |
| 17 | (39) | |
| 18 | (41) | |
| 19 | (41) | |
| 20 | (38) | |
| 21 | (39) | _ _ _ _ _ _ _ |
| 22 | (39) | _ _ _ _ _ _ _ _ _ _ _ _ _ _ _ |
| 23 | (39) | _ _ _ _ _ _ _ _ _ _ _ _ _ _ _ |
| 24 | (39) | _ _ _ _ _ _ _ _ _ _ _ _ _ _ _ |
| 25 | (39) | _ _ _ _ _ _ _ _ _ _ _ _ |
| 26 | (39) | _ _ _ _ _ _ _ _ _ _ _ _ |
| 27 | (32) | ΛΟΓΟΣ𐤄 |
| 28 | (34) | ΜΩΡΑΣΘΕΙ_ΕΝΗΜ |
| 29 | (39) | ΒΑΣΙΛΕΩΣΙΟΥΔΑ_Ο |
| 30 | (36) | ΑΛΗΜ_ _ _ΑΚΟ |
| 31 | (35) | ΚΑΙΤΟΠ ΡΩΜΑΑ |
| 32 | (39) | ΕΝΥΜΕΙΝΕΙΣΜΑΡΤΥ |
| 33 | (40) | ΟΤΙΙΔΟΥ 𐤄𐤅𐤄𐤉ΕΚΠ |
| 34 | (40) | ΚΑΤΑΒΗΣΕΤΑΙΚΑ |
| 35 | (41) | ΣΟΝ ΤΑΟΡΗΥ |
| 36 | (40) | ΓΗΣΟΝ ΙΩΣ Α |
| 37 | (38) | ΚΑΤΑΦ ΟΜΕΝΟ ΤΑΒΑ |
| 38 | (37) | ΠΑΝΤΑΤ ΥΤΑΚΑΙ ΑΡΤΙΑΝ |
| 39 | (38) | ΑΣΕΒΙΑΙΑΚΩΒΟ ΜΑΡΟΙΑ_ΚΑ |
| 40 | (37) | ΧΙΙΕΡΟΥΣΑΛΗΜΚΑ ΗΣΟΜΑΙΣΑ |
| 41 | (40) | ΡΟΦΥΛΑΚΙΟΝΤΟΥΑ ΟΥΚΑΙΕΙ |
| 42 | (40) | ΚΑΙΚΑΤΑΣΠΑΣΩΕΙΣΤΗΝΦΑΡΑΓΓΑ |
| 43 | (36) | ΚΑΙΤΑΘΕΜΕΛΙΑΑΥΤΗΣ |
| 44 | (38) | ΓΛΥΠΤΑΑΥΤΗΣΚΑΤΑΚ |
| 45 | (36) | ΜΑΤΑΑΥΤΗΣΕΝΠΡΗΣΟΥ |

TOTALS: 1753 letters/column; 45 lines, 32 (short), 43 (long), 38.95 (average) all/part of 25 lines preserved from column, average length *38.00* letters

## Column 4 Jo [4.5b]–Mi [1.7a]

[ ]
[ 6 ]
[ ]
[ ]
[ ]
[ 7 ]
[ ]
[ 8 ]
[ ]
[ ]
[ ]
[ 9 ]
[ ]
[ 10 ]
[ ]
[ ]
[ 11 ]
[ ]
[ ]
[ ]
------[-----------------------------]
---------------[---------------------]
---------------[---------------------]
---------------[---------------------]
------------[------------------------]
------------[----------------------]1.1
Λόγος יה[וה ὃς ἐγένετο πρὸς μιχαίαν τὸν]
μωρασθει ἐν ἡμ[έραις ιωθαμ, αχαζ, ἐζεκίου]
βασιλέως ιουδα, ὃ[ν εἶδεν περὶ σαμαροίας καὶ ιε-]
[ρουσ]αλημ. 2 ἀκο[ύσατε, '''''', προσεχέτω γῆ]
καὶ τὸ π[λή]ρωμα α[ὐτῆς, καὶ ἔσται κύριος יהוה]
ἐν ὑμεῖν εἰς μάρτυ[ρα, κύριος ἐκ ναοῦ ἁγίου αὐτοῦ·]
3 ὅτι ἰδοὺ יהוה ἐκπ[ορεύεται ἐκ τοῦ τόπου αὐτοῦ καὶ]
καταβήσεται κα[ὶ ἐπιβήσεται ἐπὶ ὕψη γῆς. 4 καὶ τακή-]
σον[ται] τὰ ὄρη ὑ[ποκάτωθεν αὐτοῦ, καὶ αἱ κοιλάδες ῥα-]
γήσον[τα]ι ὡς [κηρὸς] ἀ[πὸ προσώπου τοῦ πυρὸς, ὡς ὕδωρ]
καταφ[ερ]όμενο[ν ἐν κα]ταβά[σει. 5 δι' ἀσέβιαν ιακωβ]
πάντα τ[α]ῦτα καὶ [δι' ἁμ]αρτίαν [οἴκου ισραηλ. τίς ]
ἀσέβια ιακωβ; ο[ὐ σα]μάροια; κα[ὶ τίς ὕψη ιουδα; οὐ-]
χὶ ιερουσαλημ; 6 κα[ὶ θ]ήσομαι σα[μάροιαν εἰς ὀπω-]
ροφυλάκιον τοῦ ἀ[γρ]οῦ καὶ εἰ[ς φυτείας ἀμπελῶνος]
καὶ κατασπάσω εἰς τὴν φάραγγα [τοὺς λίθους αὐτῆς]
καὶ τὰ θεμέλια αὐτῆς [ἀποκαλύψω· 7 καὶ πάντα τὰ]
γλυπτὰ αὐτῆς κατακ[όψουσιν καὶ πάντα τὰ μισθώ-]
ματα αὐτῆς ἐνπρήσου[σιν ἐν πυρί, καὶ πάντα τὰ]
[ ]

## Column 5 Mi 1.7b–[2.7]

| | | ` ` ` ` ` ` ` ` ` ` ` ` ` ` ` | ` ` ` ` ` ` ` |
|---|---|---|---|
| 1 | (33) | ΔΩΛΑ ϒΤΗΣΘΗΣ | ΤΙΕΓΜΙΣ |
| 2 | (33) | Σ | ΚΑΙΕΩΣΜΙ |
| 3 | (33) | | ΙΝ_ΔΙΑΤ Ο |
| 4 | (37) | | ΑΝϒΠΟ |
| 5 | (38) | | |
| 6 | (39) | | |
| 7 | (37) | | |
| 8 | (38) | | |
| 9 | (37) | | |
| 10 | (36) | | |
| 11 | (35) | | |
| 12 | (37) | | |
| 13 | (37) | | |
| 14 | (38) | | |
| 15 | (36) | | |
| 16 | (37) | | |
| 17 | (35) | | |
| 18 | (37) | | |
| 19 | (42) | | |
| 20 | (38) | | |
| 21 | (35) | | |
| 22 | (35) | | |
| 23 | (35) | | |
| 24 | (39) | | |
| 25 | (42) | | |
| 26 | (36) | | |
| 27 | (39) | | |
| 28 | (36) | | |
| 29 | (37) | | |
| 30 | (42) | | |
| 31 | (37) | | |
| 32 | (35) | | |
| 33 | (37) | | |
| 34 | (37) | | |
| 35 | (36) | | |
| 36 | (36) | | |
| 37 | (36) | | |
| 38 | (36) | | |
| 39 | (35) | | |
| 40 | (38) | | |
| 41 | (40) | | |
| 42 | (41) | | |

TOTALS: 1553 letters/column; 42 lines, 33 (short), 42 (long), 36.98 (average) all/part of 4 lines preserved from column, average length *34.00* letters

## Column 5 Mi 1.7b–[2.7]

[ ]

[εἴ]δωλα [α]ὐτῆς θήσ̣[ω ἀφανισμόν·_ὅ]τι ἐγ μισ̣-
[θώματος πόρνης] σ[υνήγαγεν] καὶ ἕως μι[σθώ-]
[ματος πόρνης ἐπιστρέψουσ]ιν._8 διὰ τ[οῦτ]ο
[κόψομαι καὶ θρηνήσω, πορεύσομαι] ἀνυπό[δετος]
[ ]
[ 9 ]
[ ]
[ 10 ]
[ ]
[ 11 ]
[ ]
[ ]
[ ]
[ 12 ]
[ ]
[13 ]
[ ]
[ 14 ]
[ ]
[ ]
[ 15 ]
[ 16 ]
[ ]
[ ]
[ 2.1 ]
[ ]
[ 2 ]
[ ]
[ ]
[ 3 ]
[ ]
[ ]
[ ]
[ 4 ]
[ ]
[ ]
[ ]
[ ]
[ 5 ]
[ 6 ]
[ ]
[ 7 ]

## Column 6 Mi [2.7]–3.6a

| Line | Letters | | | |
|---|---|---|---|---|
| 1 | (30) | | | |
| 2 | (30) | | ΑΘΥΝΑΝΜ | |
| 3 | (36) | | ΕΝΟΥΚΑΙΕΝΠΡΟΣΘ | |
| 4 | (34) | | ΣΤΗΣΑΝ_ΚΑΤΕΝΑ | |
| 5 | (38) | Ο | ΟΛΑΙΟΝΕΞΕΔΥΣ | |
| 6 | (36) | ΕΠΙ | ΤΑΙΠΟΛΕΜΟ | |
| 7 | (36) | | | |
| 8 | (34) | | | |
| 9 | (32) | | | |
| 10 | (33) | | | |
| 11 | (37) | | | |
| 12 | (35) | | | |
| 13 | (36) | | | |
| 14 | (35) | | | |
| 15 | (34) | | | |
| 16 | (34) | | | |
| 17 | (35) | | | |
| 18 | (35) | | | |
| 19 | (36) | | | |
| 20 | (35) | | | |
| 21 | (35) | | | |
| 22 | (35) | | | |
| 23 | (35) | | | |
| 24 | (37) | | | |
| 25 | (34) | | | |
| 26 | (36) | | | |
| 27 | (35) | | | |
| 28 | (34) | | | |
| 29 | (36) | | | |
| 30 | (36) | | | |
| 31 | (36) | | | |
| 32 | (39) | | | |
| 33 | (38) | | | |
| 34 | (35) | | | |
| 35 | (37) | | | _ _ _ _ _ _ _ |
| 36 | (35) | | | ΤΟΥΣΠΛΑ |
| 37 | (33) | | | |
| 38 | (34) | | | ΟΝ` ` |
| 39 | (34) | | | ΩΝ` ` |
| 40 | (36) | | Ν_Δ | ΥΤΟΝΥΞ` ` |
| 41 | (35) | | ΑΙΣΚΟΤΑΣΘ | ΕΙΝ` ` |
| 42 | (33) | | ΥΣΕΤΑΙΟΗΛΙΟΣ | ` ` |
| | | | ` ` ` ` ` ` ` ` ` ` ` ` | ` ` |

TOTALS: 1469 letters/column; 42 lines, 30 (short), 39 (long), 34.97 (average) all/part of 12 lines preserved from column, average length *34.83* letters

# Column 6 Mi [2.7]–3.6a

[ ]
[οἱ λόγοι μου ἠγ]άθυναν μ[ετὰ τοῦ ὀρθοῦ]
[πορευομ]ένου; 8 καὶ ἔνπροσθ[εν ὁ λαός μου εἰς ἐχ-]
[θρὸν ἀντέ]στησαν, κατένα[ντι ]
[αὐτ]ο[ῦ περιβ]όλαιον ἐξεδύσ[ατε ἐλπί-]
[δα] ἐπι[στραφήσον]ται πόλεμο[ν. 9 γυναῖκες λαοῦ]
[ ]
[ ]
[ 10 ]
[ ]
[ ]
[11 ]
[ ]
[ ]
[ 12 ]
[ ]
[ ]
[ ]
[ 13 ]
[ ]
[ ]
[ ]
[ 3.1 ]
[ ]
[ ]
[ 2 ]
[ ]
[ 3 ]
[ ]
[ ]
[ ]
[ 4 ]
[ ]
[ ]
[ἐπονηρεύσαντο ἐπιτηδεύματα αὐτῶν. ]—————— 5
[Τάδε λέγει 𐤉𐤄𐤅𐤄 ἐπὶ τοὺς προφήτας] τοὺς πλα-
[νῶντας ]
[τοῖς ὀδοῦσιν αὐτῶν καὶ ἐκήρυξαν ἐπ' αὐτ]ὸν
[εἰρήνην, καὶ ὃς οὐ δώσει ἐπὶ τὸ στόμα αὐτ]ῶν,
[καὶ ἡγίασαν ἐπ' αὐτὸν πόλεμο]ν. 6 δ[ιὰ το]ῦτο νὺξ
[ὑμεῖν ἐξ ὁράσεως, κ]αὶ σκοτασθ[ήσεται ὑμ]εῖν
[ἐκ , καὶ δ]ύσεται ὁ ἥλιος [ἐπὶ τοὺς]
[ ] [ ]

## Column 7 Mi [3.6b]–4.5

| Line | Letters | | |
|---|---|---|---|
| 1 | (33) | | |
| 2 | (34) | | |
| 3 | (35) | | |
| 4 | (33) | | |
| 5 | (36) | | |
| 6 | (36) | | |
| 7 | (33) | | |
| 8 | (35) | | |
| 9 | (34) | | |
| 10 | (34) | | |
| 11 | (32) | | |
| 12 | (33) | | |
| 13 | (32) | | |
| 14 | (34) | | |
| 15 | (33) | | |
| 16 | (32) | | |
| 17 | (34) | | |
| 18 | (30) | | |
| 19 | (35) | | |
| 20 | (33) | | |
| 21 | (35) | | |
| 22 | (33) | | |
| 23 | (31) | | |
| 24 | (35) | | |
| 25 | (34) | | |
| 26 | (32) | | |
| 27 | (33) | | |
| 28 | (33) | | |
| 29 | (35) | | |
| 30 | (34) | | |
| 31 | (34) | | ΠΟΛΛΩ |
| 32 | (33) | | ΚΡΑΝΚΑΙΣΥΝΚΟΨΟΥ |
| 33 | (34) | ΜΑΧΑ | ΝΕΙΣΑΡΟΤΡΑΚΑΙΤΑΣ |
| 34 | (33) | ΣΙΒΥ ΥΤΩΝ | ΠΑΝΑΚΑΙΟΥΜΗΑΝΘΑ |
| 35 | (31) | ΡΗΕΘΝ ΦΕΘΝΟΣΜ | ΚΑΙΟΥΜΗΜΑ |
| 36 | (33) | ΘΩΣΙΝΕΤΙΠΟΛΕΜΕΙ | ΟΝΤΑΙΑΝΗΡ |
| 37 | (34) | ΥΠΟΚΑΤΩΑΜΠΕΛΟΥΑΥ | ΥΚΗΣ |
| 38 | (33) | ΑΥ ΟΥ ΙΟΥΚΕΣΤΙΝΕ | ΟΤ ΤΟΣΤΟΜΑ |
| 39 | (33) | [paleo-Hebrew] ΝΔ Μ | ΟΤ ΠΑΝ |
| 40 | (38) | ΤΕΣΟΙΛΑ ΠΟΡΕ | ΟΥΑΥΤΩΝ |
| 41 | (35) | ΗΜΕΙΣΔΕΠΟΡΕ | [paleo-Hebrew]ΘΕΟΥ |
| 42 | (30) | ΗΜ ΝΕΙΣΤΟΝ | |

TOTALS: 1407 letters/column; 42 lines, 30 (short), 38 (long), 33.50 (average) all/part of 12 lines preserved from column, average length *33.41* letters

## Column 7 Mi [3.6b]–4.5

[ ]
[ 7 ]
[ ]
[ ]
[ 8 ]
[ ]
[ ]
[ 9 ]
[ ]
[ ]
[ 10 ]
[ ]
[ 11 ]
[ ]
[ ]
[ ]
[ ]
[ 12 ]
[ ]
[ ]
[ 4.1 ]
[ ]
[ ]
[ ]
[ 2 ]
[ ]
[ ]
[ ]
[ ]
[ ]
[3 καὶ κρινεῖ ἀνὰ μέσον λαῶν] πολλῶ[ν καὶ ἐλέγ-]``
[ξει ἔθνη ἰσχυρὰ ἕως μα]κράν, καὶ συνκόψου-``
[σιν τὰς] μαχα[ίρας αὐτῶ]ν εἰς ἄροτρα καὶ τὰς``
``σιβύ[νας α]ὐτῶν [εἰς δρέ]π̣ανα, καὶ οὐ μὴ ἀνθά-``
``ρ̣η̣ ἔθν[ος ἐ]φ’ ἔθνος μ̣[άχαιραν,] καὶ οὐ μὴ μά-``
``θωσιν ἔτι πολεμε̣ῖ̣[ν. 4 καὶ καθίσ]ονται ἀνὴρ``
``ὑπ̣οκάτω ἀμπέλου αὐ[τοῦ καὶ ὑποκάτω σ]υκῆς``
``αὐ̣[τ]οῦ, [κα]ὶ οὐκ ἔστιν ἐ̣[κφοβῶν,] ὅτ[ι] τὸ στόμα``
``𐤉𐤄[𐤅𐤄 τῶ]ν δ[υνά]μ̣[εων ἐλάλησεν.____] 5 ὅτ[ι] πάν-``
``τες ο̣ἱ̣ λ̣α̣[οὶ] πορε[ύσονται ἐν ὀνόματι θε]οῦ αὐτῶν,``
``ἡμεῖς δ̣ὲ πορε[υσόμεθα ἐν ὀνόματι 𐤉𐤄]𐤅𐤄 θεοῦ``
``ἡ̣μ[ῶ]ν̣ εἰς τὸν [αἰῶνα καὶ ''''''.]______``
``````````````[``````````````]``````````````
``````````````

## Column 8 Mi 4.6–5.4(5)a

| | | |
|---|---|---|
| | | ` ` ` ` ` ` |
| 1 | (28) | ΣΥΝΑ ` ` |
| 2 | (28) | ΕΞΩΣ ` ` |
| 3 | (31) | ΗΝΕΚΑ ΘΗΣΩ ` ` |
| 4 | (28) | ΝΕΙΣΥ ΜΑ ` ` |
| 5 | (34) | ΝΗΝΕΙΣΕΘΝΟΣΙΣΧΥΡΟΝ ` ` |
| 6 | (35) | 𐤉𐤄𐤅𐤄ΕΠΑΥΤΩΝΕΝΤΩΟΡΕΙΣΕΙ ` ` |
| 7 | (32) | ΩΣΤΟΥΑΙΩΝΟΣ______ |
| 8 | (34) | ΜΩΔΗΣΘΥΓΑΤΗΡ ` ` |
| 9 | (32) | ΙΗΑΡΧΗΗ ` ` |
| 10 | (34) | ΑΛΗΜ__ ` ` |
| 11 | (32) | ΜΗΒΑΣΙ ` ` |
| 12 | (33) | ΣΟΥΑΠΩ ` ` |
| 13 | (32) | ΝΕΣΩΣΤΙ ` ` |
| 14 | (32) | ΓΑΤΕΡΣ |
| 15 | (37) | |
| 16 | (40) | |
| 17 | (39) | |
| 18 | (35) | |
| 19 | (40) | |
| 20 | (33) | |
| 21 | (33) | |
| 22 | (35) | |
| 23 | (37) | |
| 24 | (36) | |
| 25 | (36) | |
| 26 | (36) | |
| 27 | (35) | |
| 28 | (32) | |
| 29 | (30) | |
| 30 | (28) | |
| 31 | (36) | _________________ |
| 32 | (36) | `ΚΑΙΣΥΟΙΚΟ ΦΡΑΘΑΟΛΙ ΟΣΤΟΣΤΟΥ |
| 33 | (35) | ` `ΝΑΙΕΝΧ ΥΔΑ_ΕΚΣΟΥΜΟΙΕΞ |
| 34 | (33) | ` `ΤΑΙΤΟΥΕ ΝΑΙΑΡΧ ΝΤΑΕΝΤΩΙ |
| 35 | (32) | ` `ΕΞΟΔΟΙΑΥΤΟΥΑΠΑ ΧΗΣΑΦΗΜ |
| 36 | (34) | ` `ΔΙΑΤΟΥΤΟΔΩ |
| 37 | (34) | ` `ΣΗΣΤΕΞΕΤΑΙΚΑΙ |
| 38 | (37) | ` `ΑΥΤΟΥΕΠΙΣΤΡ ΨΟΥΣΙΝ_ΕΠΙΤΟ |
| 39 | (33) | ` `ΚΑΙ ΗΣΕΤΑΙΚΑΙΠΟ ΜΑΝΕΙΕΝΙ ΧΥΙ𐤉 |
| 40 | (35) | ` `ΚΑΙΕΝΤΗΕΠΑΡΣΕΙΟΝΟΜΑΤΟΣ 𐤉𐤄𐤅𐤄ΘΕΟΥ |
| 41 | (33) | ` `ΚΑΙΕΠΙΣΤΡΑΦΗΣΟΝΤΑΙΟΤΙΝΥΝΜΕΓΑΛ |
| 42 | (31) | ` `ΣΟΝΤΑΙΕΩΣΠΕΡΑΤΩΝΤΗΣΓΗΣ_ΚΑΙΕΣ |
| | | ` ` ` ` ` ` ` ` ` ` ` ` ` ` ` ` ` ` ` ` ` ` ` ` ` ` ` ` ` ` ` ` |

TOTALS: 1416 letters/column; 42 lines, 28 (short), 40 (long), 33.71 (average) all/part of 26 lines preserved from column, average length *32.84* letters

## Column 8 Mi 4.6–5.4(5)a

[`````````````````````````````]```````
[6 Ἐν τῇ ἡμέρᾳ ἐκείνῃ, λέγει 𐤉𐤄𐤅𐤄,] συνά-``
[ξω τὴν ἐκτεθλιμμένην, καὶ τὴν] ἐξωσ-``
[μένην ἀθροίσω καὶ] ἣν ἐκά[κωσα· 7 καὶ] θήσω``
[τὴν ἐκτεθλιμμένη]ν εἰς ὑ[πόλειμ]μα``
[καὶ τὴν ἐκπεπιεσμέ]νην εἰς ἔθνος ἰσχυρόν,``
[καὶ βασιλεύσει] 𐤉𐤄𐤅𐤄 ἐπ' αὐτῶν ἐν τῷ ὄρει σει-``
[ων ἀπὸ τοῦ νῦν καὶ ἕ]ως τοῦ αἰῶνος.______`` 8
[Καὶ σύ, πύργος ποιμνίου αὐχ]μώδης, θυγάτηρ``
[σειων, ἕως σοῦ ἥξει καὶ ἐλεύσετα]ι ἡ ἀρχὴ ἡ``
[πρώτη, βασιλεία τῇ θυγατρὶ ιερουσ]αλημ.__`` 9
[Νῦν ἵνα τί ''''''''''''' κακά;] μὴ βασι-``
[λεὺς οὐκ ἔστιν σοι, ἐὰν ὁ σύμβουλός] σου ἀπώ-``
[λετο, ὅτι κατεκράτησάν σου ὠδῖ]νες ὡς τι-``
[κτούσης; 10 '''''' καὶ '''''', θύ]γατερ σ[ει-]
[ων, ]
[ ]
[ ]
[ 11 ]
[ ]
[ ]
[12 ]
[ ]
[ 13 ]
[ ]
[ ]
[ ]
[ ]
[ 14(5.1) ]
[ ]
[ ]
[ ισραηλ.___]________________ 5.1(2)
`Καὶ σύ, οἶκο[ς '''''' ε]φραθα, ὀλι[γ]οστὸς τοῦ [εἶ-]
``ναι ἐν χ[ιλιάσιν ιο]υδα· Ἐκ σοῦ μοι ἐξ[ελεύσε-]
``ται τοῦ ε[ἶ]ναι ἄρχ[ο]ντα ἐν τῷ ι[σραηλ, καὶ αἱ]
``ἔξοδοι αὐτοῦ ἀπ' ἀ[ρ]χῆς ἀφ' ἡμ[ερῶν αἰῶνος.]
``2(3) διὰ τοῦτο δώ[σει αὐτοὺς ἕως καιροῦ τικτού-]
``σης τέξεται, καὶ [οἱ ἐπίλοιποι τῶν ἀδελφῶν]
``αὐτοῦ ἐπιστρ[έ]ψουσιν ἐπὶ το[ὺς υἱοὺς ισραηλ.]
``3(4) καὶ [στ]ήσεται καὶ πο[ι]μανεῖ ἐν ἰ[σ]χύι 𐤉[𐤄𐤅𐤄]
``καὶ ἐν τῇ ἐπάρσει ὀνόματος 𐤉𐤄𐤅𐤄 θεοῦ [αὐτοῦ]
``καὶ ἐπιστραφήσονται· ὅτι νῦν μεγαλ[υνθή-]
``σονται ἕως περάτων τῆς γῆς._4(5) καὶ ἔσ[ται]
`````````````````````````````````````[``]
`````````````````````````````````````

## Column 9 Mi 5.4(5)b–[6.4]

` ` ` ` ` ` ` ` ` ` ` ` ` ` ` ` ` ` `

| Line | Letters | Text |
|---|---|---|
| 1 | (33) | _ΑΣΣΟΥΡΟΤΙΕΛΘΗ Σ |
| 2 | (34) | ΝΚΑΙΟΤΙΕΠΙΒΗΕΠΙΤΑΣΒΑΡ |
| 3 | (33) | ` ` ΕΠΕΓΕΡΟΥΜΕΝΕΠΑΥΤΟΝΕΠΤΑΠ |
| 4 | (31) | ` ` ΟΚΤΩΑΡΧΟΝΤΑΣΑΝΘΡΩΠΩ |
| 5 | (30) | ` ` ΣΙΝΤΗΝΓΗΝΑΣΣΟΥΡΕΝΡ |
| 6 | (33) | ` ` ΓΗΝΝΕΒΡΩΔΕΝΠΑΡΑΞ |
| 7 | (32) | ` ` ΑΣΣΟΥΡΟΤΙΕΛΘΗΕΙΣΤ |
| 8 | (33) | ` ` ΕΠΙΒΗΕΙΣΤΑΟΡΙΑ |
| 9 | (27) | ` ` ΛΟΙΠΟΝΙΑΚΩΒ |
| 10 | (27) | ` ` ΩΣΔΡΟΣΟΣ |
| 11 | (32) | ` ` ΧΟ |
| 12 | (32) | |
| 13 | (34) | |
| 14 | (31) | |
| 15 | (37) | |
| 16 | (31) | |
| 17 | (30) | |
| 18 | (34) | |
| 19 | (34) | |
| 20 | (32) | |
| 21 | (34) | |
| 22 | (33) | |
| 23 | (33) | |
| 24 | (35) | |
| 25 | (34) | |
| 26 | (31) | |
| 27 | (34) | |
| 28 | (32) | |
| 29 | (32) | |
| 30 | (32) | |
| 31 | (32) | |
| 32 | (35) | |
| 33 | (37) | |
| 34 | (37) | |
| 35 | (33) | |
| 36 | (36) | |
| 37 | (32) | |
| 38 | (33) | |
| 39 | (33) | |
| 40 | (30) | |
| 41 | (35) | |
| 42 | (34) | |

TOTALS: 1377 letters/column; 42 lines, 27 (short), 37 (long), 32.79 (average) all/part of 11 lines preserved from column, average length *31.36* letters

## Column 9 Mi 5.4(5)b–[6.4]

[` ` ` ` ` ` ` ` ` ` ]` ` ` ` ` ` ` ` ` ` ` ` ` ` ` ` ` ` [` ` ` ` ` ` ` ]
1 [αὕτη εἰρήνη·]_Ασσουρ ὅτι ἔλθη [εἰ]ς [τὴν γῆν]
2 [ἡμῶ]ν καὶ ὅτι ἐπιβῇ ἐπὶ τὰς βάρ[εις ἡμῶν, καὶ]
3 ` `ἐπεγεροῦμεν ἐπ᾽ αὐτὸν ἑπτὰ π[οιμένας καὶ]
4 ` `ὀκτὼ ἄρχοντας ἀνθρώπω[ν. 5(6) καὶ ποιμανοῦ-]
5 ` `σιν τὴν γῆν ασσουρ ἐν ῥ[ομφαίᾳ καὶ τὴν]
6 ` `γῆν νεβρωδ ἐν παραξ[ιφι' '· καὶ ῥύσεται ἐξ ]
7 ` `Ασσουρ, ὅτι ἔλθη εἰς τ[ὴν γῆν ἡμῶν καὶ ὅτι]
8 ` `ἐπιβῇ εἰς τὰ ὅρια [ἡμῶν.___6(7) Καὶ ἔσται κατά-]
9 ` `λοιπον ιακωβ [ἐν μέσῳ λαῶν πολλῶν]
10 ` `ὡς δρόσος [παρὰ 𐤉𐤄𐤅𐤄, ὡς ' ' ' ' ' ' ἐπὶ]
11 ` `χό[ρτον, ὃς οὐκ ' ' ' ' ' ' ' ' ' ἀνδρὶ καὶ οὐ μὴ]
12 [ 7(8) ]
13 [ ]
14 [ ]
15 [ ]
16 [ ]
17 [ 8(9) ]
18 [ ]
19 [ 9(10) ]
20 [ ]
21 [10(11) ]
22 [ ]
23 [ ]
24 [ 11(12) ]
25 [ ]
26 [ 12(13) ]
27 [ ]
28 [ ]
29 [ 13(14) ]
30 [ 14(15) ]
31 [ ]
32 [ ]
33 [6.1 ]
34 [ ]
35 [ 2 ]
36 [ ]
37 [ ]
38 [ 3 ]
39 [ 4 ]
40 [ ]
41 [ ]
42 [ ]

## Column 13 Na [1.5]–[2.5a]

| Line | Letters | Text |
|---|---|---|
| 1 | (36) | |
| 2 | (33) | |
| 3 | (32) | |
| 4 | (34) | |
| 5 | (33) | |
| 6 | (36) | |
| 7 | (35) | |
| 8 | (32) | |
| 9 | (37) | |
| 10 | (31) | |
| 11 | (35) | |
| 12 | (34) | |
| 13 | (36) | |
| 14 | (34) | |
| 15 | (33) | |
| 16 | (32) | |
| 17 | (36) | |
| 18 | (33) | |
| 19 | (31) | |
| 20 | (27) | |
| 21 | (34) | ΗΞΩ |
| 22 | (36) | _ΟΥΣΠΑ ΗΣΕΤ |
| 23 | (35) | ΞΟΙΚΟΥΘ Υ |
| 24 | (37) | |
| 25 | (37) | |
| 26 | (35) | |
| 27 | (35) | |
| 28 | (34) | |
| 29 | (34) | |
| 30 | (35) | |
| 31 | (34) | |
| 32 | (35) | |
| 33 | (33) | |
| 34 | (34) | |
| 35 | (34) | |
| 36 | (36) | |
| 37 | (34) | |
| 38 | (32) | |
| 39 | (34) | |
| 40 | (35) | |
| 41 | (29) | |
| 42 | (33) | |

TOTALS: 1425 letters/column; 42 lines, 27 (short), 37 (long), 33.93 (average) all/part of 3 lines preserved from column, average length *35.00* letters

## Column 13 Na [1.5]–[2.5a]

[ 5 ]
[ 6 ]
[ ]
[ ]
[ 7 ]
[ ]
[ 8 ]
[ ]
[ ]
[ 9 ]
[ ]
[ 10 ]
[ ]
[ ]
[ 11 ]
[ ]
[12 ]
[ ]
[ 13 ]
[ καὶ τοὺς δεσ-]
[μούς σου διαρρ]ήξω. [14 καὶ ἐντελεῖται ἐπὶ σοί]
[𐤉𐤄𐤅𐤄,]_οὐ σπα̣[ρ]ή̣σετ[αι ἐκ τοῦ ὀνόματός σου ἔτι.]
[ἐ]ξ̣ οἴκου θ[εο]ῦ̣ [σου ἐξολεθρεύσω γλυπτὸν καὶ]
[ ]
[2.1(1.15) ]
[ ]
[ ]
[ ]
[ 2 ]
[ ]
[ ]
[ 3 ]
[ ]
[ ]
[ 4 ]
[ ]
[ ]
[ ]
[ 5 ]
[ ]
[ ]
[ δραμοῦν-]

## Column 14 Na 2.5b–[3.4]

| Line | Letters | Text |
|---|---|---|
| 1 | (27) | ΤΑΙΜΝΗΣΘΗΣΕΤΑΙΔΥΝΑΣΤΩΝΑΥΤΟΥ |
| 2 | (31) | ΘΕΝΗΣΟΥΣΙΝΕΝΤΑΙΣΠΟΡΕΙΑ ΣΑΥΤΩΝ |
| 3 | (35) | ΑΙΤΑΧΥΝΟΥΣΙΝΕΠΙΤΑΤΕΙΧΗΚΑΙΕΤΟΙΜΑΣΕ |
| 4 | (33) | ΟΕΠΙΚΑΛΥΜΜΑ_ _ _ _ _ _ _ _ _ _ _ _ _ _ _ _ _ _ _ _ _ |
| 5 | (33) | Α ΤΩΝΠΟΤΑΜΩΝΗΝΟΙΧΘΗΣΑΝΚΑΙΟΝΑ |
| 6 | (29) | ΛΕΥΘΗΚΑΙΗΛΑΜΠΗΝΗΑΠΕΚ ΛΥΦΘ |
| 7 | (32) | ΗΚΑΙΑΙΑΒΡΑΙΑΥΤΗΣΑΓ ΜΕΝ ΙΩ |
| 8 | (35) | ΕΡΩΝΑΠΟΦΘΕΓΓ ΜΕΝ |
| 9 | (35) | ΝΙ ΥΗΚΟΛΥΜ Σ |
| 10 | (37) | ΑΥΤΟΙΦΕΥ Η |
| 11 | (34) | ΤΡΕΦΩ ΟΝ |
| 12 | (31) | ΝΤΟΧ Ι |
| 13 | (34) | Ι |
| 14 | (33) | . |
| 15 | (36) | |
| 16 | (35) | |
| 17 | (32) | |
| 18 | (39) | |
| 19 | (31) | |
| 20 | (37) | |
| 21 | (33) | |
| 22 | (27) | |
| 23 | (33) | . |
| 24 | (30) | ΝΔΡΑΝ |
| 25 | (30) | ΕΛΕΓΕΙ |
| 26 | (27) | ΥΣΩΕΝ |
| 27 | (33) | ΤΑ Σ |
| 28 | (32) | ΘΡΕ |
| 29 | (26) | |
| 30 | (37) | |
| 31 | (35) | |
| 32 | (37) | |
| 33 | (34) | |
| 34 | (35) | |
| 35 | (34) | ΣΚΑΙ |
| 36 | (33) | ΥΣ |
| 37 | (31) | ΣΚΑΙ |
| 38 | (32) | ΘΕ |
| 39 | (32) | |
| 40 | (27) | |
| 41 | (29) | |
| 42 | (28) | |

TOTALS: 1364 letters/column; 42 lines, 26 (short), 39 (long), 32.47 (average) all/part of 24 lines preserved from column, average length *32.25* letters

# Column 14 Na 2.5b–[3.4]

ται. 6 μνησθήσεται δυναστῶν αὐτοῦ,
[ἀσ]θενήσουσιν ἐν ταῖς πορεία[ι]ς αὐτῶν
[κ]αὶ ταχυνοῦσιν ἐπὶ τὰ τείχη καὶ ἑτοιμάσε[ι]
[τ]ὸ ἐπικάλυμμα.———————————— 7
[Πύλ]α[ι] τῶν ποταμῶν ἠνοίχθησαν, καὶ ὁ να[ὸς]
[ἐσα]λεύθη, 8 καὶ ἡ λαμπήνη ἀπεκ[α]λύφθ[η,]
[΄΄΄]η, καὶ αἱ ἅβραι αὐτῆς ἀγ[ό]μεν[α]ι ὡ[ς φω-]
[νὴ περιστ]ερῶν ἀποφθεγγ[ο]μέν[ων ἐπὶ τὴν καρ-]
[δίαν αὐτῶν. 9 καὶ] νι[νε]υη κολυμ[βήθρα ὕδατο]ς
[΄΄΄΄΄΄΄΄΄ ΄΄΄΄΄΄΄΄, καὶ] αὐτοὶ φεύ[γουσιν. στ]ῆ-
[τε, στῆτε, καὶ οὐκ ἦν ἐπισ]τρέφω[ν]. 10 διήρπαζ]ον
[τὸ ἀργύριον, διήρπαζο]ν τὸ χ[ρυσίον, κα]ὶ
[ ]ι
[ 11 ].
[ ]
[ ]
[ ]
[ 12 ]
[ ]
[ ]
[ 13 ]
[ ]
[ ].
[΄΄΄΄΄΄ ΄΄΄΄΄΄ αὐτοῦ καὶ τὴν μά]νδραν
[αὐτοῦ ἁρπαγῆς. 14 ἰδοὺ ἐγὼ πρὸς σ]έ, λέγει
[𐅃𐅃 τῶν δυνάμεων, καὶ ἐκκα]ύσω ἐν
[καπνῷ τὸ ἅρμα αὐτῆς, καὶ τοὺς λέον]τά[ς] σ[ου]
[καταφάγεται ῥομφαία, καὶ ἐξολε]θρε[ύσω]
[ ]
[ ]
[3.1 ]
[ 2 ]
[ ]
[ 3 ἀνα-]
[βαίνοντος καὶ ΄΄΄΄΄΄΄΄΄΄ ῥομφαία]ς καὶ
[΄΄΄΄΄΄΄΄΄΄ ΄΄΄΄΄΄΄΄΄΄΄΄ καὶ πλήθο]υς
[τραυματίου ΄΄΄ ΄΄΄΄΄΄΄ ΄΄΄΄΄΄΄]ς· καὶ
[οὐκ ἦν πέρας ΄΄΄΄΄΄΄΄΄΄΄, καὶ ἀσ]θε-
[νήσουσιν ]
[ 4 ]
[ ]
[ ]

## Column 15 Na [3.4]–[3.18]

| Line | Letters | Text |
|---|---|---|
| 1 | (32) | |
| 2 | (32) | |
| 3 | (34) | |
| 4 | (33) | |
| 5 | (29) | |
| 6 | (28) | |
| 7 | (34) | Ι Θ Η Σ Ω |
| 8 | (34) | ˋ ˋ Σ Ε Α Π Ο Π |
| 9 | (30) | ˋ ˋ Π Ω Ρ Η Κ Ε |
| 10 | (28) | ˋ ˋ Θ Ε Ν Ζ Η Τ Η Σ Ω Π |
| | | —— |
| 11 | (30) | ˋ Μ Η Α Γ Α Θ Υ Ν Ε Ι Σ Υ Π |
| 12 | (28) | ˋ ˋ Σ Α Ε Ν Π Ο Τ Α Μ Ο Ι Σ |
| 13 | (38) | Ι Σ Χ Υ Σ Θ Α Λ Α Σ Σ Α Υ Δ Ω |
| 14 | (34) | Ι Σ Χ Υ Σ Α Υ Η Σ Κ Α Ι Α Ι Γ |
| 15 | (33) | Φ Ο Υ Δ Κ Α Ι Λ Ι Β Υ |
| 16 | (33) | Κ Α Ι Γ Ε Α Υ Τ Η Ε Ι Σ Α Π Ο Ι |
| 17 | (33) | Μ Α Λ Ω Α Κ Α Ι Γ Ε Τ |
| 18 | (31) | Η Ν Π Α Σ Ω |
| 19 | (36) | Τ Η Σ Β Α Λ Ο Υ |
| 20 | (35) | Ν Ε Σ Α Υ Η |
| 21 | (33) | Α Ι Γ Ε Μ Ε Θ |
| 22 | (34) | Ε Σ Υ Ζ Η Τ |
| 23 | (33) | Ν Τ Α Τ Α |
| 24 | (35) | Σ Κ Ο Π Σ Α Λ Ε Υ Θ |
| 25 | (33) | ˋ ˋ Σ Τ Ο Μ Ν Τ Ο Σ |
| 26 | (31) | Ν |
| 27 | (33) | Α Ν Ο Χ Θ |
| 28 | (33) | Π Υ Ρ Τ Υ Σ Μ Ο Χ |
| 29 | (34) | Ι Σ Ε Α Υ Τ |
| 30 | (35) | Ε Ι Σ Π Η Λ |
| 31 | (36) | Λ Ι Ν Θ Ε Ο Υ |
| 32 | (36) | Ε Θ Ρ Ε Υ Σ Ε Ι Σ Ε Ρ Ο Μ Φ |
| 33 | (31) | Κ Α Τ Α Β Α Ρ Υ Ν Θ Η Τ Ι Ω |
| 34 | (34) | Θ Η Τ Ι Ω Σ Α Κ Ρ Ι Σ _ Ε Π Λ |
| 35 | (34) | Ω Σ Τ Ο Υ Σ Α Σ Τ Ε Ρ Α Σ Τ |
| 36 | (33) | Α Ι Ε Ξ Ε Π Ε |
| 37 | (33) | Ο Χ Λ |
| 38 | (30) | |
| 39 | (28) | |
| 40 | (30) | |
| 41 | (33) | |
| 42 | (33) | |

TOTALS: 1370 letters/column; 42 lines, 28 (short), 38 (long), 32.61 (average) all/part of 31 lines preserved from column, average length *33.16* letters

## Column 15 Na [3.4]–[3.18]

[ 5 ]
[ ]
[ ]
[ ]
[ 6 ]
[ ]
[κα]ὶ θήσω [σε ὡς '''''', 7 καὶ ἔσται πᾶς ὁ ὁρῶν]
``σε ἀποπ[ηδήσεται ἀπὸ σοῦ καὶ ἐρεῖ τεταλαι-]
``πώρηκε[ν νινευη· τίς στενάξει αὐτῇ; πό-]
``θεν ζητήσω π[αρακαλοῦντάς σοι;___ 8]
`Μὴ ἀγαθύνεις ὑπ[ὲρ νω αμων, ἡ κατοικοῦ-]
``σα ἐν ποταμοῖς, [ὕδωρ κύκλῳ αὐτῆς, ἧς ]
ἰσχὺς θάλασσα, ὕδω[ρ τὸ τεῖχος αὐτῆς, 9 αἰθιοπία, ἡ]
ἰσχὺς αὐ[τ]ῆς καὶ αἴγ[υπτος, καὶ οὐκ ἔστιν πέ-]
[ρας· ]φουδ καὶ λίβυ[ες ἐγένοντο '''''' σου.] 10
καί γε αὐτὴ εἰς ἀποι[κίαν, ἐπορεύθη ἐν αἰχ-]
μαλω[σί]α, καί γε τ[ὰ νήπια αὐτῆς '''''''''']
[ἐπὶ κεφαλ]ὴν πασῶ[ν ὁδῶν , καὶ ἐπὶ τοὺς ἐν-]
[δόξους αὐ]τῆς βαλοῦ[σιν κλῆρον, καὶ πάντες οἱ]
[μεγιστᾶ]νες αὐ[τ]ῆ[ς '''''''''''' ἐν χειροπέ-]
[δαις.___ 11 κ]αί γε μεθ[υσθήσῃ, ἔσῃ '''''''''']
['''''', καί γ]ε σὺ ζητ[ήσεις '''''''''' ἐξ]
[ἐχθροῦ. 12 πά]ντα τὰ [ὀχυρώματά σου συκαῖ σὺν]
σκοπ[οῖς· ἐὰν] σαλευθ[ῶσιν καὶ πεσοῦνται ἐπὶ]
``στόμ[α ἔσθο]ντος. [13 ἰδοὺ ὁ λαός σου γυναῖκες]
[ἐ]ν [μέσῳ σου· τοῖς ἐχθροῖς σου ἀνοιγόμε-]
[ναι] ἀνο[ι]χθ[ήσονται πύλαι τῆς γῆς σου, ἔφα-]
[γεν] πῦρ τ[ο]ὺς μοχ[λούς σου. 14 ὕδ'' '''''''''']
[ὕδρευσα]ι σεαυτ[ῇ, '''''''' τὰ ὀχυρώματά]
[σου, ἐλθὲ] εἰς πηλ[ὸν καὶ '''''' '''''''''''',]
[κράτησον π]λινθε[ί]ου. [15 ἐκεῖ φάγεταί σε πῦρ, ἐξο-]
[λ]εθρεύσει σε ῥομφ[αία, φάγεταί σε ὡς βροῦχος,]
καταβαρύνθητι ὡ[ς βροῦχος, καταβαρύν-]
θητι ὡς ἀκρίς._16 Ἐπλ[ήθυνας '''''''''''' σου]
ὡς τοὺς ἀστέρας τ[οῦ οὐρανοῦ· βροῦχος ὥρμη-]
[σεν κ]αὶ ἐξεπε[τάσθη. 17 '''''''''''''''',]
[''''''''] ὄχλ[ος '''''''''''''''''''']
[ ]
[ ]
[ 18 ]
[ ]
[ ]

## Column 16 Na [3.18]–Ha 1.11a

| Line | Letters | Text |
|---|---|---|
| 1 | (28) | |
| 2 | (36) | |
| 3 | (37) | |
| 4 | (36) | |
| 5 | (31) | |
| 6 | (35) | |
| 7 | (35) | |
| 8 | (35) | |
| 9 | (35) | |
| 10 | (35) | |
| 11 | (35) | |
| 12 | (35) | |
| 13 | (33) | |
| 14 | (36) | |
| 15 | (36) | |
| 16 | (33) | |
| 17 | (39) | |
| 18 | (36) | |
| 19 | (37) | |
| 20 | (36) | |
| 21 | (35) | |
| 22 | (35) | Α |
| 23 | (33) | ΑΣΑΤΕΟΤΙΕΡ ˋˋ |
| 24 | (33) | ΑΙΣΥΜΩΝΟΥ ˋˋ |
| 25 | (35) | ΗΘΗ_ΟΤΙΙΔΟΥΕΓΩ ˋˋ |
| 26 | (34) | ΤΟΕΘΝΟΣΤΟΠΙΚΡΟΝ ˋˋ |
| 27 | (33) | ΕΥΟΜΕ ΝΕΙ ΤΑΠΛΑ ˋˋ |
| 28 | (34) | ΛΗΡΟΝΟ |
| 29 | (31) | _ΘΑΜΒΟΣ |
| 30 | (34) | ΜΑΑΥΤΟΥ |
| 31 | (38) | Ι_ΚΑΙΚΟΥΦ |
| 32 | (33) | ΤΟΥΚΑΙΟΞΥΤ |
| 33 | (37) | ΡΑΣΚΑΙΟΡΜΗ |
| 34 | (34) | ΠΕΙΣΑΥΤΟΥΠΩΡΡ |
| 35 | (34) | ΣΘΗΣΟΝΤΑΙΩΣΑ |
| 36 | (34) | ΑΓΕΙΝ_ ΑΝΤΑΕΙΣΑΔΙΚΙΑΝΗΞΕΙ |
| 37 | (32) | ˋˋ ΤΟΥΠΡΟΣΩΠΟΥΑΥΤΩΝΚΑΥΣΩΝ |
| 38 | (33) | ˋˋ ΩΣΑΜΜΟΝΑΙΧΜΑΛΩΣΙΑΝ_ΚΑΙΑΥΤ |
| 39 | (34) | ˋˋ ΕΥ ΠΑΙΞΕΙΚΑΙΤΥΡΑΝΝΟΙΓ |
| 40 | (31) | ˋˋ ΤΟΣΕ ΣΠΑΝΟΧΥΡΩΜΑΕΝΠΑΙ |
| 41 | (31) | ˋˋ ΑΛΕΙΧΩΜΑΚΑΙΣΥΝΑΗΜΨΕΤ |
| 42 | (35) | ˋˋ ΔΙΕΛΕΥΣΕΤΑΙΠΝΕΥΜΑΚΑΙΠΑΡ |
| | | ˋˋˋˋˋˋˋˋˋˋˋˋˋˋˋˋˋˋˋˋˋˋˋˋˋˋˋ |

TOTALS: 1442 letters/column; 42 lines, 28 (short), 39 (long), 34.33 (average) all/part of 21 lines preserved from column, average length *33.71* letters

# Column 16 Na [3.18]–Ha 1.11a

[ ]
[ ]
[ ]
[ ]
[ ]
[---------------------------------]
[---------------------------------]
[---------------------------------]
[---------------------------------]
[---------------------------------]
[---------------------------------]
[---------------------------------]
[1.1 ]
[ ]
[2 ]
[3 ]
[ ]
[ 4 ]
[ ]
[ ]
[ ]
[ 5 ]. α[ ]
[καὶ '''''', καὶ '''''', θαυμ]άσατε, ὅτι ἔρ-``
[γον '''''''''' ἐν ταῖς ἡμέρ]αις ὑμῶν. οὐ``
[μὴ πιστεύσητε ὅτι ἐκδιηγ]ηθῇ._6 ὅτι ἰδοὺ ἐγὼ``
[ἐγείρω τοὺς χαλδαίους,] τὸ ἔθνος τὸ πικρὸν``
[καὶ τὸ ταχινὸν τὸ πορ]ευόμε[νο]ν εἰ[ς] τὰ πλά-``
[τη τῆς γῆς τοῦ κατακ]ληρονο[μῆσαι σκηνώμα-]
[τα οὐκ αὐτῷ·]_7 θάμβος [καὶ φοβερὸς αὐτός,]
[ἐξ αὐτοῦ τὸ κρί]μα αὐτοῦ [ καὶ τὸ λῆμμα αὐτοῦ ]
[ἐξελεύσετα]ι·_8 καὶ κουφ[ότεροι ὑπὲρ παρδάλεις]
[οἱ ἵπποι αὐ]τοῦ καὶ ὀξύτ[εροι ὑπὲρ τοὺς λύ-]
[κους ἑσπέ]ρας· καὶ ὁρμή[σουσιν οἱ ἱππεῖς αὐτοῦ]
[καὶ οἱ ἱπ]πεῖς αὐτοῦ πώρρ[ωθεν ἐλεύσονται]
[καὶ πετα]σθήσονται ὡς ἀ[ετὸς '''''''' τοῦ]
[φ]αγεῖν._[9 π]άντα εἰς ἀδικίαν ἥξει, ['''''''']
``τοῦ προσώπου αὐτῶν καύσων, [καὶ συνάξει]
``ὡς ἄμμον αἰχμαλωσίαν._10 καὶ αὐτ[ὸς ἐν βασι-]
``[λ]εῦ[σιν ἐν]παίξει, καὶ τύραννοι γ[έλως αὐτῷ, ]
``[αὐ]τὸς ε[ἰ]ς πᾶν ὀχύρωμα ἐνπαί[ξεται καὶ]
``[β]αλεῖ χῶμα καὶ συνλήμψετ[αι αὐτό. 11 τότε]
``διελεύσεται πνεῦμα καὶ παρ[ελεύσεται καὶ]
`````````````````````````````[``````````]
`````````````````````````````

## Column 17 Ha [1.11b]–2.8a

| Line | Letters | Text |
|---|---|---|
| 1 | (35) | |
| 2 | (34) | |
| 3 | (36) | |
| 4 | (35) | |
| 5 | (33) | |
| 6 | (28) | |
| 7 | (32) | |
| 8 | (34) | |
| 9 | (33) | ΗΣΘΑΛΛΑ |
| 10 | (29) | ΤΑΗΓΟΥΜΕΝΟΝ |
| 11 | (34) | ΑΝΕΣΠΑΣΕΝ_ΚΑΙΕΣΥΡΕΝ |
| 12 | (34) | ΦΙΒΛΗΣΤΡΩΑΥΤΟΥΚΑΙΣΥΝΗΓΑ |
| 13 | (34) | ΣΑΓΗΝΗΑΥΤΟΥ_ΔΙΑΤΟΥΤΟΕΥ |
| 14 | (36) | ΙΚΑΙΧΑΡΕΙΤΑΙ_ΔΙΑΤΟΥΤΟΘΥΣΕΙ |
| 15 | (33) | ΣΤΡΩΑΥΤΟΥΚΑΙΘΥΜΙΑΣΕΙΤΗΣΑ |
| 16 | (33) | ΟΥΟ ΕΝΑΥΤΟΙΣΕΛΙΠΑΝΘΗΑΡΤΟΣ |
| 17 | (36) | ΤΟΒ ΩΜΑΑΥΤΟΥΣΤΕΡΕΟΝ_ΕΙΔΙΑΤΟΥ |
| 18 | (33) | ΩΣΕΙΜΑΧΑΙΡΑΝΑΥΤΟΥΚΑΙΔΙΑΠΑΝ |
| 19 | (39) | ΝΕΘΝΗΟΥΦΕΙΣΕΤΑΙ_ _ _ _ _ _ _ _ _ |
| 20 | (37) | ΜΟΥΣΤΗΣ ΚΑΙΣΤΗ |
| 21 | (30) | ΑΣΚΑΙΑΠΟΣΚΟΠΕΥΣΩΙΔ |
| 22 | (32) | ΝΕΜΟΙΚΑΙΤΙΑΠΟΚΡΙΘ |
| 23 | (32) | _ΚΑΙΑΠΕΚΡΙΘΗΜΟΙ |
| 24 | (36) | ΙΟΡΑΣΙΝΚΑΙΕΚΦΑΝ Ν |
| 25 | (33) | ΗΑΝΑΓΕΙΝΩΣΚΩΝ Ι |
| 26 | (37) | ΑΙΡΟΝΚΑΙΕΝΦΑΝΗΣΕΤ |
| 27 | (40) | ΙΑΨΕΥΣΕΤΑΙ_ _ΕΑΝΣΤΡΑΓ |
| 28 | (38) | ΤΟΝΟΤΙΕΡΧΟΜΕΝΟΣΗ |
| 29 | (35) | ΙΔ ΣΚΟΤΙΑΟΥΚΕΥΘΕΙΑΨΥΧΗΑΥΤΟΥ |
| 30 | (34) | ΚΑΙΟΣΕΝΠΙΣΤΕΙΑΥΤΟΥΖΗΣΕΤ |
| 31 | (41) | .ΟΣΑΝΗΡΑΛΑΖΩΝΚΑΙΟΥΓ |
| 32 | (36) | ΚΑΘΩΣΟΑΔΗΣΨΥΧΗ |
| 33 | (35) | ΤΟΣΟΥΚΕΝΠΙΠΛΑΜ |
| 34 | (33) | ΤΟΝΠΑΝΤΑΤΑΕΘΝΗΚΑΙ |
| 35 | (37) | ΑΘΡΟΙ ΤΟΝΠΑΝΤΑΣΤΟΥΣΛΑ Σ_ΟΥΧΙ |
| 36 | (34) | ΤΑΥΤΑΠΑΝ ΠΑΡΑΒΟΛΗΝΚ ΟΥΛΗΨΕ |
| 37 | (36) | ΚΑΙΠΡΟΒΛ ΑΔΙΗΓΗΣΙΣΑΥΤΟΥΚΑ ΕΙΟΥΑΙΟ |
| 38 | (32) | ΠΛΗΘΥΝΩΝΟΥΚΑΥΤΩΚ ΑΡΥΝΩΝΕΦΕΑΤΟΝ |
| 39 | (35) | ΠΑΧΟΣΠΗΛΟΥ_ΟΥΧΙΕΞΑΙ ΣΑΝΑΣΤΗΣΟΝΤΑΙ |
| 40 | (36) | ΔΑΚΝΟΝΤΕΣΣΕΚΑΙΕΓΝΗ ΙΝΟΙΣΑΛΕΥΟΝΤΕΣ |
| 41 | (39) | ΣΕΚΑΙΕΣΗΕΙΣΔΙΑΡΠΑΓΑΣΑΥΤ ΟΤΙΕΣ ΥΛΕΥΣΑΣ |
| 42 | (34) | ΕΘΝΗΠΟΛΛΑΚΑΙΣΚΥΛΕΥ ΝΤΕΣΟΙ |

TOTALS: 1453 letters/column; 42 lines, 28 (short), 41 (long), 34.59 (average) all/part of 34 lines preserved from column, average length *34.87* letters

# Column 17 Ha [1.11b]–2.8a

[ ]
[12 ]
[ ]
[ ]
[13 ]
[ ]
[ ]
[ 14 ]
[ποιήσεις ἀνθρώπους ὡς ἰχθύας τ]ῆς θαλά[σ-]
[σης ὡς ἑρπετὰ οὐκ ἔχον]τα ἡγούμενον.
[15 πάντα ἐν ἀγκίστρῳ] ἀνέσπασεν καὶ ἔσυρεν
[αὐτὸν ἐν τῷ ἀμ]φιβλήστρῳ αὐτοῦ καὶ συνήγα-
[γεν αὐτὸν ἐν τῇ] σαγήνῃ αὐτοῦ· (16) Διὰ τοῦτο εὐ-
[φρανθήσετα]ι̣ καὶ χαρεῖται . 16 Διὰ τοῦτο θύσει
[τῷ ἀμφιβλή]στρῳ αὐτοῦ καὶ θυμιάσει τῇ σα-
[γήνῃ αὐτ]οῦ, ὅ[τι] ἐν αὐτοῖς ἐλιπάνθη ἄρτος
[αὐτοῦ, καὶ] τὸ β[ρ]ῶμα αὐτοῦ στερεόν. 17 Εἰ διὰ τοῦ-
[το ἐκκεν]ώσει μάχαιραν αὐτοῦ καὶ διὰ παν-
[τὸς ἀποκτέννει]ν ἔθνη οὐ φείσεται;___________ 2.1
[Ἐπὶ τῆς φυλακῆς] μου στήσ[ομαι] καὶ στη[λώσομαι]
[ἐπὶ πέτρ]ας καὶ ἀποσκοπεύσω ἰδ[εῖν τί]
[λαλήσει ἐ]ν ἐμοὶ καὶ τί ἀποκριθ[ῶ ἐπὶ τὸν]
[ἔλεγχόν μου.] 2 Καὶ ἀπεκρίθη μοι [𐤉𐤄𐤅𐤄 καὶ]
[εἶπεν γράψα]ι ὅρασιν καὶ ἐκφαν[ ἐπὶ πυξίω]ν,
[ὅπως τρέχ]ῃ ἀναγεινώσκων [ἐν αὐτῇ. 3 ὅτι ἔτ]ι
[ὅρασις εἰς κ]αιρὸν καὶ ἐνφανήσετ[αι εἰς πέρας]
[καὶ οὐ δ]ιαψεύσεται· Ἐὰν στραγ[γεύσηται προσδέ-]
[χου αὐ]τόν, ὅτι ἐρχόμενος ἥ[ξει καὶ οὐ ]
[ .] 4 ἰδ[οὺ] σκοτία, οὐκ εὐθεῖα ψυχὴ αὐτοῦ [ἐν]
[αὐτῷ· καὶ δί]καιος ἐν πίστει αὐτοῦ ζήσετ[αι.]
[5 ].ος ἀνὴρ ἀλαζὼν καὶ οὐ χ[ ]
[ , ὃς ἐπλάτυνεν] καθὼς ὁ ᾅδης ψυχὴ[ν αὐ-]
[τοῦ, καὶ οὗτος ὡς θάνα]τος οὐκ ἐνπιπλάμ[ενος]
[καὶ συνάξει πρὸς αὐ]τὸν πάντα τὰ ἔθνη καὶ
ἀθροί[σει πρὸς αὐ]τὸν πάντας τοὺς λα[ού]ς. 6 οὐχὶ
ταῦτα πάν[τα] παραβολὴν κ[ατ' αὐτ]οῦ λήψε[ται]
καὶ πρόβλ[ημ]α διήγησις αὐτοῦ; κα[ὶ ἐρ]εῖ οὐαὶ ὁ
πληθύνων οὐκ αὐτῷ· κ[αὶ β]αρύνων ἐφ' ἑατὸν
πάχος πηλοῦ. 7 οὐχὶ ἐξαί[φνη]ς ἀναστήσονται
δάκνοντές σε, καὶ ἐγνή[ψουσ]ιν οἱ σαλεύοντές
σε, καὶ ἔσῃ εἰς διαρπαγὰς αὐτ[οῖς;] 8 ὅτι ἐσ[κ]ύλευσας
ἔθνη πολλὰ καὶ σκυλεύ[σουσίν σε πά]ντες οἱ
[ ]

## Column 18 Ha [2.8b]–2.20

| Line | Letters | Text |
|---|---|---|
| 1 | (28) | |
| 2 | (29) | |
| 3 | (32) | |
| 4 | (32) | |
| 5 | (31) | |
| 6 | (34) | |
| 7 | (32) | |
| 8 | (32) | |
| 9 | (27) | |
| 10 | (25) | |
| 11 | (28) | |
| 12 | (28) | Μ |
| 13 | (27) | ΤΗΤ |
| 14 | (28) | ΚΕΝΟΝ |
| 15 | (27) | ΘΗΣΕΤΑΙ |
| 16 | (24) | 𐤉𐤄𐤅𐤄ΩΣ |
| 17 | (27) | ΘΑΛΑΣΣ |
| 18 | (24) | Τ ΕΙΠΛ |
| 19 | (28) | ΥΑΝΑΤΡ |
| 20 | (28) | ΟΥΕΠΙΒ |
| 21 | (27) | ΥΝΗΝΑΥ Ν_ΕΝΕΠΛΗΣ |
| 22 | (30) | ΚΔΟΞΗΣ ΙΕΚΑΙΓΕΣΥΚΑΙ |
| 23 | (30) | ΚΥΚΛΩΣΕΙΕΠΙΣΕΠΟ |
| 24 | (26) | 𐤉𐤄𐤅𐤄_ΚΑΙΕΜΕΤΟΣ |
| 25 | (31) | ΤΗΝΔΟΞΑΝΣ Υ_ΟΤΙΑΔΙΚΙΑ |
| 26 | (29) | ΨΕΙΣΕΚΑΙΤΑΛΑΙΠΩΡΙΑ |
| 27 | (25) | ΕΙΣΕΔΙΑΙΜΑΤΑΑΝ |
| 28 | (25) | ΩΝΚΑΙΑΔΙΚΙΑΝΓΗΣΠΟΛΕΩΣ |
| 29 | (25) | ΑΙΠΑΝΤΩΝΤΩΝΕΝΟΙ ΟΥΝΤΩΝΕΝ |
| 30 | (26) | Η__ΤΙΩΦΕΛΗΣΕΝΓΛΥΠΤΟΝΟΤΙ |
| 31 | (29) | ΝΑΥΤΟΟΠΛΑΣΑΣΑΥΤΟΧΩΝΕΥΜΑ |
| 32 | (29) | ΝΤΑΣΙΑΝΨΕΥΔΗΟΤΙΠΕΠΟΙΘΕΝΟ |
| 33 | (28) | ΛΑΣΑΣΕΠΙΤΟΠΛΑΣΜΑΑΥΤΟΥΕΠΑΥΤΟ |
| 34 | (28) | ΟΙΗΣΑΙΕΙΔΩΛΑΚΩΦΑ__________ |
| 35 | (25) | ΙΛΕΓΩΝΤΩΞΥΛΩΕΓΝΗΨΟΝΕΞΕ |
| 36 | (26) | ΤΩΛΙΘΩΣΙΩΠΩΝΑΥΤΟΣΦΩ |
| 37 | (29) | ΑΥΤΟΣΕΣΑΓΜΕΝΟΝΧΡΥ ΥΝ |
| 38 | (25) | ΡΟΥΝΚΑΙΠΑΝ ΠΝΕΥΜΑΟΥ |
| 39 | (28) | Ε ΤΙΝΕΝΜΕΣΩΑΥΤΟΥ__ΚΑΙΟ𐤉𐤄𐤅𐤄 |
| 40 | (25) | ΕΝΝΑΩΑΓΙΩ ΥΤΟΥΣΙΩΠΗΣΟΝΑΠΟ |
| 41 | (29) | ΠΡΟΣΩΠΟΥΑΥΤΟΥΠΑΣΑΗΓΗ ______ |
| 42 | | |

TOTALS: 1146 letters/column; 42 lines, 24 (short), 34 (long), 27.95 (average) all/part of 30 lines preserved from column, average length *27.53* letters

## Column 18 Ha [2.8b]–2.20

[ ]
[ 9 ]
[ ]
[ ]
[ 10 ]
[ ]
[ 11 ]
[ ]
[12 ]
[ ]
[13 τῶν δυνά-]
``μ[εων ; καὶ '''''''''' λαοὶ ἐν ἱκανό-]
``τητ[ι πυρός, καὶ ἔθνη ἐν ἱκανότητι]
``κενὸν [''''''''''''''''. 14 ὅτι πλησ-]
``θήσεται [ἡ γῆ τοῦ γνῶναι τὴν δόξαν]
``𐤉𐤄𐤅𐤄, ὡς [ὕδ" κατακαλύψει ἐπὶ]
``θαλάσσ[ης.________________ 15 οὐαὶ]
``τ[ῷ ποτίζοντ]ει πλ[ησίον αὐτοῦ]
['''''' '''']υ ἀνατρ[οπῇ '''''''']
['''''''' διὰ τ]οῦ ἐπιβ[λέπειν ἐπὶ]
[τὴν ἀσχημοσ]ύνην αὐ[τῶ]ν._16 Ἐνεπλήσ-``
[θης ἀτιμίας ἐ]κ δόξης, [π]ίε καί γε σὺ καὶ``
['''' '''''''''''.] κυκλώσει ἐπὶ σὲ πο-``
[τήριον δεξιᾶς] 𐤉𐤄𐤅𐤄,_καὶ ἔμετος``
[ἀτιμίας ἐπὶ] τὴν δόξαν σ[ο]υ._17 ὅτι ἀδικία ``
[λιβάνου καλύ]ψει σε, καὶ ταλαιπωρία``
[κτηνῶν ˜ πτοήσ]ει σε δι' αἵματα ἀν-``
[θρώπ]ων καὶ ἀδικίαν γῆς, πόλεως``
[κ]αὶ πάντων τῶν ἐνοι[κ]ούντων ἐν``
[αὐτ]ῇ.__18 τί ὠφέλησεν γλυπτόν, ὅτι``
[ἔγλυψε]ν αὐτὸ ὁ πλάσας αὐτὸ χώνευμα``
[καὶ φα]ντασίαν ψευδῆ, ὅτι πέποιθεν ὁ``
[π]λάσας ἐπὶ τὸ πλάσμα αὐτοῦ ἐπ' αὐτὸ ``
[π]οιῆσαι εἴδωλα κωφά.____________`` 19
[Οὐα]ὶ λέγων τῷ ξύλῳ ἔγνηψον, ἐξε-``
[γέρθητι ] τῷ λίθῳ σιωπῶν· αὐτὸς φω-``
[τιεῖ· ἰδοὺ] αὐτὸ σεσαγμένον χρυ[σο]ῦν``
[καὶ ἀργυ]ροῦν, καὶ πᾶν πνεῦμα οὐ``
[μὴ] ἔ[σ]τιν ἐν μέσῳ αὐτοῦ.__20 καὶ ὁ 𐤉𐤄𐤅𐤄``
``ἐν ναῷ ἁγίῳ [α]ὐτοῦ· σιώπησον ἀπὸ``
``προσώπου αὐτοῦ πᾶσα ἡ γῆ.[___]______``
traces of letters (erased)
``````````` [`````]```````````` [`````]``
```````````

# Column 19 Ha [3.1]–3.15a

| Line | Letters | Text | |
|---|---|---|---|
| 1 | (30) | | |
| 2 | (27) | | |
| 3 | (31) | | |
| 4 | (29) | | |
| 5 | (21) | | |
| 6 | (24) | | |
| 7 | (26) | | |
| 8 | (30) | | |
| 9 | (31) | | |
| 10 | (29) | | |
| 11 | (29) | | |
| 12 | (33) | | |
| 13 | (21) | | |
| 14 | (21) | | |
| 15 | (27) | | |
| 16 | (25) | | |
| 17 | (31) | | |
| 18 | (26) | | |
| 19 | (31) | | |
| 20 | (32) | | |
| 21 | (27) | | |
| 22 | (24) | | |
| 23 | (26) | | |
| 24 | (30) | . | |
| 25 | (27) | ΕΞΕΓ ΕΙΣΤΟΤΟ | . |
| 26 | (28) | ΡΑΒΔ ΥΣ. . . . | ΜΟΙΡΑΓΗ |
| 27 | (28) | ΣΕΤΑΙΓΗ_ΕΙΔΟΣ | ΑΝΟΡΗ |
| 28 | (28) | ΕΝΤΙΝΑ ΜΑΥ | ΚΕΝ |
| 29 | (30) | ΑΒΥΣΣΟ | |
| 30 | (29) | ΣΙΣ ΥΤΟΥ | |
| 31 | (29) | ΦΕΓΓΟΣΑΣ | |
| 32 | (30) | ΣΟΝΤΑ | |
| 33 | (29) | ΕΝΕΜ | |
| 34 | (30) | ΑΛ Η | Ν |
| 35 | (28) | ΛΑΟ | |
| 36 | (29) | ΣΟΥ | ΝΕΞΟΙΚΟΥ Ε |
| 37 | (29) | Β | ΚΕΝΩΣΑ ΘΕΜΕΛΙΟΥΣΕΩΣΤΡ |
| 38 | (28) | Χ | ΣΕΛΕ_ _ _ _ _ _ _ _ _ _ _ _ _ _ _ _ _ _ |
| 39 | (30) | ΔΙΕΤΡΗ | ΣΕΝΡΑΒΔΟΙΣΑΥΤΟΥΚΕΦΑΛΗΝ |
| 40 | (30) | ΑΤΕΙ | ΤΩΝΑΥΤΟΥΣΕΙΣΘ ΣΟΝΤΑΙΤΟΥ |
| 41 | (28) | ΣΚΟ | ΑΙΗΜΑΣΤΟΓΑΥΡΙΑΜΑΑΥΤΩΝ |
| 42 | (29) | ΚΑΘ | ΘΙΩΝΠΤΩΧΟΝΚΡΥΦΗ_ΕΝΕΤΕΙ |

TOTALS: 1182 letters/column; 42 lines, 21 (short), 35 (long), 28.14 (average) all/part of 19 lines preserved from column, average length *29.00* letters

## Column 19 Ha [3.1]–3.15a

[3.1 ]
[2 ]
[ ]
[ ]
[ 3 ]
[ ]
[ ]
[ ]
[ 4 ]
[ ]
[ 5 ]
[ ]
[ ]
[ 6 ]
[ ]
[ ]
[ ]
[ 7 ]
[ ]
[ 8 ]
[ ]
[ ]
[ ]
.[καὶ ἡ ἱππασία σου σωτηρία. 9 ἐξεγείρων]
ἐξεγ[ερ]εῖς τὸ τό[ξον σου· ].
ῥάβδ[ο]υς ....[ σελε. ποτα]μοί, ῥαγή-
σεται γῆ. 10 Εἴδοσ[άν σε, ὠδίνησ]αν ὄρη,
ἐντίνα[γ]μα ὑ[δ παρῆλθεν· ἔδω]κεν
ἄβυσσο[ς φωνὴν αὐτῆς, ]
σις [α]ὐτοῦ. [11 εἰς]
φέγγος ἀσ[τραπῆς σιβύνης σου πορεύ-]
σοντα[ι .]
12 ἐν ἐμ[βριμήσει γῆν, ἐν θυμῷ]
ἀλ[ο]ή[σεις ἔθνη. 13 ἐξῆλθες εἰς σωτηρία]ν
λαο[ῦ σου, εἰς σωτηρίαν τοῦ χριστοῦ]
σου· [ κεφαλὴ]ν ἐξ οἴκου [ἀσ]ε-
β[οῦς, ἐξε]κένωσα[ς] θεμελίους ἕως τρ[α-]
χ[ήλου.] σελε.________________________ 14
Διέτρη[σα]ς ἐν ῥάβδοις αὐτοῦ κεφαλὴν
ἀτει[χίσ]των αὐτοῦ, σεισθ[ή]σονται τοῦ
σκο[ρπίσ]αι ἡμᾶς τὸ γαυρίαμα αὐτῶν
καθ[ὼς ἐσ]θίων πτωχὸν κρυφῇ. 15 Ἐνέτει-
[ ]

## Column 20 Ha [3.15b]–Zp 1.6a

| Line | Letters | Text |
|---|---|---|
| 1 | (31) | |
| 2 | (32) | |
| 3 | (30) | |
| 4 | (32) | |
| 5 | (30) | |
| 6 | (33) | |
| 7 | (30) | |
| 8 | (31) | |
| 9 | (33) | |
| 10 | (33) | |
| 11 | (32) | |
| 12 | (25) | |
| 13 | (29) | |
| 14 | (27) | |
| 15 | (32) | |
| 16 | (29) | |
| 17 | (30) | |
| 18 | (31) | |
| 19 | (31) | |
| 20 | (31) | |
| 21 | (31) | |
| 22 | (30) | |
| 23 | (26) | |
| 24 | (29) | |
| 25 | (31) | ΥΙΟΥΑ … ΝΑΓΩΓΗ |
| 26 | (29) | ΣΥΝ … ΡΟΣΩΠΟΥ |
| 27 | (30) | ΤΗΣΓ … ΡΩ |
| 28 | (31) | ΠΟΣΚΑ |
| 29 | (30) | ΤΟΥΟΥ |
| 30 | (30) | |
| 31 | (30) | |
| 32 | (27) | ΟΥΤΗΣΓΗΣΛ ΕΙ𐤉 |
| 33 | (32) | ΝΧΕΙΡΑΜΟΥΕΠΙ ΙΟΥ |
| 34 | (34) | ΑΣ ΚΑΤΟΙΚΟΥΝΤΑΣΕΝΙΕΡ |
| 35 | (32) | Α Ε ΟΛ ΣΩΕΚΤΟΥΤΟΠΟΥΤ |
| 36 | (30) | ΥΠ ΒΑΑΛΤΟΟΝΟΜΑΤΩ |
| 37 | (31) | ΡΕΙΜΜ ΕΡΕΩΝΤ ΥΣΠΡΟΣΚ |
| 38 | (31) | ΤΑΣ Π ΟΥ |
| 39 | (31) | ΝΟΥΚ Ι |
| 40 | (27) | ΟΝ ΑΣ |
| 41 | (30) | ΕΝ Ω |
| 42 | (30) | ΟΠΙΣΘΕ |

TOTALS: 1274 letters/column; 42 lines, 25 (short), 34 (long), 30.33 (average) all/part of 18 lines preserved from column, average length *30.33* letters

# Column 20 Ha [3.15b]–Zp 1.6a

[νες ]
[ 16 ]
[ ]
[ ]
[ ]
[ ]
[ 17 ]
[ ]
[ ]
[ ]
[ ]
[ 18 ]
[ ]
[ 19 ]
[ ]
[ ]
[ ]
[__________________________________]
[__________________________________]
[__________________________________]
[__________________________________]
[1.1 ]
[ ]
[ ]
``υἱοῦ α[μων βασιλέως ιουδα.\_\_2 Συ]ναγωγῇ``
``συν[αγ''' πάντα ἐπάνωθεν π]ροσώπου``
``τῆς γ[ῆς, λέγει 𐤉𐤄𐤅𐤄. 3 '''''''''' ἄνθ]ρω-``
``πος κα[ὶ κτήνη, '''''''''''' πετεινὸν]
``τοῦ οὐ[ρανοῦ καὶ ἰχθύες τῆς θαλάσσης,]
``['''''''' '''''''''''''' '''''''''']
``[καὶ ἐξολεθρεύσω τοὺς ἀνθρώπους ἀπὸ]
``[προσώπ]ου τῆς γῆς, λ[έγ]ει 𐤉[𐤄𐤅]𐤄._4 καὶ]
``[ἐκτενῶ τὴ]ν χεῖρά μου ἐπὶ ιου[δαν καὶ ἐπὶ]
``[πάντ]ας [τοὺς] κατοικοῦντας ἐν ιερ[ουσαλημ]
``[κ]α[ὶ] ἐ[ξ]ολ[εθρεύ]σω ἐκ τοῦ τόπου τ[ούτου τὸ]
``ὑπ[όλειμμα ''']βααλ, τὸ ὄνομα τῶ[ν χωμα-]
``ρειμ μ[ετὰ τῶν ἱ]ερέων, 5 τ[ο]ὺς προσκ[υνοῦν-]
``τας [ἐ]π[ὶ τὰ δώματα '''''''''' τοῦ] οὐ[ρα-]
``νοῦ κ[α]ὶ [τοὺς προσκυνοῦντας τοὺς ὀμνύ-]``
``ον[τ]ας [τῷ 𐤉𐤄𐤅𐤄 καὶ τοὺς ὀμνύοντας]``
``ἐν [τ]ῷ ['''''''' 6 καὶ τοὺς '''''''''' ἀπὸ]``
``ὄπισθε[ν 𐤉𐤄𐤅𐤄 καὶ τοὺς μὴ ζητήσαντας]``
``````````[``````````````````]``````````
``````````

## Column 21 Zp [1.6b]–1.18a

1 (35)
2 (32)
3 (32)
4 (33)
5 (33)
6 (34)
7 (31)
8 (34)
9 (33)
10 (33)
11 (33)
12 (34)
13 (35)
14 (34)
15 (33)
16 (32)
17 (35)
18 (33)
19 (34)
20 (31)
21 (36)
22 (29)
23 (32)
24 (35)
25 (32) ΚΑΙΟΥΜΗ
26 (31) ΣΟΥΣΙΝΑΜΠΕΛΩΝ
27 (28) ΟΙΝΟΝΑΥΤΩΝ_ΕΝΓΥΣ
28 (31) ΓΑΛΗΕΝΓΥΣΚΑΙΤΑΧΕΙΑ
29 (31) 𐤉𐤄𐤅𐤄ΠΙΚΡΑΕΠΙΣ
30 (27) ΑΟΡΓΗΣΗΗΜ   Ι Η ΜΕΡΑ
31 (33) ΕΝΟΧΩΡΙΑΣΗΜΕΡΑΑΠΟΡΙΑΣ
32 (32) ΜΕΡΑΣΚΟΤΟΥΣΚΑΙΣΚΟΤΙΑΣ
33 (33) Ι ΝΟΦΟΥ_   Α Ε ΑΤΙ
34 (29) ΕΠΙΤ Σ   ΕΙΣΤΑΣΟ
35 (35) ΑΣΤΑΣΥ ΗΛΑΣ_ΚΑΙΕΚ
36 (32) ΠΟΥΣΚΑΙΠΟΡΕΥΣΟΝ Ι
37 (31) 𐤉𐤄𐤅𐤄Ε   ΡΤΟ _Κ Ι
38 (33) ΝΩΣ   Α Π   Α Α
39 (33) Κ
40 (33) ΝΑ
41 (31) Ν   ΟΡ
42 (31)

TOTALS: 1361 letters/column; 42 lines, 27 (short), 35 (long), 32.40 (average) all/part of 18 lines preserved from column, average length *31.38* letters

## Column 21 Zp [1.6b]–1.18a

[ 7 ]
[ ]
[ ]
[ 8 ]
[ ]
[ ]
[ ]
[ 9 ]
[ ]
[ ]
[ 10 ]
[ ]
[ ]
[ ]
[11 ]
[ ]
[ ]
[12 ]
[ ]
[ ]
[ ]
[ 13 ]
[ ]
[ ]
κ̣αὶ ο̣ὐ μ̣ὴ [κατοικήσουσιν καὶ καταφυτεύ-]
``σουσιν ἀμπελῶν[ας καὶ οὐ μὴ πίωσιν τὸν]
``οἶνον αὐτῶν._14 ἐνγὺς̣ [ἡμέρα 𐤉𐤄𐤅𐤄 ἡ με-]
``γάλη, ἐνγὺς καὶ ταχεῖα [σφόδρα· φωνὴ ἡμέ-]
[ρας 𐤉]𐤄𐤅𐤄 πικρά, ἐπισ['''' ἐκεῖ δυνατός̣.]
[15 ἡμέρ]α ὀργῆς ἡ ἡμ[έρα ἐκε]ί[ν]η, [ἡ]μέ̣ρα̣
[θλίψεως καὶ στ]ενοχωρ̣ί̣α̣ς̣, ἡμέρα ἀπορίας``
[καὶ '''''', ἡ]μέρα̣ σκότους καὶ σκοτίας,``
[ἡμέρα νεφέλης κα]ὶ [γ]νόφου,_16 [ἡμέρ]α [κ]ε[ρ]ατί-``
[νης καὶ κραυγῆς] ἐπὶ̣ τ̣[ὰ]ς̣ πόλ]ε̣ις τὰς ὀ-
[χυρὰς καὶ ἐπὶ τὰς γωνί]α̣ς τὰς ὑ̣[ψ]ηλάς._17 Καὶ ἐκ-``
[θλίψω τοὺς ἀνθρώ]πους καὶ πορεύ̣σον[τα]ι``
[ὡς τυφλοί, ὅτι τῷ 𐤉]𐤄𐤅𐤄 ἐ̣[ξήμα]ρ̣τ̣ο̣[ν·]_Κ[α]ὶ [ἐξ-]``
[ε̣χεῖτο τὸ αἷμα αὐτῶ]ν ὡς [χοῦν κ]α[ὶ] π[τώμ]α̣[τ]α``
[αὐτῶν ὡς ''''''''.] 18 κ[αί γε τὸ ἀργύριον αὐ-]``
[τῶν καί γε̣ τὸ χρυσίο]ν α[ὐτῶν οὐ μὴ δύνηται]``
[ἐξελέσθαι αὐτοὺς ἐ]ν [ἡμέρα̣] ὀρ[γῆς 𐤉𐤄𐤅𐤄,]``
[ ]..[ ]
[``````]````````````[````````````````]

## Column 22 Zp [1.18b]–2.10

| | | |
|---|---|---|
| 1 | (28) | |
| 2 | (29) | |
| 3 | (30) | |
| 4 | (30) | |
| 5 | (28) | |
| 6 | (28) | |
| 7 | (26) | |
| 8 | (29) | |
| 9 | (29) | |
| 10 | (26) | |
| 11 | (28) | |
| 12 | (31) | |
| 13 | (26) | |
| 14 | (28) | |
| 15 | (28) | |
| 16 | (28) | |
| 17 | (30) | |
| 18 | (26) | |
| 19 | (29) | |
| 20 | (29) | |
| 21 | (30) | |
| 22 | (26) | |
| 23 | (28) | |
| 24 | (30) | |
| 25 | (30) | |
| 26 | (27) | |
| 27 | (24) | |
| 28 | (29) | |
| 29 | (28) | |
| 30 | (28) | |
| 31 | (27) | |
| 32 | (26) | |
| 33 | (33) | Δ |
| 34 | (31) | |
| 35 | (31) | |
| 36 | (33) | . |
| 37 | (28) | Ε ΠΟ ΛΑΟΥ |
| 38 | (28) | Ο ΚΑΙ ΙΕΠΙΛΟΙ |
| 39 | (27) | ΛΗ Ο Υ |
| 40 | (29) | ΑΥΤΗΑΥΤΟΙ |
| 41 | (29) | ΑΥΤΩΝΟΤΙΩΝΕΙΔΙ |
| 42 | (27) | . . . . . ΕΠΙΛΑΟΝ[illegible] |

TOTALS: 1197 letters/column; 42 lines, 24 (short), 33 (long), 28.50 (average) all/part of 8 lines preserved from column, average length *29.25* letters

## Column 22 Zp [1.18b]–2.10

[ ]
[ ]
[ 2.1 ]
[ ]
[ ]
[ 2 ]
[ ]
[ ]
[ ]
[3 ]
[ ]
[ ]
[ ]
[4 ]
[ ]
[ ]
[ 5 ]
[ ]
[ ]
[ ]
[ 6 ]
[ ]
[ 7 ]
[ ]
[ ]
[ ]
[ ]
[ ]
[ 8 ]
[ ]
[ ]
[ 9]
Δ[ιὰ τοῦτο ζῶ ἐγώ, λέγει 𐤉𐤄𐤅𐤄 τῶν δυνάμεων]
[ ]
[ ]
.[ ]
ἕ[ως τοῦ αἰῶνος· κατάλοι]πο[ι τοῦ] λαοῦ
[μ]ο[υ αὐτούς], καὶ [ο]ἱ ἐπίλοι-
[ποι τοῦ ἔθνους μου κ]λη[ρ]ο[νομήσο]υ-
[σιν αὐτούς.] 10 αὕτη αὐτοῖ[ς ἀντὶ ὕβρεως]
αὐτῶν, ὅτι ὠνείδι[σαν καὶ ]
..... ἐπὶ λαὸν 𐤉𐤄[𐤅𐤄 τῶν δυνάμεων.]
[ ] [ ]

## Column 23 Zp [2.11]–3.7

| | | |
|---|---|---|
| 1 | (33) | |
| 2 | (33) | |
| 3 | (34) | |
| 4 | (32) | |
| 5 | (34) | |
| 6 | (32) | |
| 7 | (35) | |
| 8 | (31) | |
| 9 | (34) | |
| 10 | (32) | |
| 11 | (33) | |
| 12 | (32) | |
| 13 | (35) | |
| 14 | (31) | |
| 15 | (37) | |
| 16 | (34) | |
| 17 | (32) | |
| 18 | (33) | |
| 19 | (33) | |
| 20 | (35) | |
| 21 | (30) | |
| 22 | (34) | |
| 23 | (33) | |
| 24 | (33) | |
| 25 | (31) | |
| 26 | (34) | |
| 27 | (33) | |
| 28 | (35) | |
| 29 | (32) | |
| 30 | (34) | |
| 31 | (26) | |
| 32 | (32) | |
| 33 | (30) | |
| 34 | (31) | |
| 35 | (32) | |
| 36 | (31) | ˋ ˋ Ω |
| 37 | (27) | ˋ ˋ X INANΔ |
| 38 | (29) | ˋ ˋ KOΥNTA_EIΠ |
| 39 | (29) | ˋ ˋ ΞAIΠAIΔEIAN |
| 40 | (25) | ˋ ˋ HΓH THΣΠAN O |
| 41 | (28) | HN_ΔIATOΥTOO |
| 42 | (32) | ATEΠANTATAEΠIT |
| | | ˋ ˋ ˋ ˋ ˋ ˋ ˋ ˋ ˋ ˋ ˋ ˋ ˋ ˋ ˋ |

TOTALS: 1346 letters/column; 42 lines, 25 (short), 37 (long), 32.04 (average) all/part of 7 lines preserved from column, average length *28.71* letters

## Column 23 Zp [2.11]–3.7

[11 ]
[ ]
[ ]
[ 12 ]
[ 13 ]
[ ]
[ ]
[ 14 ]
[ ]
[ ]
[ ]
[ ]
[ ]
[ 3.1(15) ]
[ ]
[ ]
[ ]
[ ]
[ ]
[1(2) ]
[ 2 ]
[ ]
[ 3 ]
[ ]
[ ]
[ 4 ]
[ ]
[ ]
[ 5 ]
[ ]
[ ]
[ 6 ]
[ ]
[ ]
[ ἀπ-]
ώ[λοντο αἱ πόλεις αὐτῶν παρὰ τὸ μὴ ὑπάρ-]
χ[ε]ιν ἄνδ[ρα, διὰ τοῦ μὴ εἶναι κατοι-]
κοῦντα._7 εἶπ[α με, δέ-]
ξαι παιδείαν, [καὶ οὐ ἡ π-]
ηγὴ [αὐ]τῆs, πάν[τα] ὅ[σα ἐξεδίκησα]
[ἐπ' αὐτ]ήν·_Διὰ τοῦτο ὀ[ρθρίσατε, δια-]
[φθείρ]ατε πάντα τὰ ἐπιτ[ηδεύματα αὐτῶν.]
[ ] [ ]

## Column 28 [Hg (end) ]–Za 1.4a

| Line | Letters | Text |
|---|---|---|
| 1 | (30) | |
| 2 | (30) | |
| 3 | (30) | |
| 4 | (30) | |
| 5 | (30) | |
| 6 | (30) | |
| 7 | (30) | |
| 8 | (30) | |
| 9 | (30) | |
| 10 | (30) | |
| 11 | (30) | |
| 12 | (30) | |
| 13 | (30) | |
| 14 | (30) | |
| 15 | (30) | |
| 16 | (30) | |
| 17 | (30) | |
| 18 | (30) | |
| 19 | (30) | |
| 20 | (30) | |
| 21 | (30) | |
| 22 | (30) | |
| 23 | (30) | |
| 24 | (30) | |
| 25 | (30) | |
| 26 | (30) | |
| 27 | (30) | |
| 28 | (30) | |
| 29 | (30) | |
| 30 | (30) | |
| 31 | (30) | |
| 32 | (30) | |
| 33 | (28) | ΟΝΕΔΔΩ |
| 34 | (38) | Ηϯ |
| 35 | (26) | ΤΟΥΣ |
| 36 | (28) | ΥΝΑΜΕΩΝ |
| 37 | (26) | ϯϰϯϩΤΩΝΔΥΝΑΜ |
| 38 | (28) | ΗΣΟΜΑΙΠΡΟΣΥΜΑΣΕΙΠΕΝϯ |
| 39 | (25) | ΝΑΜΕΩΝ_ _ΜΗΓΕΙΝΕ ΚΑ |
| 40 | (32) | ΕΣΥΜΩΝΟΥΣΕΚΑΛΟΥΝΠΡΟΣΑ |
| 41 | (33) | ΤΑΙΟΙΕΝΠΡΟΣΘΕΝΛΕΓΟΝΤΕΣ |
| 42 | (27) | ϯϰϯϩΤΩΝΔΥΝΑΜΕΩΝ ΠΙ |

TOTALS: 1251 letters/column; 42 lines, 25 (short), 38 (long), 29.78 (average) all/part of 10 lines preserved from column, average length *29.10* letters

## Column 28 [Hg (end) ]–Za 1.4a

[ ]
[ ]
[ ]
[ ]
[ ]
[ ]
[ ]
[ ]
[ ]
[ ]
[ ]
[ ]
[ ]
[ ]
[ ]
[ ]
[ ]
[ ]
[ ]
[ ]
[ ]
[ ]
[ ]
[ ]
[ ]
[________________________]
[________________________]
[________________________]
[________________________]
[1.1 ]
[ ]
[ ]
[υἱ]ὸν εδδω [τὸν προφήτην λέγων____]
[2 ὠργίσθ]η 𐤉[𐤄𐤅𐤄 ἐπὶ πατέρας ὑμῶν ὀργήν. 3 καὶ ἐρεῖς]
[πρὸς αὐ]τούς [___Τάδε λέγει 𐤉𐤄𐤅𐤄]
[τῶν δ]υνάμεων [ἐπιστρέψατε πρός με,]
[λέγει] 𐤉𐤄𐤅𐤄 τῶν δυνάμ[εων, καὶ ἐπι-]
[στραφ]ήσομαι πρὸς ὑμᾶς, εἶπεν 𐤉[𐤄𐤅𐤄]
[τῶν δυ]νάμεων.__4 μὴ γείνε[σθε] κα-
[θὼς οἱ πατέρ]ες ὑμῶν, οὓς ἐκάλουν πρὸς α[ὐ-]
[τοὺς οἱ προφῆ]ται οἱ ἔνπροσθεν λέγοντες
[Τάδε λέγει] 𐤉𐤄𐤅𐤄 τῶν δυνάμεων [ἐ]πι-
[ ]

## Column 29 Za [1.4b]–[1.15a]

| Line | Letters | Text |
|---|---|---|
| 1 | (31) | |
| 2 | (29) | |
| 3 | (27) | |
| 4 | (30) | |
| 5 | (29) | |
| 6 | (30) | |
| 7 | (32) | |
| 8 | (31) | |
| 9 | (33) | |
| 10 | (29) | |
| 11 | (32) | |
| 12 | (30) | |
| 13 | (32) | |
| 14 | (28) | |
| 15 | (31) | |
| 16 | (30) | |
| 17 | (29) | |
| 18 | (30) | |
| 19 | (32) | |
| 20 | (27) | |
| 21 | (32) | |
| 22 | (31) | |
| 23 | (30) | |
| 24 | (30) | |
| 25 | (30) | |
| 26 | (29) | |
| 27 | (30) | |
| 28 | (33) | |
| 29 | (28) | |
| 30 | (32) | |
| 31 | (31) | |
| 32 | (27) | |
| 33 | (34) | |
| 34 | (30) | |
| 35 | (31) | ` ` Π |
| 36 | (27) | ` ` ΜΗ |
| | | ——— |
| 37 | (30) | ` ` ΤΩ |
| 38 | (32) | ` ` ΑΓΑ |
| 39 | (32) | ` ` ΠΡΟΣ |
| 40 | (29) | ` ` ΓΕΛ |
| | | ——— |
| 41 | (31) | ` ` Α |
| 42 | (30) | ` ` ΣΕ |
| | | ` ` ` ` ` |

TOTALS: 1271 letters/column; 42 lines, 27 (short), 34 (long), 30.26 (average) all/part of 8 lines preserved from column, average length *30.25* letters

## Column 29 Za [1.4b]–[1.15a]

[στρέψατε ]
[ ]
[ ]
[ 5 ]
[ ]
[ 6 ]
[ ]
[ ]
[ ]
[ ]
[ ]
[ ]
[ 7 ]
[ ]
[ ]
[ ]
[ ]
[ 8 ]
[ ]
[ ]
[ ]
[ ]
[9 ]
[ ]
[ 10 ]
[ ]
[ ]
[ 11 ]
[ ]
[ ]
[ ]
[ 12 ]
[ ]
[ ]
π[όλεις ιουδα, ἃς τοῦτο ἑβδο-]
μη̣[κοστὸν ἔτος; 13 καὶ ἀπεκρίθη 𐤉𐤄𐤅𐤄 ]
τῷ̣ [ἀγγέλῳ τῷ λαλοῦντι ἐν ἐμοὶ ῥήματα]
ἀγα[θά, λόγους παρακλητικούς. 14 καὶ εἶπεν]
πρός [με ὁ ἄγγελος ὁ λαλῶν ἐν ἐμοί ἀνάκρα-]
γε λ[έγων___Τάδε λέγει 𐤉𐤄𐤅𐤄 τῶν δυν-]
ά[μεων ἐζήλωκα τὴν ιερουσαλημ καὶ τὴν]
σε[ιων ζῆλον μέγαν 15 καὶ ὀργὴν μεγάλην]
[ ]

## Column 30 Za [1.15b]–2.12(8)a

| Line | Letters | Text |
|---|---|---|
| 1 | (37) | |
| 2 | (36) | |
| 3 | (30) | |
| 4 | (36) | |
| 5 | (32) | |
| 6 | (37) | |
| 7 | (36) | |
| 8 | (33) | |
| 9 | (32) | |
| 10 | (35) | |
| 11 | (34) | |
| 12 | (39) | |
| 13 | (36) | Ν Τ Α Υ Τ |
| 14 | (34) | Τ Α Λ Ι Κ Μ Η |
| 15 | (34) | Ι Ε Ρ Ο Υ |
| 16 | (34) | Ρ Ε Σ |
| 17 | (33) | Υ |
| 18 | (33) | Α |
| 19 | (37) | |
| 20 | (34) | |
| 21 | (38) | |
| 22 | (35) | |
| 23 | (39) | |
| 24 | (36) | |
| 25 | (37) | |
| 26 | (37) | |
| 27 | (38) | . |
| 28 | (30) | Ο Λ Α |
| 29 | (33) | Λ Ο Σ Ε Τ Ε |
| 30 | (34) | |
| 31 | (33) | — — — Ρ Ο Σ |
| 32 | (34) | Τ Α Σ Τ Ι |
| 33 | (26) | Υ Σ |
| 34 | (32) | Ε Ι Σ |
| 35 | (27) | Υ |
| 36 | (34) | |
| 37 | (29) | |
| 38 | (33) | |
| 39 | (32) | |
| 40 | (34) | Α Τ Ο Ι Κ Θ Γ Α |
| 41 | (31) | Ε Λ Ε Γ Ε |
| 42 | (31) | Ξ Η Σ Α Σ Τ Ε Ι Λ Ε Ν |

TOTALS: 1425 letters/column; 42 lines, 26 (short), 39 (long), 33.92 (average) all/part of 22 lines preserved from column, average length *32.50* letters

## Column 30 Za [1.15b]–2.12(8)a

[ ]
[ ]
[ 16 ]
[ ]
[ ]
[ ]
[ 17 ]
[ ]
[ ]
[ ]
[ 2.1(1.18) ]
[ 2(1.19) ]
[ἄγγελον τὸν λαλοῦντα ἐν ἐμοί τί ἐστι]ν ταῦτ[α; ]
[καὶ εἶπεν πρός με ταῦτα τὰ κέρατα] τὰ λικμή-
[σαντα τὸν ιουδαν τὸν ισραηλ καὶ τὴν] ιερου-
[σαλημ.____3(1.20) Καὶ ἔδειξέν μοι 𐤉𐤄𐤅𐤄 τέσσα]ρες
[τέκτονας. 4(1.21) καὶ εἶπα τί οὗτοι ἔρχονται το]ῦ
[ποιῆσαι; καὶ εἶπεν λέγων ταῦτα τὰ κέρατ]α
[ ]
[ ]
[ ]
[ ]
[ 5(1) ]
[ ]
[ 6(2) ]
[ ]
[ ].
[τὸ μῆκος αὐτῆς. 7(3) καὶ ἰδοὺ ὁ ἄγγελος] ὁ λα-
[λῶν ἐν ἐμοὶ ἐκπορεύεται, καὶ ἄγγε]λος ἕτε-
[ρος ἐκπορεύεται εἰς συνάντησιν αὐτῷ.]___ 8(4)
[Καὶ εἶπεν πρὸς αὐτόν δράμε λάλησον π]ρὸς
[τὸν νεανίαν ἐκεῖνον λέγων ἀτειχίσ]τας τι-
[θήσεις ιερουσαλημ ?? ἀπὸ πλήθο]υς
[ . 9(5) καὶ ἐγὼ ἔσομαι] εἰς
[αὐτήν, λέγει 𐤉𐤄𐤅𐤄, τεῖχος πυρὸς κ]υ-
[κλόθεν καὶ εἰς δόξαν ἔσομαι ἐν μέσῳ αὐτῆς.]
[10(6) Οὐαὶ οὐαὶ καὶ φεύγετε ἀπὸ γῆς βορρᾶ,]
[λέγει 𐤉𐤄𐤅𐤄, ὅτι ὡς τοὺς τέσσαρες ἀνέμους]
[τοῦ οὐρανοῦ ὑμᾶς, λέγει 𐤉𐤄𐤅𐤄.]
[11(7) Οὐαὶ εἰς σειων ἀνασῴζου, κ]ατοικ[οῦσα] θ[υ]γα-
[τέρα βαβυλῶνος.__12(8) ὅτι τάδ]ε λέγε[ι 𐤉𐤄𐤅𐤄]
[τῶν δυνάμεων ὀπίσω δό]ξης ἀ[πέ]στειλέν
[ ] [ ]

# Column 31 Za [2.12(8)b]–3.7a

```
 1  (28)
 2  (28)
 3  (33)
 4  (32)
 5  (36)
 6  (35)
 7  (33)
 8  (39)
 9  (22)
10  (31)
11  (28)
12  (31)
13  (34)
14  (33)       .
15  (34)    ``ΞΕΤΑΙ
            ____
16  (30)    ``ΣΑΡΞΑ
17  (34)    ``ΤΑΙ
            ____
18  (33)    `ΚΑΙΕ
19  (34)
20  (31)    ``ΔΙ                              ΝΑΥΤ
21  (27)                                ΑΙΕΙΠΕΝ
22  (34)                                ΠΙΤΙ
23  (36)
24  (36)
25  (30)
26  (34)
27  (32)                  . . .
28  (34)        ΑΙΕΙΠΕΝΠΡ
29  (34)         ΥΛΕΓΩΝΑ
30  (32)         ΑΥΤΟΥ_ΚΑ
31  (30)         ΑΑΠΟΣΟΥ
32  (30)         ΣΕΜΕΤΕ        ΤΑ
33  (32)    ``ΚΙΔΑΡΙΝΚΑ     ΑΝΕΠΙΤ
34  (31)    ``ΚΑΙΕΠΕΘΗΚ   ΤΗΝΚΙΔ
35  (34)    ``ΕΠΙΤΗΝΚ      ΗΝΑΥΤΟΥΚ
36  (33)    ``ΕΙΜΑΤΙΑ      ΓΓΕΛΟΣ𐤅𐤄
37  (35)    ``ΜΑΡΤΥΡΑ     ΓΓΕΛΟΣ𐤄
            ____
38  (32)    `ΤΑΔΕΛΕΓΕΙ 𐤉𐤄𐤅𐤄ΤΩΝΔΥ
39  (33)    ``ΤΑΙΣΟΔΟΙΣΜΟΥΠΟΡΕΥΘΗΣ
40  (33)    ``ΚΗΝΜΟΥΦΥΛΑΞΗΣΚΑΙΓΕΣΥ
41  (32)    ``ΟΙΚΟΝΜΟΥΚΑΙΓΕΦ    ΑΞΕΙΣΤ
42  (31)    ``ΚΑΙ     ΩΣΟΙΕΝΠ     Π
            ``
              —.
            `````
```

TOTALS: 1358 letters/column; 42 lines, 22 (short), 39 (long), 32.33 (average) all/part of 25 lines preserved from column, average length *33.32* letters
```

# Column 31 Za [2.12(8)b]–3.7a

[με ]
[ ]
[ 13(9) ]
[ ]
[ ]
[14(10) ]
[ ]
[ 15(11) ]
[ ]
[ ]
[ ]
[ 16(12) ]
[ ]
.[ ἐκλέ-]
``ξεται [ἔτι ἐν ιερουσαλημ._17(13) σιώπησον πᾶσα]
``σὰρξ ἀ[πὸ προσώπου 𐤉𐤄𐤅𐤄, ὅτι ἐξεγήγερ-]
``ται [ἐκ τοῦ κατοικητηρίου ἁγίου αὐτοῦ.___3.1]
`Καὶ ἔ[δειξέν μοι τὸν ἰησοῦν τὸν ἱερέα τὸν]
[ ]
``δι[άβολος ἕστηκεν ἐκ δεξιῶ]ν αὐτ[οῦ τοῦ]
[διαβάλλειν αὐτόν. 2 κ]αὶ εἶπεν [𐤉𐤄𐤅𐤄]
[πρὸς τὸν διάβολον ἐ]πιτι[μήσαι 𐤉𐤄𐤅𐤄 ἐν σοί,]
[ ]
[ ]
[ 3 ]
[ ]
[ ]...[ 4 ]
[κ]αὶ εἶπεν πρ[ὸς τοὺς ἑστηκότας ἐνώπιον αὐ-]
[το]ῦ λέγων ἀ[φέλετε τὰ ειμάτια τὰ ````````]
[ἀπ'] αὐτοῦ._κα[ὶ εἶπεν πρὸς αὐτόν ἰδοὺ ἀφή-]
[ρηκ]α ἀπὸ σοῦ [τὴν ἀνομίαν σου, καὶ ἔνδυ-]
[σαί] σε μετε[κδύμα]τα. 5 [καὶ εἶπα ἐπίθετε]
``κίδαριν κα[θαρ]ὰν ἐπὶ τ[ὴν κεφαλὴν αὐτοῦ.]
``καὶ ἐπέθηκ[αν] τὴν κίδ[αριν τὴν καθαρὰν]
``ἐπὶ τὴν κ[εφαλ]ὴν αὐτοῦ κ[αὶ ἐνέδυσαν αὐτὸν]
``ειμάτια, [καὶ ἄ]γγελος 𐤉𐤄[𐤅𐤄 ἕστηκεν. 6 καὶ ἐ-]
``μαρτύρα[το ἄ]γγελος 𐤉[𐤄𐤅𐤄 ```` ἰησ``` λέγων 7]
`Τάδε λέγει 𐤉𐤄𐤅𐤄 τῶν δυ[νάμεων___ἐὰν ἐν]
``ταῖς ὁδοῖς μου πορευθῇς [καὶ ἐὰν τὴν φυλα-]
``κήν μου φυλάξῃς, καί γε σὺ [διακρινεῖς τὸν]
``οἶκόν μου· καί γε φ[υλ]άξεις τ[ὰς αὐλάς μου]
``καὶ [δώσ]ω σοι ἐνπ[ερι]π[ατοῦντας ἐν μέσῳ]
``_.[ ]
`````[```````````````````````````]
`````

## Column B1 Za [8.18]–[8.23a]

| Line | Letters | Text |
|---|---|---|
| 1 | (22) | |
| 2 | (22) | |
| 3 | (22) | |
| 4 | (22) | |
| 5 | (22) | |
| 6 | (23) | T E I |
| 7 | (21) | I K Ω |
| 8 | (22) | N _ K A I |
| 9 | (24) | K A I _ T H N _ A |
| 10 | (22) | E I P H N H N _ A |
| 11 | (23) | _ _ _ _ _ _ _ _ _ |
| 12 | (22) | ƶ _ T Ω N _ Δ Υ N A |
| 13 | (26) | Θ Ω Σ I N _ Λ A O I _ K A I |
| 14 | (23) | _ Π O Λ E I Σ _ Π O Λ |
| 15 | (22) | Σ O N T A I _ K A T O |
| 16 | (18) | Σ M I A N |
| 17 | (23) | M E N Π O |
| 18 | (17) | |
| 19 | (20) | |
| 20 | (22) | |
| 21 | (21) | |
| 22 | (21) | |
| 23 | (19) | |
| 24 | (22) | |
| 25 | (19) | |
| 26 | (18) | |
| 27 | (20) | |
| 28 | (21) | A I Σ E K E I |
| 29 | (20) | N T A I Δ E |
| 30 | (20) | Ω N _ T Ω N _ |
| 31 | (20) | N Ω N _ K |
| 32 | (18) | |
| 33 | (20) | |

TOTALS: 697 letters/column; 33 lines, 17 (short), 26 (long), 21.12 (average) all/part of 17 lines preserved from column, average length *21.88* letters

## Column B1 Za [8.18]–[8.23a]

[ 18 ]
[ ]
[ 19 ]
[ ἡ τετάρ-]``
[τη καὶ νηστεία ἡ πέμπτη καὶ]``
[νηστεία ἡ ἑβδόμη καὶ νησ]τεί-``
[α ἡ δεκάτη ἔσονται τῷ ο]ἴκῳ``
[ιουδα εἰς εὐφροσύνη]ν_καὶ``
[εἰς ἑορτὰς ἀγαθάς, ] καὶ_τὴν_ἀ-``
[λήθειαν καὶ τὴν] εἰρήνην_ἀ-``
[γαπήσατε.____]_________`` 20
[Τάδε λέγει 𐤉𐤄𐤅𐤄]ꝛ_τῶν_δυνά-``
[μεων ἕως '' ἔλ]θωσιν_λαοὶ _καὶ``
[κατοικοῦντες]_πόλεις_πολ̣-``
[λάς. 21 καὶ ἐλεύ]σονται̣_κατο[ι-]``
[κοῦντες ?? μίαν πρὸ]ς μίαν
[λέγοντες πορευθῶ]μεν πο[ρευ-]
[όμενοι ]
[ ]
[ ]
[ 22 ]
[ ]
[ ]
[ ]
[ ]
[ 23 ]
[ ]
[ἐν ταῖς ἡμέρ]αις ἐκεί[ναις]
[ἐὰν ἐπιλάβω]νται δέ[κα ἄν-]
[δρες ἐκ πασ]ῶν_τῶν_[γλωσ-]
[σῶν τῶν ἐθ]νῶν_κ[αὶ ἐπιλά-]
[βωνται ]
[ ]

## Column B2 Za 8.23b–[9.7]

ˋ ˋ ˋ ˋ ˋ ˋ ˋ ˋ ˋ ˋ ˋ ˋ ˋ ˋ ˋ

| Line | Letters | Text |
| --- | --- | --- |
| 0 | | |
| 1 | (22) | ΡΕΥΣΟΜΕΘΑ_ΜΕΘΥΜ |
| 2 | (25) | ΚΗΚΟΑΜΕΝ_ΘΕΟΣ_ΜΕΘ |
| 3 | (25) | ˋΛΗΜΜΑΛΟΓΟΥ_𐤄𐤅𐤄𐤉 _ΕΝ |
| 4 | (28) | ˋˋΚΑΙ_ΔΑΜΑΣΚΟΥ_ΚΑΤΑΠΑΥ |
| 5 | (22) | ˋˋΟΤΙ_ΤΩ_𐤄𐤅𐤄𐤉_ΟΦΘΑΛ |
| 6 | (24) | ˋˋΘΡΩΠΩΝ_ΚΑΙ_ΠΑΣΩΝΦ |
| 7 | (26) | ˋˋΙΣΡΑΗΛ_ΚΑΙ_ΓΕ_ΕΜΑΘ |
| 8 | (24) | ˋˋΤΗΝ_ΤΥΡΟΣ_ΚΑΙ_ΣΕΙΔ |
| 9 | (23) | ˋˋΦΡΟΝΗΣΕΝ_ΣΦΟΔΡΑ |
| 10 | (24) | ˋˋΜΗΣΕΝ_ΤΥΡΟΣ_ΟΧΥ |
| 11 | (24) | ˋˋΚΑΙ_ΕΒΟΥΝΙΣΕΝ_ΑΡ |
| 12 | (23) | ˋˋΧΟΥΝ_ΚΑΙ_ΧΡΥΣΙΟΝ |
| 13 | (23) | ˋˋΕΞΟΔΩΝ_ΙΔΟΥ_𐤄𐤉 |
| 14 | (25) | ˋˋΜΗΣΕΙ_ΑΥΤΗΝ_ΚΑΙΠ |
| 15 | (23) | ˋˋΘΑΛΑΣΣΑΝΔΥΝΑΜΙ |
| 16 | (25) | ˋˋΑΥΤΗ_ΕΝ_ΠΥΡΙ_Κ ΤΑΝ |
| 17 | (23) | ˋˋΤΑΙ_Κ ΙΟ |
| 18 | (24) | |
| 19 | (20) | |
| 20 | (22) | |
| 21 | (22) | |
| 22 | (22) | |
| 23 | (22) | |
| 24 | (22) | |
| 25 | (22) | |
| 26 | (22) | |
| 27 | (22) | |
| 28 | (22) | |
| 29 | (22) | |
| 30 | (22) | |
| 31 | (22) | |
| 32 | (24) | |
| 33 | (23) | |

TOTALS: 764 letters/column; 33 lines, 20 (short), 28 (long), 23.15 (average) all/part of 17 lines preserved from column, average length *24.05* letters

## Column B2 Za 8.23b–[9.7]

[`````]```````````````•`````[```]
[πο]ρευσόμεθα_μεθ' ὑμ[ῶν, ὅτι]
[ἀ]κηκόαμεν_θεὸς_μεθ' [ὑμῶν.____9.1]
`Λῆμμα λόγου_𐤉𐤄𐤅𐤄·_ἐν [γῇ αδραχ]
``καὶ_δαμασκοῦ_κατάπαυ[σις αὐτοῦ,]
``ὅτι_τῷ_𐤉𐤄𐤅𐤄_ὀφθαλ[μὸς ἀν-]
``θρώπων_καὶ_πασῶν φ[υλῶν τοῦ]
``ισραηλ._2 καί_γε_εμαθ [ὁρίζει αὐ-]
``τήν,_τύρος_καὶ_σειδ[ών, ὅτι ἐ-]
``φρόνησεν_σφόδρα. [3 καὶ ᾠκοδό-]
``μησεν_τύρος_ὀχύ[ρωμα ἑαυτῇ]
``καὶ_ἐβούνισεν_ἀρ[γύριον ὡς]
``χοῦν_καὶ_χρυσίον [ὡς πηλὸν]
``ἐξόδων._4 ἰδοὺ_𐤉𐤄[𐤅𐤄 κληρονο-]
``μήσει_αὐτὴν_καὶ π[ατάξει εἰς]
``θάλασσαν δύναμι[ν αὐτῆς, καὶ]
``αὐτὴ_ἐν_πυρὶ_κ[α]ταν[αλωθήσε-]
``ται._5 κ[α]ὶ ὄ[ψεται ασκαλων καὶ]

6

7

# Additional Fragments (unidentified)

## 1. (PAM 40.566)
Zp 2:10 (col 22, l.42)?

1 ]ων``
2 ]__``

## 2. (PAM 40.566)

1 ].μ[
2 ].[

## 3. (PAM 40.566)

1 ]ω̣``
2 ]ο``
3 ]θη``

## 4. (PAM 40.559)
Mi 1:5?

1 ]τ̣αυ̣[τα

## 5. (PAM 40.566)
see notes in D on Mi 1:1 and Na 3:9-10

1 ]``
2 ]ου``
3 ]αι``

## 6. (PAM 40.559 [hand B])
Za 4:7–8?

1 [ ]``
2 [πρὸ προσώπου Ζοροβαβ]ελ``
3 [εἰς ''''' καὶ ἐξήγαγεν] τ̣ὸν``
4 [λίθον τὸν κεφάλαιον ? ]...``
5 [χάρις χάρις αὐτῇ__καὶ]_ἐ-``
6 [γένετο ]

# D. NOTES ON PALAEOGRAPHY AND IDENTIFICATION

**Cols. 2–4** (plates I–IV)—Due to deterioration of the leather at the edges and to a slightly different arrangement there are some differences between plate I, representing a recent photograph (not including the fragments published by B. Lifshitz), and plates II–IV, representing earlier photographs.

**Col. 3**, ll. 10–11 (Jo 3:3)—The identification of fragment b on plate III is based on the assumption that the tetragrammaton on l. 11 together with the spaces on both sides amount to some 6–7 letters (cf. col. 18, l. 24). The identification is further supported by the fact that three other fragments from the same lot (published by B. Lifshitz) have been preserved for these lines (fragms. a, c, d on plate III). Note also the similarity between these fragments in the colour of the leather and the thinness of the letters. Note that fragment b has been identified by Lif. (fragm. 6) as Na 2:8–9 (l. 2: *καὶ Ν̣[ινευη]*).His reconstruction, however, is not possible as part of the text reconstructed by him has actually been preserved in a different position. Nor does the omega on l. 1 fit the preserved part of the omega of [*περιστ*]*ερῶν* (col. 14, l. 8). The space between the lines on this fragment is larger than that on the main fragment of col. 14, where Na 2:8–9 would have belonged.

**Col. 3**, l. 35 (Jo 4:1) *ἠθ̣[ύμησεν]*—Barth. 163 notes that some letters were lost in Jo 4:1. He probably refers to this word, of which now only the first two letters are visible, although the word itself is transcribed by him as *ἠ*[*θύ*]*μησεν*.

**Col. 4**, l. 24—What looks on the photograph like *Ν̣Ο̣Ι̣* and could, with some imagination, be taken as *Ι̣Ο̣Ν̣*(*Α*) written upside down in the space after the book of Jonah, actually represents mere holes in the leather.

**Col. 4**, ll. 28–9 (Mi 1:1)—At the end of these lines additional fragment 5 could be placed (note [*ἐζεκίου*] at the end of l. 28 and [*καὶ*] at the end of l. 29 as well as a short l. 27). However, at the beginning of l. 30 there is no room for [*ιε*] (now reconstructed at the end of l. 29) and furthermore on the fragment there is more room between the lines than on the main text of col. 4.

**Col. 4**, l. 38—See note on additional fragment 4.

**Col. 6**, ll. 40–2—The right and left sides of these lines do not occur on the same level on plate V due to shrinkage of fragment b.

**Col. 7**, l. 41 (Mi 4:5)—The base of the preserved part of the delta of *δ̣ὲ* is slanted. In view of the MT, LXX and the available space, *δέ* is nevertheless the only possible reconstruction.

**Col. 13**, l. 21 [*διαρρ*]*ήξω*—Reconstructed differently by Lif. (fragm. 5 [Na 1:9]): [*λογ*]*ίζε̣σ̣*[*ε*]. The cross-bar of the first letter (eta) is clearly visible. The second letter is a xi.

**Col. 13**, l. 22 *οὐ σπα̣*[*ρ*]*ή̣σετ*[*αι*]—Reconstructed differently by Lif. (fragm. 3): [*πρεσβυτέρ*]*ους πά̣*[*ντας*]. The latter reconstruction (Jl 1:14) is impossible as there is a large space before *οὐ*.

**Col. 14**, l. 36 [*πλήθο*]*υς*—Reconstructed differently by Lif. (fragm. 8 [Za 4:8–9]):

*Zo*[ροβαβελ]. The reconstruction of this fragment as Na 3:3 is based on the reading of these two letters. Upsilon and sigma are clearly visible.

**Col. 15**, ll. 15–16 (Na 3:9–10)—Additional fragment 5 can be placed at the ends of these lines (note [σου] at the end of l. 15) only if the chi, now reconstructed at the end of l. 16, would be written at the beginning of the next line. However, there is no room for that letter and the division of the word in the middle of a syllable would be unusual for hand A. At present the text is reconstructed as [αἰχ-](16)μαλω[σί]ạ.

**Col. 15**, l. 28—π̣ῦρ τ[ο]ὺς—Reconstructed differently by Lif. (fragm. 1): ẹὕρη (*sic*). Lifshitz's reconstruction (Ho 2:8) differs mainly in one letter from ours: the last letter on the fragment clearly is part of a tau.

**Col. 17–22**—There are slight differences between plate XVIII (recent photograph) and plates XI–XV. See the note on cols. 2–4.

**Col. 17**, ll. 23–5—Fragment c (plate XI) can be placed at the ends of the lines because of the structure of the margin and the gluing of the two columns.

**Col. 18**, l. 18 (Ha 2:15) τ[ῷ]—Less likely: π̣[οτίζοντ]ẹι based on an unusual pi.

**Col. 18**—The text of this column has one line less than the two adjacent columns (see plate XIX). There are a few traces of letters on l. 42 and it appears that it had been inscribed previously and then erased, probably because the scribe wanted to start the new section (Ha 3:1) at the beginning of a new column.

**Col. 19**, l. 26 (Ha 3:9) ῥάβδ̣[ο]υ̣ς̣—Traces of some four letters are visible after this word. Barth. reads λέγει te[tr] (= LXX), but this reconstruction creates too long a text. Reconstruction according to MT requires a different text.

**Col. 19**, l. 35—Traces of additional letters are visible on the leather.

**Col. 20**, ll. 35–42—In these lines a thinner pen is used.

**Col. 21**, ll. 35–9—There are faint traces of several additional letters on the leather.

**Col. 22**, l. 42—The traces of the letters occur at a higher level than the remainder of the words, but this may be due to the shrinking of the leather.

**Col. 23**, ll. 39–40 [π-](40)ηγὴ—See note on the reconstruction.

**Col. 30**, l. 41 [τάδ]ε λέγẹ[ι]—Reconstructed differently by Lif. (fragm. 9 [Za 8:21]): ἔλεγο[ν]. The remnant of the third epsilon appears a little higher than the previous letter, so that an omicron would be possible as well.

**Col. 30**, l. 42 [δό]ξης ἀ[πέ]σ̣τ̣ẹι̣λεν—Reconstructed differently by Lif. (fragm. 9 [Za 8:21]): [καὶ ζη]τῆσα[ι]. The first preserved letter clearly is a xi and cannot be a tau.

**Col. 31**, l. 35—κ[αὶ]—For shape of preserved bottom part of kappa, cf. l. 41.

**Col. B2**—Above the first line of the text, at a distance of what would have been four lines of text, appears a partial semicircle turning downwards. In col. 18 a similarly shaped sign (letter) occurs one line below the text at the far right, but this is probably a remnant of a completely erased line (see above). Furthermore, on the photograph of col. 31 appears a similar shape, but this is a mere shadow not visible on the leather. Probably this letter (sign) has no significance and like the minuscule line in the margin between cols. 8 and 9 (opposite l. 1) it merely presents a 'trying out' of the scribe's pen. For a similarly shaped sign, see the top margin of 4Q491,5 (*DJD* VII, plate V).

**Col. B2**, l. 14 *μήσει*—All letters are clearly visible on photograph 41.690A.

**Additional fragment 4**—The shape and content of the fragment fit Mi 1:5 (col 4, l. 38).

**Additional fragment 5**—See above on Mi 1:1 (col. 4) and Na 3:9–10 (col. 15). Another possibility is col. 16, ll. 33–4 (Ha 1:8).

# E. NOTES ON THE RECONSTRUCTIONS

THE reconstructed text of the scroll (R) not only completes words of R which have been partially preserved, but it also reconstructs most words in the lacunae. In both matters, the reconstruction follows as much as possible the known orthography, vocabulary and translation technique of R. Since the biblical text is known and the length of the lines of the scroll and the column structure are rather fixed, frequently the contents of the lacunae are reconstructed on the basis of these data. As a rule, R is rather consistent, so that its vocabulary and system of translation can be identified in other instances as well (see F11). Such supporting evidence is provided in the following notes. In these notes constant reference is made to section F, containing a discussion of the translation technique, language and text of R. A reference such as 'see F11' refers to paragraph 11 of that section. The reliance on a presumed consistency can, of course, be misleading. Thus, if [σα]μάροια in Mi 1:5 is a mere mistake, reconstructions based on this spelling (Mi 1:1,6) rather than σαμάρεια (LXX) are incorrect.

The text of R is reconstructed in accordance with the supposition that this translation followed MT as closely as possible (see most sections in F1, especially F10, F14.1). However, since only limited knowledge on the vocabulary and translation technique of R can be derived from the scroll, and since R sometimes follows the LXX even when R could have found a more literal (consistent) rendering (see F0.2, 11.2,3), the text of the LXX forms the starting point for the reconstructions in the lacunae. That text has been deviated from whenever adherence to MT in the widest sense of the word would require a different rendering. At the same time, if R would have offered a rendering different from the LXX, but when that equivalent is not known, no equivalent is included in the reconstruction.

The text in the lacunae is reconstructed on the basis of their size and our knowledge of the translation technique and vocabulary of R and without reference to any external sources. While studies by Barth. and others have made it very plausible that there exists a close connection with other known translations such as sections of the so-called 'LXX' of 1–4 Kingdoms, the vocabulary of those sections has not been invoked in our reconstruction in order to avoid circular reasoning. By the same token, even though a remarkable similarity has been recognized with some of the other Greek versions of the Min. Proph. (see F16.2), this evidence is, as a rule, not used in the reconstruction itself. An exception is made for the quotations from Mi in Justin Martyr which show a remarkable resemblance to R (see H. Koester, *Septuaginta und Synoptischer Erzählungsstoff im Schriftbeweis Justins des Märtyrers*, Habilitationsschrift, Theol. Fak. Heidelberg 1956, pp. 26–32 and [independently] Barth. 203–11).

In several instances the transcription deviates from the one published by Barth. 169–178. Differences consisting of the amount of certainty ascribed to letters visible on the leather (questionable letters, etc.) are disregarded in the notes. On the other hand, differences in readings are mentioned. 'Barth.' refers to *Devanciers*, and 'Barth. (notes)' to unpublished notes. The latter reference occurs rarely. Several fragments which Barth. could not place and letters visible on the fragments overlooked by him have now been identified. These additions to Barth. have not been noted separately.

As elsewhere in this monograph, the 'LXX' is quoted from the best available reconstruction of the Old Greek translation, viz., the edition of Ziegler. On the implications of this use of the term 'LXX', see F0.1.

## Jonah

Jo 1:16 [τὸν 𐤉𐤄]𐤅𐤄 (LXX: τὸν κύριον)—For the use of the article rendering את, see F6.

Jo 2:1 [𐤉𐤄𐤅𐤄] (LXX: κύριος)—See F5.4.1.

Jo 2:1 [κ]αταπιεῖν = LXX—Article not included (calc. of space), cf. F2.3.1.

Jo 2:1 [ιωνα] (LXX: Ιωνας)—See Jo 4:1. Similar reconstructions in 2:2; 3:3,4.

Jo 2:1 [ἐν κοιλίᾳ] (LXX: ἐν τῇ κοιλίᾳ)—According to F3.5 R would have omitted the article. Similarly 2:2 [ἐκ κοιλίας]. However, calc. of space would allow for the addition of the article.

Jo 2:1 [τοῦ κήτου]ς = LXX—Also possible here (and elsewhere in vv. 1–2): [τοῦ ἰχθύο]ς (MT: [ה]הדג).

Jo 2:2 [𐤉𐤄𐤅𐤄] (LXX: κύριον)—See above on 1:16.

Jo 2:2 [τὸν θεὸν αὐτο]ῦ = LXX—For use of article, see F4.1.

Jo 2:2 [ἐκ κοιλίας] (LXX: ἐκ τῆς κοιλίας)—According to F3.5 R would have omitted the article, but no certainty is possible here.

Jo 2:3 [ἐν] = LXX—The dative of [θλίψ]ει requires the preposition ἐν (= LXX) reflecting -ב as against -מ in MT מצרה.

Jo 2:3 [ἐπεκαλεσάμην] (LXX: κραυγῆς μου)—instead of MT שִׁוַּעְתִּי, the LXX read שַׁוְעָתִי (nominal form), thus wrongly adding a second complement to the verb. R probably recognized the verbal form of the Hebrew, reconstructed as ἐπεκαλεσάμην. For R's interest in using the same part of speech as the Hebrew, see F10.3.

Jo 2:3 [τῆς φωνῆς μου] (LXX: φωνῆς μου)—Article added in accordance with F4.1.

Jo 2:4 [καὶ ἀ]πέρρειψάς (LXX: ἀπέρριψάς)—καὶ added in accordance with MT ותשליכני. Cf. F14.1.

Jo 2:4 βάθ[ος] (LXX: βάθη)—Adapted to the singular of MT (מצולה), cf. F10.4.1. Barth.: βά[θη].

Jo 2:4 [ἐν καρδίᾳ θαλασσῶν] (LXX: καρδίας θαλάσσης)—Adapted to MT בלבב ימים. For approximations according to the grammatical number of the Hebrew, see F10.4.1.

Jo 2:6 π[εριεχύθησάν] (LXX: περιεχύθη)—For approximations to MT in grammatical number, see F10.4.1. Considerations of space make it likely that R would have used the longer plural form as reconstructed here. For the use of verbal forms with a neuter plural, see F7.11.

Jo 2:7 ἡ [γῆ] (LXX: εἰς γῆν)—Corrected according to MT הארץ. See F10.4.2.

Jo 2:7 [γῆ ---] (LXX: γῆν, ἧς)—Omission reconstructed according to MT (see F14.1) and supported by calc. of space.

Jo 2:7 [μοχλο]ὶ αὐτῆς (LXX: οἱ μοχλοὶ αὐτῆς)—Article omitted because of calc. of space. Cf. F4.3,5.

Jo 2:7 εἰς [αἰῶνα] (LXX: αἰώνιοι)—Adapted to MT לעולם. See F10.3 for the exact representation of MT.

Jo 3:2 [πρὸς αὐτὴν] (LXX: ἐν αὐτῇ)—Adapted to MT אליה (see F11.1[2]).

Jo 3:2 [τὸ κήρυγμα---] (LXX: τὸ κήρυγμα τὸ ἔμπροσθεν)—Omitted with MT הקריאה.

Jo 3:3 ]πορείας (LXX: ὡσεὶ πορείας)—Omission of ὡσεὶ in accordance with MT מהלך, also in v. 4 (LXX: ὡσεὶ πορείαν). See F10.6.

Jo 3:5 [ἐπίσ]τευσα[ν] (LXX: ἐνεπίστευσαν)—Reconstructed with many MSS of the LXX in accordance with F8.1.

Jo 3:5 [ἄνδρες νινευη] (LXX: οἱ ἄνδρες Νινευη)—For omission of articles, see F3.4 and F5.3.

Jo 3:7 [οἱ βόες] (LXX: καὶ . . .)—Adapted to MT הבקר. For similar omissions, see F14.1.

Jo 3:7 [νεμέσθωσαν] = LXX. The reconstructed line is short, so that a longer verbal form with a preverb would also be possible. Alternatively, the verb may have been preceded by a word like μηδὲ (unlike MT אל).

Jo 3:7 [καὶ ὕδ'' μὴ] (LXX: μηδὲ ὕδωρ)—Adapted to MT ומים אל with many MSS of the LXX. For the addition of καὶ see F14.1. For καὶ ... μὴ instead of μηδὲ, see F10.7. It is hard to know whether R would have read here the singular or plural form of ὕδωρ since he is not consistent in this matter. For ὕδωρ changed to plural, see Jo 2:6. For ὕδωρ retained, see Na 2:9; 3:8 and Mi 1:4. In Ha 2:14; 3:10 no reconstruction has been attempted. The reconstructed line here is short, so that the plural form may be preferred as it gives one more letter.

Jo 3:8 [οἱ ἄνθρωποι] = LXX—For the reconstruction (MT האדם), cf. v. 7 and Ha 2:17.

Jo 3:8 [ἐν ἰσχύι] (LXX: ἐκτενῶς)—Adapted to MT בחזקה. For the use of the same part of speech as the Hebrew, see F10.3. For the rendering of -ב by R, see F9.3.

Jo 3:9 ἐπι[σ]τ[ρέψει] (LXX: εἰ)—εἰ omitted with MT ישוב (although there would have been room for this word at the end of l. 29).

Jo 3:9 [καὶ] παρ[ακληθήσετα]ι (LXX: μετανοήσει)—Adapted to MT ונחם.

Jo 3:9 [ἐπιστ]ρέψ[ει] (LXX: ἀποστρέψει)—The usual equivalent of שוב in R is ἐπιστρέφω, see vv. 8, 10. For the use of different preverbs, see F8.3. Note the alternation of the (reconstructed) ἐπιστρέφω and the preposition ἀπό, for which cf. v. 10 in R: ἐπέστρεψαν ἀπὸ.

Jo 3:9 [θυμοῦ] (LXX: ὀργῆς)—Reconstructed on the basis of the following word in R, viz., [ὀργ]ῆς (cf. θυμοῦ in the LXX).

Jo 3:10 τ[οῦ ποιῆσαι] = LXX. Barth.: [ποιῆσαι].

Jo 4:1 Κ[αὶ ἐ]λ[υπήθη ι]ωνα = LXX (Ιωνας).

Jo 4:2 Space reconstructed after εἶπεν in accordance with the 'paragraphos' occurring after l. 36. See A4a.

Jo 4:2 [οὗτος] (LXX: οὗτοι)—Adapted to MT זה דברי. Reconstructed on the basis of the following words in R, ὁ λόγος μου. For approximations to MT in grammatical number, see F10.4.1.

Jo 4:2 [ἐπὶ τῆς γῆς μου] (LXX: ἐν τῇ γῇ μου)—Adapted to MT על אדמתי. For the prepositions, see F9.3. For the use of the article, see F4.1.

Jo 4:2 [ὅτι[1]] (LXX: διότι)—See F9.3.

Jo 4:2 [θεὸς] (LXX: ---)—Adapted to MT אל. See 14.1.

Jo 4:5 [ἑαυτῷ] = LXX or ἑατῷ (cf. F12.14).

## Micah

Mi 1:1 Λόγος 𐤉[𐤄𐤅𐤄 ὃς ἐγένετο or ἐγενήθη] (LXX: καὶ ἐγένετο λόγος κυρίου)—Reconstructed with MT דבר יהוה אשר היה on the basis of the first two words preserved in R. Cf. LXX to Ho 1:1; Am 1:1; Jl 1:1; Zp 1:1.

Mi 1:1 [τὸν] μωρασθει (LXX: τὸν Μωρασθι)—MT המרשתי. The reconstructed line 27 of col. 4 is short, possibly because the scribe did not want to break up μωρασθει now written as the first word of l. 28.

Mi 1:1 [ιωθαμ] (LXX: Ιωαθαμ)—Reconstructed according to MT יותם. Cf. the note on the transliteration of יונה in Jo 2:1.

Mi 1:1 —In the reconstruction καί of the LXX is omitted twice with MT, leaving a somewhat short line 28. Cf. F14.1. There is room for one occurrence of καί.

Mi 1:1 ὃ[ν] (LXX: ὑπὲρ ὧν)—Reconstructed with MT אשר, referring to λόγος.

Mi 1:1 [σαμαροίας] (LXX: Σαμαρείας)—Cf. v. 5 [σα]μάροια. The reconstruction is based on the assumption that R would have been consistent in this spelling. Cf. F12.2. For the non-representation of the article, see F5.3.

Mi 1:1 [καὶ ιερουσ]αλημ (LXX: καὶ περὶ Ιερουσαλημ)—Adapted to MT וירושלם (calc. of space). See F10.6.1 for approximations to MT by omission.

Mi 1:2 ['''''] (LXX: λόγους)—MT has here עמים כלם, but in the reconstructed text of R there is only room for one of the two words.

Mi 1:2 [--- προσεχέτω] (LXX: καί[1])—Omitted with MT הקשיבי, see F14.1.

Mi 1:2 [γῆ] (LXX: ἡ γῆ)—For the omission of the article (MT: ארץ), see F1.3.

Mi 1:2 [κύριος 𐤉𐤄𐤅𐤄] (LXX: κύριος), MT אדני יהוה—In the lacuna there is sufficient room for two words, so that R probably had κύριος for אדני and the tetragrammaton for יהוה (see F5.4.1). See also note on אדני in v. 2b.

Mi 1:2 εἰς μάρτυ[ρα] (LXX: εἰς μαρτύριον)— Adapted to MT לעד. For lexical approximations of nouns to MT, see F10.1.

Mi 1:2 [κύριος] = LXX, MT אדני—R probably distinguished between the tetragrammaton (𐤉𐤄𐤅𐤄) and אדני (κύριος). In Za 9:4 אדני (MT)—𐤉𐤄[𐤅𐤄] probably reflects יהוה.

Mi 1:2 [ναοῦ] (LXX: οἴκου)—Reconstructed according to the rendering in R of the same word (היכל) in Jo 2:5; Na 2:7.

Mi 1:3 *ἐκπ[ορεύεται]* = LXX, MT יצא—Based on the assumption that the Hebrew participle would be reflected by the Greek praesens. Barth.: *ἐκπ[ορευόμενος]*.

Mi 1:3 *κα[ὶ ἐπιβήσεται]* = LXX—Future tense reconstructed according to the preceding verb in R (MT: וירד ודרך).

Mi 1:3 *[ἐπὶ ὕψη γῆς]* (LXX: *ἐπὶ τὰ ὕψη τῆς γῆς*)—Articles omitted in accordance with F3.4. This assumption is supported by calc. of space, although one of the two articles could have been included in the text.

Mi 1:4 *[τακή]σον[ται]* (LXX: *σαλευθήσεται*)—Reconstructed according to the frequent LXX equivalence of *τήκω* מסס and the identical reading of *α′* ad loc. (cf. also *θ′*). Note that in the same verse יתבקעו is rendered in R by *[ῥα]γήσον[τα]ι* and in the LXX by *τακήσονται*.

Mi 1:4 *ἀ[πὸ προσώπου]* = LXX—For a similar rendering in R, see Ha 2:20.

Mi 1:4 *[τοῦ πυρὸς]* (LXX: *πυρὸς*)—Article added with MT האש.

Mi 1:4 *[ὡς ὕδωρ]* (LXX: *καὶ ὡς ὕδωρ*)—Adapted to MT כמים. For omission of *καὶ* in R to conform with MT, see F10.6a. For the grammatical number of *ὕδωρ*, see on Jo 3:7. The next word in R ending in *-μενο[ν]* necessitates the singular rather than the plural form of *ὕδωρ*.

Mi 1:5 *[δι']* (LXX: *διὰ*) twice—Cf. Ha 2:17 and see F12.6 for this orthography. Preposition reconstructed according to the case ending of the noun.

Mi 1:5 *[ἀσέβιαν]* (LXX: *ἀσέβειαν*)—Cf. *ἀσέβια* later in the verse in R.

Mi 1:5 *]ἀσέβια* (LXX: *ἡ ἀσέβεια*)—Article omitted in accordance with F3.4.

Mi 1:5 *ο[ὐ]* = LXX—According to R's rendering of הלוא later in the verse as well as in Ha 2:7, *οὐχί* would have been expected here, too. However, there does not seem to be room for *οὐχί*, so that R probably followed the LXX.

Mi 1:5 *[σα]μάροια* (LXX: *Σαμάρεια*)—Barth. reads *[σα]μάρεια* like the LXX, but the reading of the omicron is certain. See F12.2.

Mi 1:5 *[ὕψη]* (LXX: *ἡ ἁμαρτία οἴκου*)—Adapted to MT במות. For the use of the article, see F3.4. For the use of *ὕψη* (rather than *ὑψηλά*), see v. 3.

Mi 1:6 *σα[μάροιαν]* (LXX: *Σαμάρειαν*)—Cf. on v. 1. Barth. reconstructs R as the LXX. See F12.2.

Mi 1:6 *[φυτείας]* (LXX: *φυτείαν*)—Adapted to MT למטעי. See F10.4.1 for approximations to the Hebrew in grammatical number.

Mi 1:7 *κατακ[όψουσιν]* = LXX (*-σι*)—For the verbal form, cf. the next verb in the verse. See F12.13 for use of *ν* movable.

Mi 1:7 *θήσ[ω]* (LXX: *θήσομαι*)—Based on placing of the fragment and count of letters (cf. also Mi 4:7 and Na 3:6). On the other hand, *[θ]ήσομαι* is used in the previous verse.

Mi 1:7 *[ἀφανισμόν]* (LXX: *εἰς ἀφανισμόν*)—Adapted to MT שממה. See F10.6.1 for approximations to MT by omission.

Mi 1:7 *[ὅ]τι* (LXX: *διότι*)—Reconstructed according to R's preference, see F9.3.

Mi 1:7 *ἐγ μισ[θώματος]* (LXX: *ἐκ μισθωμάτων*)—Adapted to MT מאתנן. For approximations to MT in grammatical number, see F10.4a. For the orthographic interchange *ἐκ* > *ἐγ*, see F12.4.

Mi 1:7 *[πόρνης]* (LXX: *πορνείας*) twice—Adapted to MT זונה (thus also the Lucianic MSS).

Mi 1:7 *[ἐπιστρέψουσ]ιν* (LXX: *συνέστρεψεν*)—Adapted to MT ישובו (for the equivalent, see note on 2:8). See F10.4a for approximations to MT through a change in grammatical number and F7.5 for the change of tense. Barth.: *[συστρέψουσ]ιν*.

Mi 1:8 *[κόψομαι καὶ θρηνήσω, πορεύσομαι]* (LXX: *κόψεται καὶ θρηνήσει, πορεύσεται*)—Adapted to MT אספדה ואילילה אילכה. See F10.4c for approximations to MT in grammatical person.

Mi 2:7 *[οἱ λόγοι μου]* (LXX: *οἱ λόγοι αὐτοῦ*)—Reconstructed with MT דברי. See F10.4.3 for approximations to MT in grammatical person.

Mi 2:7 *μ[ετὰ τοῦ ὀρθοῦ]* (LXX: *μετ' αὐτοῦ καὶ ὀρθοὶ*)— Adapted to MT עם הישר. See F10.6.1, 14.1 for omission of *καὶ* and *αὐτοῦ*, F1.2 for the article, and F10.4.1 for the grammatical number.

Mi 2:8 *[εἰς ἐχθρὸν]* (LXX: *εἰς ἔχθραν*)—Reconstructed with MT לאויב.

Mi 2:8 *ἐπι[στραφήσον]ται* (LXX: *συντριμμὸν*)—Reconstructed as translation of a variant ישובו (see F15.3) for which cf. MT שובי. For the equivalent, see R in Jo 3:8,10; Mi 5:3(4); Za 1:4.

Mi 2:8 πόλεμο̣[ν] (LXX: πολέμου [diff. constr.])—Based on the preceding verb ἐ̣πι̣[στραφήσον]ται. Less likely: πολέμο̣[υ].

Mi 2:9 [γυναῖκες] (LXX: ἡγούμενοι)—Adapted to MT נשי.

Mi 3:4 [ἐπιτηδεύματα αὐτῶν] (LXX: ἐν τοῖς ἐπιτηδεύμασιν αὐτῶν)— Reconstructed with MT מעלליהם (thus also α′).

Mi 3:5 [Τάδε λέγει יהוה] = LXX—For reconstruction of R see Za 2:12(8) and 3:7 (MT: כה אמר יהוה). Similar reconstructions: Za 1:4,14; 8:20.

Mi 3:5 [καὶ ἐκήρυξαν] (LXX: καὶ κηρύσσοντας)—Adapted to MT וקראו (for the lexical choice cf. R in Jo 3:2,5). A form of καλέω is possible as well.

Mi 3:5 [ἐπ' αὐτ]ὸ̣ν = LXX—Reconstructed on the basis of the LXX and not MT. In the reconstruction of this column all lines have approximately 35 characters, so that also this line (38) would have had the same number of characters. ‴]ο̣ν could reflect κηρύσσ]ο̣ν[τας as in the LXX, but then the line, reconstructed without αὐτὸν, would be too short, and the verbal form would not have equalled MT.

Mi 3:5 [καὶ ὃς] (LXX: καὶ)—Adapted to MT ואשר. For the use of the same part of speech as in the Hebrew, see F10.3.

Mi 3:5 [δώσει] (LXX: ἐδόθη)—Adapted to MT יתן.

Mi 3:5 [ἐπὶ] (LXX: εἰς)—Adapted to MT על (cf. F10.2).

Mi 3:5 [καὶ ἡγίασαν] (LXX: ἤγειραν)—Adapted to MT וקדשו (cf. F10.1).

Mi 3:6 [ὑμεῖν] (LXX: ὑμῖν)—Cf. the same form later in the verse and see F12.1.

Mi 3:6 [ὑμεῖν ---], [ὑμ]εῖν (LXX: ἔσται)—Omitted in accordance with MT (supported by calc. of space). See F10.6.

Mi 3:6 [ὁράσεως] = LXX. For equivalent of R, cf. Ha 2:2.

Mi 4:3–7—For a full reconstruction of the text of these verses according to R, see Barth. 206.

Mi 4:3 [λαῶν] = LXX (MT: עמים)—For equivalent of R, cf. Mi 4:5; Ha 3:13; Zp 2:9,10; Za 8:20.

Mi 4:3 [καὶ ἐλέγξει]—A reconstructed compositum ἐξελέγξει (= many MSS of the LXX) is possible as well (not prohibited by calc. of space). However, in accordance with F8.5, R would have preferred the simplex.

Mi 4:3 [ἕως] (LXX: ἕως εἰς), MT עד—For the reconstruction, see Mi 1:7, 4:7, 5:3(4) and Just ad loc.

Mi 4:3 μ[άχαιραν] (LXX: ῥομφαίαν)—The remaining part of the letter makes the present reconstruction (cf. the same equivalence [MT: חרב] earlier in the verse) more likely than ῥ̣[ομφαίαν] for which cf. Mi 5:5(6); Na 3:15.

Mi 4:4 [καὶ καθίσ]ονται (LXX: καὶ ἀναπαύσεται)—Adapted to MT וישבו (cf. also Just). For lexical approximations of verbs to MT, see F10.1. For approximations to the grammatical number of the Hebrew, see F10.4.1.

Mi 4:4 [καὶ² ---] (LXX: καὶ ἕκαστος)—Omitted with MT (and Just) on the basis of calc. of space. See F10.6.1.

Mi 4:4 ἐ̣[κφοβῶν] (LXX: ὁ ἐκφοβῶν)—Article omitted with MT מחריד. Barth. 206: ὁ ἐκφοβῶν (indeed, ὁ̣ [ἐκφοβῶν] is possible as well).

Mi 4:4 [ἐλάλησεν. ---] (LXX: ἐλάλησε ταῦτα)—Omitted in accordance with MT (and Just). See F10.6.1. In this place a closed section is reconstructed since the scroll must have included something between the last word of v. 4 (ἐλάλησεν) and the beginning of v. 5. Alternatively, the text may have read ταῦτα as in the LXX.

Mi 4:5 πορε[ύσονται ---] (LXX: πορεύσονται ἕκαστος)—Note that in the scroll there is no room for this word, also lacking in Just. See F15.3.

Mi 4:5 [ἐν ὀνόματι θε]οῦ αὐτῶν (LXX: τὴν ὁδὸν αὐτοῦ)—based on MT בשם אלהיו and in agreement with Just. For substitutions of nouns, see F10.1. For the omission of the article in front of the nomen regens, see F3.4.

Mi 4:5 [′′′′′]—For MT ועד are possible either [καὶ ἔτι] for which cf. Just ad loc. and Barth. 206 or [καὶ ἐπέκεινα] = LXX.

Mi 4:6 [λέγει] = LXX, MT נאם—Cf. R in Na 2:14; Zp 1:3. Similar reconstructions in Zp 1:2; 2:9; Za 1:3; 2:9(5),10(6).

Mi 4:6 [τὴν ἐκτεθλιμμένην] and in v. 7 [τὴν ἐκτεθλιμμένη]ν̣ (in both cases LXX: συντετριμμένην)—both reflecting MT הצלעה—, based on Just, Dial. 110.5; cf. also 109.3. Both ll. 2 and 4 of col. 8 are somewhat short, so that either the reconstructed word must be longer than indicated or the writing of this word took more space (note the wide letters in this word).

Mi 4:6 [ἀθροίσω] (LXX: εἰσδέξομαι)—Adapted to MT אספה (cf. equivalent of R in Ha 2:5). For lexical approximations of verbs to MT, see F10.1.

Mi 4:7 ὑ[πόλειμ]μα = LXX (MT: (ל)שארית)—Cf. Zp 1:4 ὑπ[όλειμμα].

Mi 4:7 [ἐκπεπιεσμέ]νην (LXX: καὶ τὴν ἀπωσμένην), MT: והנהלאה—Based on Just.

Mi 4:8 [αὐχ]μώδης = LXX. The first letter after the lacuna is a mu enabling the present reconstruction. A tau would have enabled a reconstructed [σκο]τώδης as in α′.

Mi 4:8 [σειων] (LXX: Σιων)—For this orthography, see F12.1. The article is not reconstructed with F5.3 and the LXX.

Mi 4:8 [ἕως σοῦ] (LXX: ἐπὶ σὲ)—Adapted to MT עדיך (for R, cf. F9.3).

Mi 4:8 [καὶ ἐλεύσετα]ι (LXX: καὶ εἰσελεύσεται), MT ובאה—Based on the regular equivalent of the root בא. See F8.1 concerning the replacement of compound verbs in the LXX with the simplex in R.

Mi 4:8 [βασιλεία ---] (LXX: βασιλεία ἐκ Βαβυλῶνος)—Omitted in accordance with MT. See F14.1.

Mi 4:8 [ιερουσ]αλημ = LXX—The article is not reconstructed with F5.3 and the LXX (also calc. of space).

Mi 4:9 [--- Νῦν] (LXX: καὶ νῦν)—Omitted with MT עתה. For omission of καὶ, see F14.1.

Mi 4:9 [οὐκ ἔστιν σοι] (LXX: οὐκ ἦν σοι)—Adapted to MT אין בך. Cf. 4:4; Ha 2:19. See F10.4.4 for approximations to Hebrew in tenses.

Mi 4:9 [ἐὰν] (LXX: ἤ)—Adapted to MT אם (cf. R in Ha 2:3).

Mi 4:9 [ὁ σύμβουλός] σου (LXX: ἡ βουλή σου)—Adapted to MT יועצך. Cf. passim in the LXX. For the article, see F4.1. For lexical approximations of nouns to MT, see F10.1.

Mi 4:9 [κατεκράτησάν] = LXX—Plural form of the verb reconstructed on the basis of the plural of [ὠδῖ]νες in spite of the singular of MT (החזיקך).

Mi 4:10 σ[ειων] (LXX: Σιων)—For this orthography, see F12.1.

Mi 5:1 οἶκο[ς′′′′′] (LXX: Βηθλεεμ οἶκος)—In the lacuna there is room for just βηθλεεμ (thus Barth. with W *Ach Sa*) or ἄρτου (with or without τοῦ). For approximations to MT by omission of elements, see F14.1.

Mi 5:1 [ιο]υδα = LXX—Article not reconstructed with F5.3 and the LXX (also calc. of space).

Mi 5:2 [τικτού]σης = LXX—Syntax of LXX = R is not clear (cf. σ′) and possibly a comma ought to be added after this word (against Ziegler).

Mi 5:3 [αὐτοῦ] (LXX: αὐτῶν)—Adapted to MT אלהיו. See F10.4.1 for the approximation of pronouns to MT.

Mi 5:4 [εἰ]ς [τὴν γῆν ἡμῶ]ν (LXX: ἐπὶ τὴν γῆν ἡμῶν)—Reconstruction of [εἰ]ς is based on the same rendering of בארצנו in the next verse. See F9.3 for synonymous prepositions.

Mi 5:4 βάρ[εις ἡμῶν] (LXX: χώραν ἡμῶν [Ziegler; MSS: ὑμῶν])—Adapted to MT ארמנתינו. See F10.1.

Mi 5:4 π[οιμένας] (LXX: ποιμένες)—Reconstructed thus since ἐπιγείρειν requires the accusative case, whereas in the LXX the noun is the subject of the verb.

Mi 5:5 παραξ[ιφι′′] (LXX: τάφρῳ)—Possible are either the singular παραξ[ιφίδι] (thus Barth.) or the plural παραξ[ιφίσιν] (thus Barth. in his earlier study of the text: 'Redécouverte...', *RB* 60 [1953] 27), both based on a different spelling and vocalization of the Hebrew, derived from a noun פְּתִחָה, similar in meaning to חרב in the parallel stich.

Mi 5:5 [---] after παραξ[ιφι′′ (LXX: αὐτῆς)—Omission postulated on grounds of count of letters.

Mi 5:5 [ἐξ] (LXX: ἐκ τοῦ)—Omitted on the basis of MT מאשור. See F5.3 for the omission of the definite article before proper names.

Mi 5:5 [ἡμῶν¹] = LXX (Ziegler; MSS: ὑμῶν) and MT בארצנו.

Mi 5:5 [ὅτι²] (LXX: ὅταν). Based on the same set of equivalents earlier in this verse and see further F9.3.

Mi 5:6 —In accordance with the prevalent custom of the scroll three spaces would have been left in front of v. 6 corresponding with a 'closed space' of MT.

Mi 5:6 [κατά]λοιπον (LXX: ὑπόλειμμα)—Based on the LXX in Zp 2:9. For the lack of the article, see F3.4. If the space mentioned in the preceding note would not be reconstructed, there would be room for an article in the lacuna.

Mi 5:6 [---] (after ιακωβ) (LXX: ἐν τοῖς ἔθνεσιν)—Omitted with MT on the basis of count of letters.

Mi 5:6 [---] (after [paleo-Hebrew]) (LXX: πίπτουσα)—Omission based on MT where this plus of the LXX has no equivalent.

Mi 5:6 [ὃς οὐκ '''''''' ἀνδρὶ καὶ οὐ μὴ] (LXX: ὅπως μὴ συναχθῇ μηδεὶς μηδὲ)—Reconstructed with MT אשר לא יקוה לאיש ולא (cf. α′θ′).

## Nahum

Na 1:14 [ἐπὶ σοί] (LXX: ὑπὲρ σοῦ)—Adapted to MT עליך.

Na 1:14 [γλυπτὸν] (LXX: τὰ γλυπτὰ)—Adapted to MT פסל, cf. F10.4.1.

Na 2:5 [δραμοῦν]ται (LXX: διατρέχουσαι)—Adapted to the future tense of MT (ירוצצו).

Na 2:6 --- (after αὐτοῦ) (LXX: καὶ φεύξονται ἡμέρας)—Omitted in conformity to MT. See F14.1.

Na 2:6 ἑτοιμάσε[ι] (LXX: ἑτοιμάσουσι)—Based on the assumption that MT וְהֻכַן (sing.) was read as an active form both by the LXX (plur.) and R (sing.). See F10.4.1 for differences in number.

Na 2:7 [Πύλ]α[ι] = LXX, MT שערי—No article has been reconstructed (calc. of space). See F3.2.

Na 2:8 ['''']η (LXX: καὶ αὕτη ἀνέβαινε)—For the omission of καὶ (MT העלתה), see F14.1. R could be reconstructed as [ἀνέβ]η parallel to the form of the LXX. Barth. (notes): [ἠνήχθ]η.

Na 2:8 ὡ[ς φωνὴ] (LXX: καθὼς ---)—Adapted to MT כקול. For the preposition, see F9.3.

Na 2:8 ἀποφθεγγ[ο]μέν[ων] (LXX: φθεγγόμεναι)—Barth. reconstructs the nominative for R: ἀποφθεγ[γό]μεν[αι] (cf. LXX).

Na 2:8 [ἐπὶ τὴν καρδίαν αὐτῶν] (LXX: ἐν καρδίαις αὐτῶν)—Adapted to MT על לבבהן. See F10.2. Article added on the basis of F4.1 (also calc. of space).

Na 2:9 φεύ[γουσιν] (LXX: φεύγοντες)—Adapted to MT נסים. The LXX translated this verb in conjunction with the next one as a participle.

Na 2:9 [στ]ῆ[τε, στῆτε] (LXX: οὐκ ἔστησαν)—Reconstructed in agreement with MT עִמְדוּ עֲמֹדוּ. The remnants of ll. 10–11 do not allow for the text of the LXX if indeed the last letter of l. 10 is an eta. In that case there is no room in front of the last word of l. 10 for οὐκ of the LXX, and a reconstructed [ἔστ]η[σαν] with [σαν] at the beginning of l. 11 leaves too short a text until the middle of l. 11.

Na 2:9 [---] (after ἦν) (LXX: ὁ)—Omitted with MT מפנה. See F1.3.

Na 2:10 [τὸ ἀργύριον] = LXX—Article reconstructed in accordance with the parallel phrase τὸ χ[ρυσίον] in spite of MT כסף.

Na 2:13 [καὶ τὴν μά]νδραν [αὐτοῦ] (LXX: καὶ τὸ κατοικητήριον αὐτοῦ)—For the article before a noun with a pronominal suffix, see F4.1.

Na 2:14 [πρὸς σ]έ (LXX: ἐπὶ σέ)—Adapted to MT אליך. For the equivalent of R, see F11.1(2).

Na 2:14 [τῶν δυνάμεων] (LXX: παντοκράτωρ)—Adapted to MT צבאות. See F1.5 for a complete list. For lexical approximations of nouns to MT, see F10.1.

Na 2:14 [καὶ ἐκκα]ύσω = LXX, MT והבערתי. Compositum reconstructed with the LXX because of calc. of space.

Na 2:14 [τὸ ἅρμα αὐτῆς] (LXX: πλῆθός σου)—Adapted to MT רכבה (the LXX read a form of רב, viz., רבכה). For lexical approximations of nouns to MT, see F10.1. For the article see F4.4, and for the pronoun F10.4.3.

Na 3:3 [ἀναβαίνοντος] = LXX—For this and the following words genitives are reconstructed (as in the LXX), supported by [πλήθο]υς in l. 36, *si vera lectio*.

Na 3:3 [ῥομφαία]ς = LXX (MT: חרב)—Cf. Mi 5:5(6); Na 3:15. [μάχαιρα]ς is possible, too (cf. Mi 4:3).

Na 3:3 [τραυματίου] (LXX: τραυματιῶν)—The singular form is adapted to MT חלל. See F10.4.1 for approximations to MT in grammatical number.

Na 3:3 ['''']ς—For MT פגר, R possibly read [πτώσεω]ς as in the LXX, or otherwise [πτώματο]ς or [σώματο]ς.

Na 3:3 [καὶ ἀσ]θε[νήσουσιν] = LXX—For the sake of convenience R is reconstructed as the LXX reflecting the Qere וכשלו.

Na 3:6 [ὡς] (LXX: εἰς)—Reconstructed with MT -כ (כראי). See F9.3.

Na 3:7 [αὐτῇ] (LXX: αὐτήν)—Reconstructed (hebraistically) with MT לה.

Na 3:7 π[αρακαλοῦντάς] (LXX: παράκλησιν)—Adapted to MT מנחמים. See F10.4.1 for approximations to MT in grammatical form.

Na 3:7 [σοι] (LXX: αὐτῇ)—Adapted to MT לך. For approximations of pronouns to MT, see F10.4.3.

Na 3:8 Before this verse, at the end of l. 10 of col 15, a space must have been left in the scroll corresponding with an 'open section' of MT. This space is indicated in the scroll by a 'paragraphos' and by the 'capital' letter starting the next line (l. 11) to the left of the margin. See A4a.

Na 3:8 --- μὴ ἀγαθύνεις (LXX: ἅρμοσαι χορδήν, ἑτοίμασαι)—The first two words of the difficult text of the LXX are omitted with MT התיטבי (calc. of space). For the third word R has an alternative translation.

Na 3:8 ὑπ[ὲρ νω] (LXX: μερίδα)—Reflecting MT מנא. LXX reflects an etymological understanding according to מנה.

Na 3:8 [ἧς] ἰσχὺς (LXX: ἧς ἡ ἀρχή)—For the omission of the Greek article in accordance with MT חיל, cf. F1.3.

Na 3:8 [τὸ τεῖχος αὐτῆς] (LXX: τὰ τείχη αὐτῆς)—Adapted to MT חומתה. See F10.4.1 for approximations to MT in grammatical number.

Na 3:9 [---] (before [αἰθιοπία]) (LXX: καὶ)—Adapted to MT כוש. For omission of καί, see F14.1.

Na 3:9 [---] φουδ (LXX: τῆς φυγῆς)—Adapted to MT פוט. See F5.3 for the omission of the article before proper nouns.

Na 3:9 [σου] (LXX: αὐτῆς)—Adapted to MT בעזרתך.

Na 3:10 [ἐπορεύθη] (LXX: πορεύσεται)—Adapted to MT הלכה. See F7.1.1.

Na 3:10 [ἐν αἰχ]μαλω[σί]ạ (LXX: αἰχμάλωτος)—Adapted to MT בשבי. See F10.3 for the exact representation of all elements of the Hebrew. For equivalents of -ב, see F9.3.

Na 3:10 [ἐπὶ κεφαλ]ὴν (LXX: ἐπ' ἀρχὰς)—Adapted to MT בראש according to the frequent (hebraistic) equivalent of ראש. [ἐπ' ἀρχ]ὴν (cf. Barth.) is also possible. ἐπὶ is secured by the case ending of the next word (cf. also R in Mi 5:4[5]).

Na 3:10 [ὁδῶν ---] (LXX: τῶν ὁδῶν αὐτῆς)—Article and pronoun omitted with MT חוצות. See F10.6.1, 14.1.

Na 3:10 [---] (after ἐπί$^{2}$) (LXX: πάντα)—Omitted with MT. For approximations to MT by omission, see F14.1.

Na 3:10 [τοὺς ἐνδόξους αὐ]τῆς (LXX: τὰ ἔνδοξα αὐτῆς), MT נכבדיה—Adapted to the parallel phrase [μεγιστᾶ]νες (MT גדוליה).

Na 3:10 [κλῆρον] (LXX: κλήρους)—Reconstructed according to MT גורל. See F10.4a for approximations in grammatical number.

Na 3:10 [ἐν χειροπέδαις] (LXX: χειροπέδαις)—Adapted to MT בזקים. For representation of all elements of the Hebrew, see F10.3 and for the equivalent of -ב, see F9.3. In view of the uncertainty, the space reconstructed before v. 11 is tentative.

Na 3:11 [--- ἔσῃ] (LXX: καὶ ἔσῃ)—Omitted with MT תהי, see F14.1.

Na 3:11 [ἐξ ἐχθροῦ] (LXX: ἐξ ἐχθρῶν)—Reconstructed with MT מאויב. Cf. F10.4.1.

Na 3:12 [σὺν] σκοπ[οῖς] (LXX: σκοποὺς ἔχουσαι)—Adapted to MT עם בכורים. See F10.2 for approximation to Hebrew prepositions. See F10.7 for transpositions of the LXX.

Na 3:12 [ἔσθο]ντος = LXX or [ἐσθίο]ντος (cf. R in Ha 3:14).

Na 3:13 [--- γυναῖκες] (LXX: ὡς γυναῖκες)—Omitted with MT נשים. See F10.6.

Na 3:13 [ἐ]ν [μέσῳ σου] (LXX: ἐν σοί)—Adapted to MT בקרבך (see equivalent of R in Ha 2:19). See F10.2 for approximations to the lexical meaning of Hebrew prepositions.

Na 3:13 [ἔφαγεν] (LXX: καταφάγεται)—Reconstructed because of calc. of space. See F8.1 for the use of the simplex instead of a compositum and F7.1 for the tense.

Na 3:14 [ὕδρευσα]ι (LXX: ἐπίσπασαι)—For lexical choice of R, cf. passim in the LXX and see F10.1.

Na 3:14 [τὰ ὀχυρώματά σου] (LXX: τῶν ὀχυρωμάτων σου)— For the lexical choice, cf. Ha 1:10. For the article, see F4.5. The difference in case ending is reconstructed in accordance with the assumption that the LXX reflects חִזְקִי, while R reflects MT (חַזְּקִי).

Na 3:14 [ἐλθὲ] (LXX: ἔμβηθι)—Adapted to MT באי. See F9.1.1 for synonymous verbs.

Na 3:14 [κράτησον] (LXX: κατακράτησον), MT החזיקי—See F8.1 for the use of the simplex instead of a compositum.

Na 3:15 [φάγεταί] (LXX: καταφάγεταί) (twice)—Preverb omitted in accordance with F8.1 (calc. of space).

Na 3:15 [βροῦχος[1]] (LXX: ἀκρίς)—The reconstruction (MT: ילק) is based on the equivalence ארבה—ἀκρίς in R in the same verse. See F9.2 for substitution with synonymous nouns. Note that R has the last two stichs of MT, while the LXX lacks one, probably the first one (note the different equivalents for ילק and ארבה), even though a later revision (MSS VLC+) filled in the last phrase.

Na 3:15 [--- καταβαρύν]θητι (LXX: καὶ βαρυνθήσῃ)—καὶ omitted with MT התכבדי. See F14.1. For the use of a compositum, see the context and F8.2.

Na 3:16 [ὥρμησεν] = LXX, MT פשט—Cf. R in Ha 1:8 (root: פרש) (MT: ופרשיו).

Na 3:17 ὄχλ[ος]—If the reconstruction is correct, it is not clear which Hebrew word would be represented by it (גוב?). Note the possible Coptic equivalent of this word as quoted by Barth. 233.

## Habbakuk

Ha 1:5 ]. α[—The clearly visible alpha stands at a place where we would expect an equivalent for either בגוים or ראו, neither of which would have an alpha (ἴδετε ἐν τοῖς ἔθνεσιν). It is therefore not impossible that R had here the equivalent of the LXX (καταφρονηταί), representing a different Hebrew text.

Ha 1:5 --- (after [θαυμ]άσατε) (LXX: καὶ ἀφανίσθητε)—Double reading of the LXX not reconstructed for R. See 14.1.

Ha 1:5 ἔρ[γον ''''''''''] (LXX: ἔργον ἐγὼ ἐργάζομαι)—R may have read the same verb as the LXX, since its root corresponds with that of ἔργον (MT: פעל פעל), but the exact form (first or third person) cannot be determined. If R's Hebrew text was identical with that of MT, he would not have read ἐγὼ as in the LXX. On the other hand, there is room in the lacuna for a short word in addition to the verb.

Ha 1:5 [---] (before [ἐκδιηγ]ηθῇ) (LXX: τις)—Omitted with MT (diff. construction). See F10.6 for approximation to MT through omission.

Ha 1:5 [ἐκδιηγ]ηθῇ (LXX: ἐκδιηγῆται)—Text of R reconstructed according to the assumption that it would contain an aor. subj. rather than an ind. (which would not be compatible with MT יְסֻפַּר, viz., [ἐξεδιηγ]ήθη [it is not clear which form Barth. had in mind: [ἐκδιηγ]ήθη ]). The subj. would probably depend on a conjunction like ἐάν as in the LXX.

Ha 1:6 [ἐγείρω] (LXX: ἐξεγείρω)—In accordance with F8.1, R would have preferred the simplex. Considerations of space strengthen this assumption. On the other hand, in Mi 5:4(5) R (following the LXX) uses the compositum ἐπεγείρω in accordance with the context there (ἐπ' αὐτόν).

Ha 1:6 [---] (after ἐγείρω) (LXX [Rahlfs]: ἐφ' ὑμᾶς)—Omitted with MT (calc. of space). The text of R agrees with that of most MSS of the LXX and the edition of Ziegler against that of Rahlfs.

Ha 1:6 [---] (after ἐγείρω) (LXX: τοὺς μαχητάς)—Omitted with MT on the basis of the assumption that [τοὺς χαλδαίους] equals MT. The LXX contains a doublet.

Ha 1:6 [τῆς γῆς] = LXX in spite of MT ארץ. The article is reconstructed because of calc. of space. Cf. F1.4.

Ha 1:6 [αὐτῷ] (LXX: αὐτοῦ)—Adapted to MT לו, cf. Ha 2:6 and see F10.2.

Ha 1:7 [φοβερὸς] (LXX: ἐπιφανής)—Adapted to MT ונורא (cf. the equivalence of R for ירא and φοβέομαι in Jo 1:16). For lexical approximations of adjectives to MT, see F10.1.

Ha 1:7 [αὐτός] (LXX: ἐστιν)—Cf. Ha 1:10, 2:19. See F10.3 for use of the same part of speech as in the Hebrew.

Ha 1:7 [---] (after αὐτοῦ[1]) (LXX: ἔσται)—Omitted with MT. See F10.6.1 for omission of elements possibly involving a short Hebrew text.

Ha 1:7 [---] (after αὐτοῦ[2]) (LXX: ἐξ αὐτοῦ[2])—Omitted with MT because of calc. of space. See F10.6.1 for omission of elements possibly involving a short Hebrew text.

Ha 1:8 καὶ κουφ[ότεροι] (LXX: καὶ ἐξαλοῦνται), MT: וקלו—Cf. the parallel rendering of וחדו by ὀξύτ[εροι] in R in the same verse. Also possible: κουφ[ιοῦσιν]. See F10.1 for lexical approximations to the Hebrew.

Ha 1:8 [ὑπὲρ] = LXX—Twice in this verse ὑπὲρ is reconstructed with the LXX for the comparative מן of MT (for the equivalent, cf. R in Na 3:8).

Ha 1:8 [--- ? ἑσπέ]ρας (LXX: τῆς Ἀραβίας)—See F10.1 for lexical approximations to the Hebrew. R would have omitted the article, since MT ערב has no article (see F1.3) and this is supported by calc. of space.

Ha 1:8 [καὶ οἱ ἱπ]πεῖς αὐτοῦ (LXX: καὶ ὁρμήσουσι), MT: ופרשיו—For the use of the article before nouns with pronominal suffixes, see F4.4. For approximations to MT using the same part of speech as the Hebrew, see F10.3.

Ha 1:8 [ἐλεύσονται] (LXX: ---)—Reconstructed according to MT יבאו.

Ha 1:8 [καί[5]] = LXX—R probably agrees with the LXX in adding καί to MT יעפו or possibly in reading ועפו (calc. of space).

Ha 1:8 [τοῦ φ]αγεῖν (LXX: εἰς τὸ φαγεῖν)—See F2.1 for the rendering of the *lamed* of the inf. by τοῦ.

Ha 1:9 —At the end of l. 36 of col. 16, R would have had an equivalent for MT מגמת such as πρόσοψις (σ′).

Ha 1:10 γ[έλως] (LXX: παίγνια)—For the reconstruction, see α′ and σ′. See F9.2 for synonymous nouns.

Ha 1:10 [αὐτῷ] (LXX: αὐτοῦ)—Adapted to MT לו (see F10.2).

Ha 1:10 [--- αὐ]τ̣ὸς (LXX: καὶ αὐτὸς[2])—καί omitted with MT הוא (see F14.1).

Ha 1:10 [ἐν]παίξει (LXX: ἐντρυφήσει)—Adapted to MT יתקלס. See F10.1.

Ha 1:10 ἐνπαι̣[ξεται] (LXX: ἐμπαίξεται)—For the orthographic change μ > ν, see F12.3.

Ha 1:10 [β]α̣λ̣ε̣ῖ̣ = LXX—There is room for a preverb such as ἐπι- at the end of the preceding line. Barth. (notes): [β]ουνίσει (for the equivalent, cf. R in Za 9:3).

Ha 1:10 [αὐτό] (LXX: αὐτοῦ)—Adapted to the syntax of the verb in R.

Ha 1:11 παρ[ελεύσεται] (LXX: διελεύσεται)—Cf. the frequent LXX equivalent of עבר.

Ha 1:14 [ἀνθρώπους] = LXX τοὺς ἀνθρώπους—Reconstructed in plural with Jo 3:7 [ἄνθρω]ποι̣ and Ha 2:17 ἀν[θρώπ]ων (MT: אדם). Article omitted (cf. Ha 2:17) with MT.

Ha 1:14 [ἰχθύας] (LXX: τοὺς ἰχθύας)—Article omitted with F3.4.

Ha 1:14 θαλά[σσης]—Reconstructed as θαλά[σ-](10)[σης] on lines 9–10 of col. 17 because the usual practice was to divide between geminate consonants. There is no trace of the sigma on l. 9 and the reconstructed letter would extrude into the margin. However, also on l. 17 the scribe wrote two letters beyond his right hand margin.

Ha 1:14 [---] (before [ὡς]) (LXX: καί)—Omitted with MT כרמש. See F14.1.

Ha 1:14 [--- ἑρπετὰ] (LXX: τὰ ἑρπετὰ)—Article omitted with MT כְּרֶמֶשׂ.

Ha 1:14 [---] (before [οὐκ]) (LXX: τὰ[2])—Omitted with MT לא. See F1.3 and F10.6.1.

Ha 1:15 [πάντα]—(LXX: συντέλειαν)—Adapted to MT כֻּלֹּה; cf. v. 9 in MT, LXX and R. See F10.2.

Ha 1:15 [τῷ ἀμ]φιβλήστρῳ αὐτοῦ (LXX: ἐν ἀμφιβλήστρῳ)—Article added in accordance with added pronoun (cf. MT בחרמו), cf. F4.

Ha 1:15 [ἐν τῇ] σαγήνῃ αὐτοῦ (LXX: ἐν ταῖς σαγήναις αὐτοῦ)—Article reconstructed in the singular to agree with the noun. See F4.1.

Ha 1:16 [τῷ ἀμφιβλή]στρῳ αὐτοῦ (LXX: τῇ σαγήνῃ αὐτοῦ)—For the use of the article, see F4.1.

Ha 1:17 [ἀποκτέννει]ν̣ = LXX—τοῦ not reconstructed before this word (cf. MT להרג) because of calc. of space. See F2.3.1.

Ha 2:1 [ἐπὶ πέτρ]ας (LXX: ἐπὶ πέτραν)—Case ending of [πέτρ]ας continued from previous preposition. The LXX used a different verb. Barth. 220: [ἐπὶ περιφερεί]ας reconstructed from α′ε′ (circinum) reflecting etymological exegesis of MT על מצור. Calc. of space make this reconstruction unlikely.

Ha 2:2 ἐκφαν['']—E.g., ἐκφαν[εῖν] parallel to the previous verb or ἐκφάν[ηθι].

Ha 2:2 [ἐπὶ πυξίω]ν (LXX: ἐπὶ πυξίον), MT: על הלחות—All elements of the reconstruction are uncertain. Our point of departure is the assumption that the same word is used as in the LXX and that R would have preserved the plural of MT instead of the singular of the LXX (see F10.4.1). This change requires the employment of the genitive case with ἐπί which is more frequent in the LXX with verbs of writing than either the accusative or dative case. At the same time, there is no room in the lacuna for an article required by MT so that in this matter R probably followed the LXX. For the placing of the fragment at the ends of ll. 23–5 of col. 17, see note in D.

Ha 2:2 [τρέχ]η̣ (LXX: διώκῃ)—For lexical approximations of verbs to MT, see F10.1. The reconstructed reading is identical with α′σ′.

Ha 2:2 [ἐν αὐτῇ] (LXX: αὐτά)—Reconstructed (hebraistically) with MT בו (feminine form adapted to ὅρασις).

Ha 2:3 [ὅτι] (LXX: διότι)—See F9.3. The shorter ὅτι is preferred because of calc. of space.

Ha 2:3 [ὅρασις] = LXX—Reconstruction probable because of identical equivalent (MT: חזון) in R in v. 2. On the other hand, [αὐ]τόν later in the verse should probably refer to this noun, so that a masculine noun may be expected here (ὕπνος; ὁραματισμός of α′ is too long for the lacuna). However, the same problem obtains in the

LXX, so that the problem of grammatical agreement may have been overlooked by both the LXX and R.

Ha 2:3 [οὐ] (LXX: οὐκ)—Reconstructed on the basis of the next word: [δ]ιαψεύσεται.

Ha 2:3 [προσδέχου] (LXX: ὑπόμεινον)—Thus α′. See F9.1.1 for synonymous verbs.

Ha 2:4 [καὶ[1]] (LXX: ὁ δὲ)—Adapted to MT וצדיק. καὶ also replaces δὲ in Jo 3:3, Ha 2:20 and Mi 4:5 and is reconstructed in Jo 3:7. For omission of the article in accordance with MT, see F1.3.

Ha 2:5 [′′′].ος—Calc. of space make it probable that the scroll lacks one or more of the words of MT, such as ואף כי which are also lacking in the LXX. [′′′].ος could represent בוגד e.g., [ἀσύνθε]τος, for which cf. οι λ in Jer. 3:7; α′σ′θ′ in Ps. 77(78):57 and α′θ′ in Ps. 118(119):158.

Ha 2:5 οὐ γ[′′] (LXX: οὐδὲν μὴ περάνῃ)—Barth. οὐδ[έν...]. The letter cannot be a delta (Barth.) or mu (οὐ μ[ὴ]) or kappa (οὐκ). Possible, but not likely, is a nu (νομεύω or νέμω equalling the root נוה?), but the most likely candidates are a pi (cf. LXX περάνῃ) and even more so a gamma (οὐ γ[).

Ha 2:5 [συνάξει] (LXX: ἐπισυνάξει)—Based on Ha 1:15; Mi 4:6 (MT: ויאסף). See F8.1 concerning the replacement of compounds with simplex forms in R. Tense reconstructed in accordance with the parallel verb.

Ha 2:5 [πρὸς[2]] = LXX—Barth.: [εἰς]. Cf. F11.1.

Ha 2:13 [πυρός] (LXX: ἐν πυρί)—Adapted to MT אש. For approximations to MT in case endings, see F10.4b. For omission of elements, see F10.6. If the same construction was used in both stichs, πῦρ must be reconstructed rather than πυρός (cf. κενὸν in the accusative).

Ha 2:13 [ἐν ἱκανότητι] κενὸν (LXX: πολλὰ)—Adapted to MT בדי ריק. For ἐν ἱκανότητι cf. context in R. See F10.3 for the exact representation of all elements of the Hebrew.

Ha 2:14 [πλησ]θήσεται (LXX: ἐμπλησθήσεται)—For reconstructed simplex, see F8. Barth.: [ἐνπλησ]θήσεται.

Ha 2:14 [τὴν] = LXX—For the use of the Greek article for את with nouns, see F6.

Ha 2:14 [ὕδ′′] (LXX: ὕδωρ)—See on Jo 3:7.

Ha 2:14 [κατακαλύψει] = LXX—Reconstructed in spite of R's probable preference for the simplex (cf. v. 17) because of calc. of space.

Ha 2:14 [ἐπὶ] θαλάσσ[ης] (LXX: αὐτούς)—Reconstructed according to MT על ים.

Ha 2:15 Before this verse a 'closed' section is reconstructed in accordance with the Masoretic practice and following calc. of space. See A4a.

Ha 2:15 [οὐαὶ] τ[ῷ] (LXX: ὦ)—MT הוי. Cf. Ha 2:6. Barth.: [ο]ὐα[ί].

Ha 2:15 [′′′′]υ— ἀνατρ[οπῇ] occurs also in the LXX for מספח of MT, so that it is difficult to determine the equivalent in MT represented by the preceding word [′′′′]υ. Barth. 216–17 reconstructs [ἐξ ἀπροσδοκήτο]υ and ἀνατρ[οπῆς] as in ε′ and the Sahidic translation (see p. 230). G. Howard, *Biblica* 55 (1974) 18 suggests: [αὐτο]ῦ.

Ha 2:15 [τ]οῦ ἐπιβ[λέπειν] (LXX: ὅπως ἐπιβλέπῃ)—For a similar rendering of למען, see the LXX in Jud 2:22 and 2 Chr 25:20. For the article with the infinitive, see F2.4.

Ha 2:15 [τὴν ἀσχημοσ]ύνην αὐ[τῶ]ν (LXX: τὰ σπήλαια αὐτῶν)—For the article before the noun with a pronominal suffix, see F4.1.

Ha 2:16 —In the lacuna at the beginning of l. 23 of col. 18 there is probably room for only one of the two verbs of the LXX (καὶ διασαλεύθητι καὶ σείσθητι) representing one word in MT, והערל.

Ha 2:16 —At the beginning of l. 24 of col. 18 there is room for τῆς before [δεξιᾶς] or for τοῦ before the tetragrammaton.

Ha 2:16 καὶ ἔμετος [ἀτιμίας] (LXX: καὶ συνήχθη ἀτιμία)—Genitive case required by preceding noun (based on וקיקלון of MT taken by R as two words).

Ha 2:17 [--- λιβάνου] (LXX: τοῦ Λιβάνου)—See F5.3 for the omission of the article before proper nouns.

Ha 2:17 [κτηνῶν] (LXX: θηρίων)—For this equivalent, cf. Jo 3:7,8.

Ha 2:18 [καὶ φα]ντασίαν (LXX: φαντασίαν)—Adapted to MT ומורה. For the addition of καὶ, see F14.1 (calc. of space).

Ha 2:19 [Οὐα]ἰ = LXX—Cf. Ha 2:6 for equivalent of R.

Ha 2:19 --- λέγων (LXX: ὁ λέγων)—Article omitted with MT אמר. See F1.3.

Ha 2:19 [---] τῷ λίθῳ (LXX: καὶ τῷ λίθῳ)—καὶ omitted with MT לאבן (calc. of space). See F14.1.

Ha 2:19 [ἰδοὺ] (LXX: τοῦτο δέ)—Adapted to MT הנה. For lexical approximation of particles, see F10.2. For approximations to MT by omission, see F10.6a.

Ha 2:19 οὐ [μή] ἔ[σ]τιν (LXX:οὐκ ἔστιν)—Although the construction itself is not likely (cf. R in Mi 4:4 אין—οὐκ ἔστιν), it is reconstructed because the sequence οὐ ἔ[σ]τιν is not probable and because there is room for two letters in front of ἔ[σ]τιν.

Ha 3:9 [ἐξεγείρων] ἐξεγ[ερ]εῖς (LXX: ἐντείνων ἐντενεῖς)—Participle reconstructed on the basis of the preserved verb. MT: עריה תעור.

Ha 3:9 —See note in D on the word after ῥάβδ[ο]υς.

Ha 3:9 [σελε] (LXX: διάψαλμα)—Cf. Ha 3:13 for equivalent of R. For lexical approximations of nouns to MT, see F10.1.

Ha 3:9 [ποτα]μοί (LXX: ποταμῶν)—Probably the only possible way to understand the syntax of R is by adding a comma after this word on the assumption that תבקע was read as a passive verb (see F13.2).

Ha 3:10 [--- ὠδίνησ]αν (LXX: καὶ ὠδινήσουσι)—καὶ omitted with MT יחילו. See F10.6.1.

Ha 3:10 ὑ[δ''] (LXX: ὕδατα)—See on Jo 3:7.

Ha 3:10 [παρῆλθεν] (LXX: πορείας; MSS add αὐτοῦ, thus Rahlfs)—Adapted to MT עבר (frequent equivalent in the LXX; see also σ′). See F10.3 for use of the same part of speech as as the Hebrew.

Ha 3:10 ['']σις [α]ὐτοῦ—These words are taken as an equivalent of ידיהו in v. 10, although they could also represent זבלה in the next verse. This view is based on a partial reconstruction of ll. 29–32 of col. 19. See next note.

Ha 3:11 [εἰς] φέγγος ἀσ[τραπῆς] = LXX—These words are taken as equivalents of לנגה ברק of MT לאור חציך יהלכו לנגה ברק חניתך, because the two Greek words are regular equivalents of these Hebrew words. They cannot reflect לאור חציך, and the scroll thus reflects a different Hebrew text. In this different text after the first word in l. 32 of col. 19 there probably followed a translation of לאור חציך. In other words, the scroll represents לאור חציך and לנגה ברק חניתך in a reverse order. Furthermore, it looks as though there is no space in l. 29 for a translation of (10) נשׂא and (11) שמשׁ ירח עמד זבלה, so that in this regard also R reflects a different text.

Ha 3:11 [σιβύνης] (LXX: ὅπλων)—MT חניתך. Cf. Mi 4:3. See F9.2 for synonymous nouns and F12.12 for the orthography.

Ha 3:12 ἐν ἐμ[βριμήσει] (LXX: ἐν ἀπειλῇ)—For the reconstruction (MT: בזעם), cf. Lam 2:6.

Ha 3:12 [--- ἐν θυμῷ] (LXX: καὶ ἐν θυμῷ)—καὶ omitted with MT באף. See F14.1.

Ha 3:13 [εἰς σωτηρίαν²] (LXX: τοῦ σῶσαι)—Adapted to MT לישע. For the use of the same part of speech as the Hebrew, see F10.3.

Ha 3:13 [τοῦ χριστοῦ] σου (LXX: τοὺς χριστούς σου)—Reconstructed according to MT את משיחך (sing.), adapted to the preceding word. Barth. 218: [σωτηρία]ν σ[ὺν τῷ χριστῷ].

## Zephaniah

Zp 1:2 —Spaces are reconstructed before this verse in accordance with the 'paragraphos' occurring after l. 25 of col. 20. See A4a.

Zp 1:2 συν[αγ'']—e.g., συν[άγαγε].

Zp 1:2 [πάντα] (LXX: ---)—Added according to MT כל.

Zp 1:2 [ἐπάνωθεν] (LXX: ἀπὸ)—MT מעל. Calc. of space favour the choice of [ἐπάνωθεν] in v. 2 (for the equivalent cf. Barth. 54–59) and of [ἀπό] (cf. R in Za 3:4) in v. 3, although ἐπάνωθεν is not impossible for v. 3. In both cases the article is omitted (cf. F3.1).

Zp 1:3 [πετεινὸν] (LXX: τὰ πετεινὰ)—Adapted to MT עוף.

Zp 1:3 [ἰχθύες] = LXX (οἱ ἰχθύες)—Nominative reconstructed in accordance with the case ending of [ἄνθ]ρωπος. Article of the LXX omitted in accordance with F3.5.

Zp 1:3 According to the space available in l. 30 of col. 20, R must have contained a rendering of MT והמכשלות את הרשעים not represented in the LXX. Possible reconstruction: [καὶ αἱ ἀσθένειαι σὺν τοῖς ἀσέβεσι].

Zp 1:4 [καὶ ἐκτενῶ] = LXX (MT: ונטיתי)—Cf. α′ passim.

Zp 1:4 [τοὺς] = LXX—Probably R retained the article because of [πάντ]ας (supported by calc. of space). For a similar instance in the preserved text, see Ha 2:8 כל יתר—[πά]ντες οἱ [''].

Zp 1:4 [τὸ] ὑπ[όλειμμα] (LXX: τὰ ὀνόματα)—For the article rendering את, see F6. For the equivalent, see Mi 4:7 ὑ[πόλειμ]μα as well as frequently in the LXX. See F10.1 for lexical approximations to MT.

Zp 1:4 [''] βααλ—Either [τῆς] as in the LXX or [τοῦ].

Zp 1:4 μ[ετὰ] (LXX: ---)—Adapted to MT עם.

Zp 1:5 κ[α]ὶ [τοὺς προσκυνοῦντας] (LXX: καὶ ---)—Added according to MT ואת המשתחוים[2] (calc. of space). For the equivalent, see the beginning of the verse.

Zp 1:5 [τῷ 𐤉𐤄𐤅𐤄] (LXX: κατὰ τοῦ κυρίου)—Adapted to MT ליהוה. For lexical approximations of prepositions to MT, see F10.2. For the article before the divine name, see F5.4.

Zp 1:5–6 —Reconstruction of l. 41 of col. 20 is difficult. If the word in the beginning of v. 6 is reconstructed as [καὶ τοὺς ἐκκλίνοντας] (= LXX, MT: ואת הנסוגים), even without the preverb there is not enough room for ἐν [τ]ῷ [βασιλεῖ αὐτῶν] at the end of v. 5 (MT: בְּמַלְכָּם). It is therefore not impossible that a shorter text such as ἐν [τ]ῷ [μελχομ] (cf. many MSS of the LXX) should be reconstructed.

Zp 1:14 [ἡμέρα] = LXX (Ziegler; Rahlfs reads the article with many MSS of the LXX)—For the omission of the article with nouns in the construct state, see F3.5.

Zp 1:14 ἐπισ[''']—Almost certainly this word stands for צרח in the MT and σκληρά in the LXX. Barth.: ἐπίσ[ημος].

Zp 1:14 [ἐκεῖ δυνατός] (LXX: τέτακται δυνατή)—Adapted to MT שם גבור. See F10.2.

Zp 1:17 Κ[α]ὶ [ἐξεχεῖτο] (LXX: καὶ ἐκχεεῖ)—Adapted to MT וְשֻׁפַּךְ.

Zp 1:17 π[τώμ]α[τ]α (LXX: σάρκας), MT ולחמם—See F9.2 for synonymous nouns.

Zp 1:18 κ[αί γε] (LXX: καὶ)—Adapted to MT גם. Cf. F10.2 for the equivalent of R.

Zp 2:9 ἕ[ως τοῦ αἰῶνος] (LXX: εἰς τὸν αἰῶνα), MT: עד עולם—Reconstructed on the basis of R in Mi 1:7; 4:7.

Zp 2:9 [κατάλοι]πο[ι] (LXX: καὶ οἱ κατάλοιποι)—καὶ omitted with MT שארית. Calc. of space do not allow for the inclusion of the article (alternatively [τοῦ] should be omitted in the reconstruction of the preceding phrase).

Zp 2:9 [τοῦ] λαοῦ [μ]ο[υ] (LXX: λαοῦ μου)—For the addition of the article before nouns with a pronominal suffix (calc. of space), see F4.5. The same applies to the reconstruction of [τοῦ ἔθνους μου].

Zp 2:9 [τοῦ ἔθνους μου] = LXX (ἔθνους μου) and Qere גויי.

Zp 2:9 [κ]λη[ρ]ο[νομήσο]υ[σιν] = LXX—Calc. of space favour the simplex rather than a compositum (κατα). See F8.5.

Zp 2:10 [ἀντὶ ὕβρεως] αὐτῶν (LXX: ἀντὶ τῆς ὕβρεως αὐτῶν)—Article omitted because of calc. of space (MT: גאונם). See F4.3.

Zp 2:10 —Five (?) letters are visible at the beginning of the last line of col. 22 representing ויגדלו. They cannot represent -θησαν of ἐμεγαλύνθησαν (for equivalent, see Mi 5:3[4] and LXX ad loc.).

Zp 3:6 [ἀπ]ώ[λοντο] (LXX: ἐξέλιπον)—This is a mere conjecture, not supported by any evidence, as the Hebrew verb (צדה) does not occur elsewhere in the O.T.

Zp 3:6 [παρὰ τὸ μὴ ὑπάρ]χ[ε]ιν (LXX: παρὰ τὸ μηδένα ὑπάρχειν)—Preposition reconstructed according to the LXX ad loc. and the most frequent equivalent in the LXX of מבלי in this construction.

Zp 3:6 [διὰ τοῦ μὴ εἶναι] (LXX: μηδὲ)—Reconstructed in accordance with the frequent LXX equivalent of מאין in this construction. The use of an infinitive is necessary before [κατοι]κοῦντα.

Zp 3:7 [--- δέ]ξαι (LXX: καὶ δέξασθε)—Adapted to MT תקחי. For omission of καὶ, see F14.1.

Zp 3:7 [π-]ηγὴ—This type of division is unusual for scribe A so that one's first inclination is to reconstruct a pi at the beginning of l. 40 of col. 23 and not at the end of l. 39 as in our reconstruction. However, with the exception of a minute dot which could be ink there are no signs on the leather which could be taken as remnants of such a letter. More importantly, if there would have been such a letter, it would have been protruding too much into the left margin without any contextual reason. The leather at this point is as smooth as the surrounding surface and shows no signs that a section would have peeled off.

Zp 3:7 ὀ[ρθρίσατε] (LXX: ὄρθρισον)—Adapted to the consonantal framework of MT השכימו . See next entry and F10.4.1 for approximations in grammatical number.

Zp 3:7 [διαφθείρ]ατε (LXX: διέφθαρται)—Compositum reconstructed with the LXX because of calc. of space (in spite of F8.1).

# Zechariah

Za 1:2 [πατέρας ὑμῶν] (LXX: τοὺς πατέρας ὑμῶν)—Reconstruction of l. 34 of col. 28 is not certain. In its present form the reconstructed line is longer than the other lines, so that against F3.5 the article before πατέρας is left out. Possibly [ὀργὴν] (= MT קצף) was lacking as well, and certainly μεγάλην of the LXX.

Za 1:3 [Τάδε λέγει] = LXX—Cf. also R in Za 3:7.

Za 1:3 [λέγει] 𐤉𐤄𐤅𐤄 (LXX: ---)—Adapted to MT נאם יהוה (cf. R in Na 2:14; Zp 1:3). See above on Mi 4:6.

Za 1:4 [ἐ]πι[στρέψατε]—[ἀ]πο[στρέψατε] = LXX is possible as well. For R, see note on Mi 2:8.

Za 1:13 [--- λόγους] (LXX: καὶ λόγους)—Adapted to MT דברים. For omission of καὶ to correspond with MT, see F14.1.

Za 1:14 —Space reconstructed after λ[έγων] in accordance with 'paragraphos' occurring after l. 40 of col. 29. See A4a.

Za 1:14 [τῶν δυν]ά[μεων]—Word division in the middle of a syllable (ll. 40–1 of col. 29: [δυν-](41)ά[μεων]) is unusual for scribe A who otherwise usually breaks off words at the ends of syllables. The reconstruction is therefore not certain.

Za 1:14 [τὴν ιερουσαλημ καὶ τὴν] σε[ιων] = LXX (Σιων)—Articles reconstructed because of calc. of space. See F5.1.

Za 2:2 [ἐστι]ν = LXX—Governed by ταῦτ[α]. [εἰσι]ν is equally possible, cf. F7.11.

Za 2:2 [---] (before καὶ[1]) (LXX: κύριε)—Omitted with MT.

Za 2:2 [καὶ τὴν] ιερου[σαλημ] (LXX: ---)—Adapted to MT וירושלם. For the addition of καὶ, see F14.1. The article is reconstructed because of calc. of space, but the argument is not decisive.

Za 2:3 —Space reconstructed before this verse (cf. 'closed section' in MT). See A4a.

Za 2:4 [λέγων] (LXX: πρός με)—Adapted to MT לאמר (calc. of space).

Za 2:7 [ἐκπορεύεται] (LXX: εἱστήκει)—For the equivalent (MT: יצא), cf. Mi 1:3. For lexical approximations to MT, see F10.1.

Za 2:8 [δράμε] (LXX: λέγων δράμε καὶ)—Adapted to MT רץ (calc. of space).

Za 2:8 [ἀτειχίσ]τας (LXX: κατακάρπως)—Reconstructed for MT פרזות because of a similar form in α′ (ἀτειχιστῶς) and R in Ha 3:14, even though the exact form is not clear in the context (ιερουσαλημ is construed as a plural feminine noun, probably on the basis of פרזות).

Za 2:8 τι[θήσεις] may reflect תשים for MT תשב, and it would furthermore explain the accusative of [ἀτειχίσ]τας mentioned above.

Za 2:8 [ἀπὸ πλήθο]υς = LXX (MT מרב)—Reconstruction yields too short a l. 33 of col. 30 and too long a l. 34. [ἀνθρώπο]υς would not fit the context. Either the reconstruction is wrong or the verse was shorter in R's text.

Za 2:10 [Οὐαὶ οὐαὶ καὶ] (LXX: ὦ ὦ)—Reconstructed (here as well as in v. 11) according to MT הוי הוי ו-. For R, cf. Ha 2:6,19.

Za 2:10 [ὅτι] (LXX: διότι)—Cf. F9.3 (MT: כי).

Za 2:10 [ὡς τοὺς τέσσαρες ἀνέμους] (LXX: ἐκ τῶν τεσσάρων ἀνέμων)—Adapted to MT כארבע רוחות השמים. Calc. of space do not necessitate the inclusion of τοὺς. For the reconstructed τέσσαρες, cf. R in 2:3.

Za 2:11 [εἰς σειων] (LXX: εἰς Σιων)—For the reconstructed spelling, see F12.1, for the non-representation of the article, see F5.3.

Za 2:11 [ἀνασῴζου] (LXX: ἀνασῴζεσθε)—Adapted to MT המלטי. See F10.4.1 for approximations to MT in grammatical number.

Za 2:11 [κ]ατοικ[οῦσα] (LXX: κατοικοῦντες)—Adapted to MT יושבת. See F10.4.1 for approximations to MT in grammatical number. For the omission of the article, see F3.4.

Za 2:11 θ̣[υ]γα[τέρα] (= LXX)—θ̣[υ]γά[τηρ] and θ̣[ύ]γα[τερ] are also possible.

Za 2:12 —Space reconstructed before this verse (cf. 'closed section' in MT). See A4a.

Za 2:12,17 [ὅτι] (LXX: διότι), MT: כי—See F9.3.

Za 2:12 [τῶν δυνάμεων] (LXX: παντοκράτωρ)—See F1.5 for the full evidence. For lexical approximations of nouns to MT, see F10.1.

Za 2:16 [ἐν ιερουσαλημ] (LXX: τὴν Ιερουσαλημ)—Preposition reconstructed with MT ובחר ... בירושלם. For this Hebraistic rendering, see the LXX of 2 Chr (6:5,6,34 and passim) and see P. Walters, *The Text of the Septuagint* (Cambridge 1973) 142–3. For the non-representation of the article, see F5.4.

Za 2:17 —Space reconstructed before this verse in accordance with the 'paragraphos' occurring after l. 15 of col. 31. See A4a.

Za 2:17 [σιώπησον] (LXX: εὐλαβείσθω)—MT הס. Cf. Ha 2:20 for equivalent of R. See F10.1 for lexical approximations to MT.

Za 2:17 [ἐκ τοῦ κατοικητηρίου ἁγίου αὐτοῦ] (LXX: ἐκ νεφελῶν ἁγίων αὐτοῦ)—Adapted to MT ממעון קדשו. For the root, cf. σ' ἐκ κατοικήσεως ἁγίας αὐτοῦ and the frequent equivalent of the LXX and α'. R's presumed equivalent probably differed from that for היכל, ναός (see Na 2:7). See F10.1 for lexical approximations to MT. For the addition of the article, see F4.4.

Za 3:1 Space reconstructed before this verse because of calc. of space. Cf. 'closed section' in MT and see A4a.

Za 3:1 [ἕστηκεν] (LXX: εἱστήκει)—Reconstructed (here and in v. 5) for the participle of MT (עמד).

Za 3:1 [τοῦ διαβάλλειν αὐτόν]—(LXX: τοῦ ἀντικεῖσθαι αὐτῷ), MT: לשטנו —Reconstructed in accordance with διάβολος (שטן) occurring earlier in the sentence. For a similar rendering, see the LXX of Num 22:22.

Za 3:4 [ἐνώπιον] (LXX: πρὸ προσώπου...)—For R a shorter word has been reconstructed because otherwise the line would have been too long. The longer reconstruction is, however, not impossible.

Za 3:4 [ειμάτια]—Orthography reconstructed as in v. 5. See F12.1.

Za 3:4 [τὴν ἀνομίαν σου] (LXX: τὰς ἀνομίας σου)—Adapted to MT עונך. For approximations to MT in grammatical number, see F10.4.1.

Za 3:5 [καὶ εἶπα] (LXX: καὶ ---)—Added according to MT ואמר.

Za 3:5 The sequence of the two sentences in R agrees with the LXX as in MSS BS+ (Ziegler's edition) and disagrees with MSS WAQL+ (Rahlfs).

Za 3:5 κ[αὶ ἐνέδυσαν αὐτὸν] (LXX: καὶ περιέβαλον αὐτὸν)—Reconstructed according to the frequent equivalent of MT וילבשהו.

Za 3:5 [καὶ ἄ]γγελος 𐤉𐤄[𐤅𐤄] (LXX: καὶ ὁ ἄγγελος κυρίου)—For the omission of the article in construct nouns, see F3.5.

Za 3:6 [ἐ]μαρτύρα[το] (LXX: διεμαρτύρατο)—The preverb is not reconstructed for R because of calc. of space. See F8.1. Barth.: [διε]μαρτύρα[το].

Za 3:6 [---] (before [ἄ]γγελος) (LXX: ὁ)—See on F3.4.

Za 3:7 —Space reconstructed after δυ[νάμεων] in accordance with the 'paragraphos' occurring before l. 38 of col. 31. See A4a.

Za 3:7 [τὴν φυλα]κήν μου (LXX: τὰ προστάγματά μου)—For the article rendering את, see F6. Barth.: τ[ὴν ...].

Za 3:7 τ[ὰς αὐλάς μου] (LXX: τὴν αὐλήν μου)—Adapted to MT את חֲצֵרָי. See F10.4.1.

Za 3:7 ἐνπ̣[ερι]π[ατοῦντας] (LXX: ἀναστρεφομένους), MT: מַהְלְכִים—Reconstructed from the preserved letters according to the equivalent of α' elsewhere. In this reconstruction the Hebrew is taken in the same way as in the LXX (possibly reflecting a different vocalization: מְהַלְּכִים). At the same time, the Hebrew could also have been understood abstractly (BDB: 'goings') as ἐνπ̣[ερι]π[ατήματα] (word not found in the LXX).

Za 8–9 —Spaces between words have not been indicated for the reconstructed words in the lacunae, since they are not predictable, even though they occur in most instances in the text written by scribe B.

Za 8:19 [ἡ τετάρτη] (LXX: ἡ τετρὰς)—Reconstructed according to MT הרביעי (thus also α'σ'θ': ἡ τοῦ τετάρτη).

Za 8:19 [ἔσονται] = LXX—Reconstructed because of Greek syntax as well as of calc. of space. MT is in the singular: יהיה.

Za 8:19 [---] (before εἰς) (LXX: εἰς χαρὰν καὶ)—Omitted against MT (calc. of space).

Za 8:19 [---] καὶ[5] (LXX: καὶ εὐφρανθήσεσθε, καὶ)—Omitted with MT (calc. of space).

Za 8:20 [Τάδε λέγει] = LXX—Thus also R in Za 3:7.

Za 8:20 [ἕως] (LXX: ἔτι)—Reconstructed on the basis of the mood of [ἔλ]θωσιν which would not have suited ἔτι. [ἕως] is reconstructed from MT עֹד read as עַד. The next word in R (MT: אשר) was probably ἄν.

Za 8:21 [ἐλεύ]σονται̣ (LXX: συνελεύσονται)—For the replacement of composita of the LXX with simplex forms in R, see F8.1.

Za 8:21 [πρὸ]ς (LXX: εἰς)—Reconstructed with F11.1(2). Barth.: [εἰ]ς.

Za 8:21 —l. 16 of col B1 is somewhat short, and there is room for an added word such as [*πόλιν*], possibly required as supplement to [*μίαν*[1]].

Za 8:21 *πο[ρευόμενοι]* (LXX: ---)—Reconstructed with MT הלוך on the basis of the assumption that in this construction of the infinitive absolute (נלכה הלוך) the participle would be used (cf. the addition in Lucianic and other MSS). Also possible is *πο[ρεύσει]* (thus Barth. with the corrector of codex S).

Za 8:23 [*ὅτι*] (LXX: *διότι*)—See F9.3 (MT: כי).

Za 8:23 [---] (after last word) (LXX: *ἐστιν*)—Omitted with MT. For approximations to MT by omission, see F10.6.

Za 9:1 —'Open' section reconstructed before this verse because of calc. of space and the 'capital' letter in l. 3 of col. B2. Cf. the 'closed section' in MT and see A4a.

Za 9:1 [*αδραχ*] (LXX: *Σεδραχ*)—MT חדרך.

Za 9:1 [*τοῦ*] *ισραηλ* = LXX—Article included because of calc. of space.

Za 9:2 [*ὁρίζει αὐ*]*τήν* (LXX: *ἐν τοῖς ὁρίοις αὐτῆς*)—Adapted to MT תגבל בה. For the use of the same part of speech as the Hebrew, see F10.3. The rendering of the preposition בה has been adapted to the verb: [*αὐ*]*τήν*.

Za 9:2 [*ὅτι*] (LXX:*διότι*)—See F9.3.

Za 9:3 *ὀχύ[ρωμα]* (LXX: *ὀχυρώματα*)—Adapted to MT מצור. For approximations to MT in grammatical number, see F10.4.1.

Za 9:3 [*ἑαυτῇ*] = LXX—According to the orthography of *ἑατὸν* in Ha 2:6, [*ἑατῇ*] is possible as well.

Za 9:3 [*ὡς πηλὸν*] = LXX and MT—For equivalent of R, cf. Na 3:14; Ha 2:6.

Za 9:4 [*εἰς*] = LXX for -ב in MT—Reconstruction secured by the case ending of the next word. For similar renderings in R, see Jo 3:4; Na 3:14 (both = LXX).

# F. TRANSLATION TECHNIQUE, ORTHOGRAPHIC PECULIARITIES AND TEXTUAL RELATIONS

## Contents

5.4.1 General practice (18 ×)
5.4.2 Article before *κύριος*/𐤉𐤄𐤅𐤄: R (= LXX) has article (2 × + 2 ×)
5.4.3 Article before *κύριος*/𐤉𐤄𐤅𐤄: R omits (1 ×)

6. את
6.1 את—Greek article: R = LXX (7 × + 12 ×)
6.2 Conclusions

7. Tenses of the verb
7.0 קטל translated by historic present, when R = LXX (2 × + 4 ×)
7.1 קטל translated by past (usually aorist), when R = LXX (19 ×)
7.1.1 Idem, when R differs from LXX (13 × + 5 ×)
7.2 קטל translated by future, when R = LXX (3 ×)
7.2.1 Idem, when R differs from LXX (1 ×)
7.3 וְקטל translated by future, when R = LXX (14 ×)
7.3.1 Idem, when R differs from LXX (11 × + 4 ×)
7.4 וְקטל translated by past by R and LXX (0 × + 1 ×)
7.5 יקטל translated by ind. fut., when R = LXX (19 ×)
7.5.1 Idem, when R differs from LXX (9 × + 10 ×)
7.6 יקטל translated by ind. of past or present tense by both R and LXX (5 ×)
7.6.1 Idem, when R differs from LXX (1 ×)
7.7 יקטל translated after conjunctions or negations by aorist subj. by R = LXX (5 ×)
7.7.1 Idem, when R differs from LXX (5 × + 2 ×)
7.8 וַיקטל translated by past by both R and LXX (11 × + 3 ×)
7.8.1 Idem, when R differs from LXX (5 × + 1 ×)
7.9 ויקטל translated by future by both R and LXX (5 ×)
7.9.1 Idem, when R differs from LXX (6 × + 1 ×)
7.10 Conclusions
7.11 The use of verbs with neuter plural nouns

8. The verb: simplex and composita
8.1 Simplex in R for compositum in LXX (5 × + 11 ×)
8.2 Compositum in R for simplex of LXX (2 × + 1)
8.3 Different preverbs (5 × + 1 ×)
8.4 Same preverb, different verb (and number) (4 ×)
8.5 Conclusions

9. Synonymous parts of speech
9.1 Synonymous verbs
9.1.1 Different verbs (stems) (13 ×; 4 ×)
9.1.2 Synonymous verbs—different form (4 ×)
9.2 Synonymous nouns and adjectives (33 × + 9 ×)
9.3 Synonymous prepositions, conjunctions and particles

10. Approximations to the Hebrew text/language
10.1 Lex. meaning of the Hebr.: adjectives, nouns, verbs (43 × + 15 ×)
10.2 Lex. meaning of the Hebr.: prepositions and particles (9 × + 14 ×)
10.3 Exact representation of elements of the Hebrew (15 × + 9 ×)
10.4 Form
10.4.1 Number (in nouns, pronouns and verbs) (19 × + 22 ×)
10.4.2 Case endings (7 × + 1 ×)

10.4.3 Person: nouns, pronouns, verbs (5× +2×)
10.4.4 Tenses (1× +1×)
10.5 Addition of element(s) (3×)
10.6 Omission of element(s) (12× +6×)
10.6.1 Omission of elements possibly involving different Hebrew text (0× +11×)
10.7 Stylistic transpositions of the LXX (7× +1×)

11. Consistency and inconsistency
11.1 Consistency
11.2 Inconsistency
11.3 Non-stereotyped renderings

12. Orthographic and (morpho)phonological peculiarities
12.1 ι = ει (12× +4×)
12.2 ει = οι (1× +2×)
12.3 Preverbs and prefixes with final nasal (9× +1×)
12.4 ἐκ before nasals (3×)
12.5 γγ = νγ (2×)
12.6 διά = δι' (1× +2×)
12.7 τ = θ (1×)
12.8 ἐπ' = ἐφ' (2×)
12.9 λαμβάνω (2×)
12.10 α = ε (1× +1×)
12.11 ο = ω (1×)
12.12 Sibilants (1×)
12.13 ν movable
12.14 αυ = α (1×)
12.15 Augment

## III. Textual Relations (13–15)

13.1 R = LXX against MT (14× +1×)
13.2 R = LXX against MT in vocalization (21×)

14.1 R = MT against LXX (59× +35×)
14.2 R = MT against LXX in vocalization (15× +5×)

15.1 LXX = MT against R (16× +3×)
15.2 LXX = MT against R in vocalization (2× +1×)
15.3 R differs from both LXX and MT (6×)
15.4 Indecisive (1×)

16. Relation between R and MSS of the LXX and the Hexaplaric sources
16.1 Data
16.2 Conclusions

# I. Introduction

0.1 *General*

The following paragraphs analyse some of the issues in the translation technique and language of R, its relationship to MT and the LXX, and its relation to individual MSS and revisions of the LXX. While a fuller treatment of these issues must await another occasion, the present discussion centres on matters which need to be clarified for the reconstruction of the full text of R.

For each entry the text of MT is written in the left-hand column. The right-hand column contains the text of the LXX (edition of Ziegler) as a lemma with the text of the scroll (R) recorded or referred to in second position.

Five different relationships between these texts are denoted by square brackets:

(*a*) One bracket after the LXX lemma without any following text: R is identical with the LXX.

(*b*) One bracket with following text: R is identical with the LXX, but some letters are reconstructed. Reconstructed letters are indicated throughout in square brackets.

(*c*) Two brackets after the LXX text with text following: R differs from the LXX (including orthographical differences and the writing of the tetragrammaton in palaeo-Hebrew characters).

(*d*) Three brackets after the LXX text with text following: R differs from the LXX (as in *c*), but the difference is reconstructed.

(*e*) Text of the LXX without brackets: presumed text of R is identical with the LXX. Since the two presumably are identical, the text is not repeated.

In addition, the following notations are used:

| | |
|---|---|
| [ ] | after the brackets: reconstructed text of the scroll |
| {...} | text of the LXX rearranged in order to represent equivalent of MT |
| {..~} | idem, stylistic transposition |
| {d} | doublet |
| +++ | plus element of the LXX |
| --- | minus element of the LXX |
| K, Q | Ketib, Qere |
| (Hebr) | reconstructed Hebrew *Vorlage* of the LXX (supplement to the left column) or R (supplement to the right column) |

The last-mentioned notations employ the system of the CATSS data base, on which see in greater detail: J. Abercrombie et al., *Computer Assisted Tools for Septuagint Studies (CATSS), Vol. 1, Ruth*, Septuagint and Cognate Studies 20 (Scholars Press: Atlanta, 1986) and E. Tov, *A Computerized Data Base for Septuagint Studies, The Parallel Aligned Text of the Greek and Hebrew Bible, CATSS Vol. 2*, Journal of Northwest Semitic Languages, Supplementary Series 1 (1986).

In accordance with the CATSS system, the morphological components of the Hebrew words are separated by a slash (/). This system facilitates the analysis of the representation of the individual morphemes of the Hebrew in the Greek translations. In the use of these slashes, convenience for the purpose of comparison rather than linguistic correctness has sometimes guided their location.

The text of the "LXX" is quoted from the edition of Ziegler which contains the best modern reconstruction of the Old Greek translation: J. Ziegler, *Duodecim prophetae, Septuaginta, Vetus Testamentum graecum auctoritate societatis litterarum gottingensis*², vol. XII (Göttingen 1967 [basically identical with the first edition of 1943]). This edition is superior to that of Rahlfs from which the text (as opposed to the apparatus) deviates in 22 details in the section covered by the scroll as well as in 43 cases of orthography (mainly the ν movable). In some of these instances it would have made a difference if the text of Rahlfs had been chosen as the base text, since what appears as a change in R from the "LXX" according to one edition may be identical with the text of the LXX in the other one. These details have been remarked upon in the notes on the reconstruction (E). In any event, study of the best single ancient source, codex B, shows that because of the idiosyncracies and mistakes of this source it is still better to choose a modern reconstruction of the Old Greek, with all its subjectivity, than an available ancient source such as codex B.

In the following analysis conclusions are drawn from the detailed comparison of R with the LXX. In this analysis the only possible procedure is to compare R with the best available reconstruction of the so-called original text of the LXX, contained in the aforementioned edition of Ziegler. This procedure implies some imprecisions, for if the text of the LXX in fact known to the reviser differed from this modern edition, to the same degree our analysis and statistics will be slightly imprecise as well. This margin of error must be kept in mind. Naturally, this imprecision applies to the study of all revisions of the LXX.

This imprecision is felt especially in those few cases in which R is presented as changing the text of the LXX, while some MSS of the LXX actually agree with R (see 16.1). In those instances R possibly did not insert the change. Rather, R copied the text from ancestors of MSS which have not been chosen as the text of Ziegler's edition, and such "variants" may be irrelevant to the discussion. At the same time, caution is in order in the other direction, since the MS tradition of the LXX may have been influenced secondarily by the reading of R which is often identical with that of the Hexapla or α′σ′θ′ (see 16.2 and Barth. 203–65).

### 0.2 *R is a revision of the LXX*

That R is a revision of the LXX, rather than an independent translation of the Hebrew, is established by two sets of data:

(1) R depends on the LXX, as is shown by those special (unusual, idiosyncratic) renderings of the LXX which for some reason were left untouched by R.

(2) R revises the LXX in a certain direction.

Evidence of consistent recensional activity is provided in sections F10 (involving inner-Greek revisional activity) and F14.1 (involving the reviser's correcting of the LXX towards a Hebrew text close to MT). Secondary proof of inner-Greek recensional activity is found in sections F1–9 and 11–12.

In what follows, evidence of the common basis of the LXX and R is provided. Examples are given of shared translation equivalents which are rare, unusual or even unique within the LXX as a whole, shared additions of elements or omissions against MT, all of which show the special relationship between the two translations which is explained here in terms of a translation and its revision. Agreements of the LXX and R against MT involving a different Hebrew text (F13.1) are not included in this category, for while they show that the two texts were based on the same Hebrew text, they do not necessarily prove that both were derived from a common inner-Greek origin. The evidence is subdivided into two categories: shared equivalents (0.2.1) and shared translation technique (0.2.2). The exact reasoning for adducing a particular example is not quoted in detail, but is based on an analysis of the vocabulary and translation technique elsewhere in the LXX.

The evidence adduced here is not exhaustive.

The text is quoted according to the sequence and numbering of MT. Different numbers of the LXX, if any, are added in parenthesis after the text of the LXX.

### 0.2.1 *Shared equivalents*

The following shared equivalents are rare, unusual or unique within the LXX, thus showing a dependence of R upon the LXX. In several instances the revision shares only one aspect of a LXX rendering, while changing another. Thus in Ha 2:6 חידות R did not change the translation option of the LXX, but omitted the preposition and changed the case ending. Likewise, in Ha 2:16 R, like the LXX, took קיקלון as being composed of two elements, but changed the translation options.

| | | |
|---|---|---|
| Jo 2:5 | נגרשתי | ἀπῶσμαι ] ἀ̣πῶ[σμαι] (hapax translation) |
| Jo 2:6 | סוּף (reed) | ἐσχάτη ]] [ἐσχά]τη, {d} ἔλος (vocal.) (סוֹף—ending, סוּף) |
| Jo 4:1 | ו/ירע אל | καὶ ] κ[αὶ] |
| | | ἐλυπήθη ] [ἐ]λ̣[υπήθη] |
| Jo 4:1 | רעה | λύπην ] λύ[πην] |
| Mi 1:4 | מגרים | καταφερόμενον ] καταφ[ερ]όμενο[ν] |
| Mi 1:6 | ל/עי | εἰς |
| | | ὀπωροφυλάκιον ] [ὀπω]ροφυλάκιον (rendering עי also in Ps. 79 (78):1; Mi 3:12; Jer 26 (33):18; meaning unclear) |
| Mi 1:6 | ו/הגרתי | καὶ ] |
| | | κατασπάσω ] |
| Mi 1:8 | שילל (K) שולל (Q) | ἀνυπόδετος ] ἀνυπό[δετος] (hapax translation) (barefoot) |
| Mi 2:8 | ו/אתמול | καὶ ] |
| | | ἔμπροσθεν ]] ἔνπροσθ[εν] |
| Mi 3:6 | ו/באה | καὶ |
| | | δύσεται ] [δ]ύσεται |
| Mi 4:7 | ל/שארית | εἰς ] |
| | | ὑπόλειμμα ] ὑ[πόλειμ]μα |
| Mi 4:8 | עֹפֶל (hill) | αὐχμώδης ] [αὐχ]μώδης (hapax translation; vocalization; wrongly connected with preceding word) (dry—based on עֹפֶל = אָפֵל?; cf. also α′) |
| Mi 4:8 | ה/ממשלה | ἡ ] |
| | | ἀρχὴ ] |
| Na 3:10 | גדול/יה | οἱ |
| | | μεγιστᾶνες] [μεγιστᾶ]νες |
| | | αὐτῆς ] αὐ[τ]ῆ̣[ς] |
| Na 3:12 | בכורים (first-ripe figs) | σκοποὺς ]]] σκοπ[οῖς] (hapax translation) (watchers, guards; meaning unclear) |
| Na 3:16 | ו/יעף | καὶ ] [κ]αὶ |
| | | ἐξεπετάσθη ] ἐξεπε[τάσθη] |
| Ha 1:10 | ו/רזנים | καὶ ] |
| | | τύραννοι ] (hapax translation) |
| Ha 1:10 | ישחק | ἐμπαίξεται ]] ἐνπαι̣[ξεται] |
| Ha 1:10 | ו/יצבר (and he heaped up) | καὶ |
| | | βαλεῖ ] [β]α̣λε̣ῖ (hapax translation) (and he threw) |
| Ha 1:14 | {ו/ב ~..} | ἔχοντα ] [ἔχον]τα |
| | משל | ἡγούμενον ] |
| | ב/ו | {...} ]] > |

| | | |
|---|---|---|
| Ha 1:15 | העלה | ἀνέσπασε ]] ἀνέσπασεν (hapax translation) |
| Ha 2:1 | ו/אצפה | καὶ ] |
| | | ἀποσκοπεύσω ] |
| Ha 2:5 | יהיר | ἀλαζὼν ] (rare translation) |
| Ha 2:6 | ו/מליצה | καὶ ] |
| | | πρόβλημα ] πρόβλ[ημ]α |
| Ha 2:6 | חידות | διήγησιν ]] διήγησις |
| Ha 2:7 | ו/יקצו (also v. 19) | καὶ ] |
| | | ἐκνήψουσιν ]] ἐγνή[ψουσ]ι̣ν (rare) |
| Ha 2:15 | מספח | ἀνατροπῇ ]] [...]υ ἀνατρ[οπῇ] (hapax word in LXX; meaning unclear—LSJ: pouring out) |
| Ha 2:18 | ו/מורה | --- ]]] [καὶ] |
| | | φαντασίαν ] [φα]ντασίαν (hapax; rare word; based on etym. ראה) |
| Ha 2:18 | יצר/ו | τὸ ] |
| | | πλάσμα ] |
| | | αὐτοῦ ] αὐτοῦ |
| Za 1:4 | ה/ראשנים | οἱ ἔμπροσθεν ]] οἱ ἔνπροσθεν |
| Za 1:14 | קרא | ἀνάκραγε ] [ἀνάκρα]γε |
| Za 9:2 | חכמה | ἐφρόνησαν ]] [ἐ]φρόνησεν |

## 0.2.2 *Shared translation technique*

| | | |
|---|---|---|
| Jo 3:4 | ל/בוא | τοῦ |
| | | εἰσελθεῖν ]] [πορεύεσθ]αι |
| | ב/עיר | ε̣ἰς ] (prep.) |
| | | τὴν ] |
| | | πόλιν ] πό̣[λιν] |
| Jo 3:7 | ה/אדם | οἱ |
| | | ἄνθρωποι ] [ἄνθρω]ποι̣ (number) |
| Jo 4:2 | עד | ἔτι ] |
| | היות/י | ὄντος ] ὄ[ντος] (construction) |
| | | μου |
| Mi 4:3 | ילמדון | μάθωσι ]] μάθωσιν |
| | עוד | {...} ]] ἔτι |
| | מלחמה | πολεμεῖν ] πολεμε̣ῖ̣[ν] (construction) |
| Mi 5:1 | צעיר | ὀλιγοστὸς (2) ] ὀλι[γ]οστὸς |
| Mi 5:2 | עת | (3) καιροῦ |
| | יולדה | τικτούσης ] [τικτού]σης |
| | ילדה | τέξεται ] (identical construction; possibly a comma has to be added after τικτούσης) |
| Na 2:6 | חומת/ה | ἐπὶ ] |
| | | τὰ ] |
| | | τείχη ] (vocalization) |
| Na 2:10 | זהב | τὸ ] |
| | | χρυσίον ] χ[ρυσίον] |
| Na 3:14 | באי | ἔμβηθι ]]] [ἐλθὲ] |
| | ב/טיט | εἰς ] (prep.) |
| | | πηλὸν ] πηλ[ὸν] |
| Ha 2:5 | ישבע | ἐμπιπλάμενος ]] ἐνπιπλάμ[ενος] |
| Ha 2:6 | חידות | εἰς ]] > |
| | | διήγησιν ]] διήγησις |
| | ל/ו | αὐτοῦ] (preposition) |
| Ha 2:16 | ו/קיקלון | καὶ ] |
| | | συνήχθη ]] ἔμετος (two words) |
| | | ἀτιμία ]]] [ἀτιμίας] |
| Ha 2:17 | מ/דמי | διὰ ]] δι' (preposition) |
| | | αἵματα ] |
| Ha 3:13 | יסוד | δεσμοὺς ]] θ̣εμελίους (number) |
| Ha 3:14 | ל/אכל | ἔσθων ]] [ἐσ]θίων (participle instead of infinitive) |
| Zp 3:6 | מ/בלי איש | παρὰ |
| | | τὸ |
| | | μηδένα ]] [μὴ] --- |
| | | ὑπάρχειν ] [ὑπάρ]χ[ε]ιν (construction) |
| | | {...μηδένα} ]] ἄνδ̣[ρα] |

| | | |
|---|---|---|
| Za 9:1 | ו/דמשק | καὶ Δαμασκοῦ ] |
| | מנחת/ו | θυσία αὐτοῦ ]] κατάπαυ[σις αὐτοῦ] |

See further all instances of *shared vocalization* of the LXX and R (F13.2).

## II. Translation Technique and Orthographic Peculiarities

### 1. *Hebrew article*

#### 1.1 *Hebrew article: R=LXX has Greek article (34× +27×)*

The most frequent (and expected) equivalence for the Hebrew article is the Greek article: Jo 3:7,8 והבהמה, 3:8 החמס, 3:9 האלהים, 3:10 [2]הרעה, 4:5 לעיר; Mi 1:4 ההרים, 3:5 המתעים, 3:6 השמש, 4:5 העמים, 4:8 הממשלה הראשנה; Na 2:7 הנהרות, 3:16 השמים; Ha 1:6 הגוי המר, 1:14 הים, 2:5 העמים, 2:6 המרבה, 2:19 לעץ, 2:20 הארץ; Zp 1:2 האדמה, 1:3 השמים, האדמה, 1:4 המקום, 1:5 ואת המשתחוים, 1:15 היום, 1:16 הערים הבצרות, הגבהות; Za 1:4 הראשנים, 1:13 את המלאך, 2:7 הדבר, 8:19 והאמת. In all these cases R=LXX.

Also in the following cases both have the Greek article, though a different one: Jo 3:10 [1]הרעה; Na 2:6 הסכך, 2:7 וההיכל.

RECONSTRUCTIONS (27×)

In the following instances the article is reconstructed for R (=LXX), often supported by calc. of space:

Jo 1:15 הים, 1:16 האנשים, 2:1 הדג, 2:2 הדגה, 3:7 האדם, הבקר, והצאן, 3:8 האדם, 3:10 האלהים; Mi 1:1 המרשתי (calc. of space), 2:7 הישר, 4:6 הצלעה (calc. of space), והנדחה (calc. of space), 4:7 הצלעה (calc. of space), והנהלאה; Na 3:8 הישבה; Ha 1:6 ההולך; Zp 1:4 הכהנים (calc. of space); 1:5 הנשבעים, 1:14 הגדול, 1:16 הפנות, 1:17 לאדם (calc. of space); Za 1:4 הנביאים, 2:4 (1:21) הקרנות, 8:19 והשלום (calc. of space), 8:23 בימים, הגוים.

#### 1.2 *Hebrew article: R adds to LXX in conformity with MT (2×)*

| | | |
|---|---|---|
| Mi 1:6 | ה/שׂדה | --- ]] τοῦ |
| | | ἀγροῦ ] ἀ[γρ]οῦ |
| Za 3:5 | ה/צניף | --- ]] τὴν |
| | | κίδαριν ] κίδ[αριν] |

#### 1.3 *R (=MT) omits article of LXX (2× +6×)*

| | | |
|---|---|---|
| Ha 1:11 | רוח | τὸ ]] > |
| | | πνεῦμα ] |
| Ha 2:2 | קורא | ὁ ]] > |
| | | ἀναγινώσκων ]] ἀναγεινώσκων |

RECONSTRUCTIONS (6×)

| | | |
|---|---|---|
| Mi 1:2 | ארץ | ἡ ]]] > |
| | | γῆ |
| Na 2:9 | מפנה | ὁ ]]] > |
| | | ἐπιβλέπων ]] [ἐπισ]τρέφω[ν] |
| Na 3:8 | חיל | ἡ ἀρχὴ ]] ἰσχὺς |

| | | |
|---|---|---|
| Ha 1:14 | כ/רמש | καὶ ]]] > |
| | | ὡς |
| | | τὰ ]]] (vocal.) |
| | | ἑρπετὰ |
| | | τὰ ]]] > |
| | לא | οὐκ |
| Ha 2:4 | ו/צדיק | ὁ δὲ ]]] [καὶ] |
| | | δίκαιος ] [δί]καιος |
| Ha 2:19 | אמר | ὁ ]]] > |
| | | λέγων ] λ̣έγων |

## 1.4 *R=LXX adds article against MT (10× + 2×)*

| | | |
|---|---|---|
| Mi 4:5 | ל/עולם | εἰς ] |
| | | τὸν ] |
| | | αἰῶνα (phrase) |
| Mi 4:7 | ו/עד | καὶ |
| | | ἕως ] [ἕ]ως |
| | | εἰς ]] > |
| | עולם | τὸν ]] τοῦ |
| | | αἰῶνα ]] αἰῶνος (phrase) |
| Mi 5:3 | אפסי | ἄκρων (4) ]] περάτων |
| | ארץ | τῆς ] |
| | | γῆς ] |
| Na 2:8 | ו/הצב | καὶ ] |
| | | ἡ ] |
| | | ὑπόστασις ]] λαμπήνη |
| Na 2:10 | זהב | τὸ ] |
| | | χρυσίον ] χ[ρυσίον] |
| Ha 2:5 | כ/שאול | καθὼς ] |
| | | ὁ ] |
| | | ᾅδης ] (vocalization) |
| Ha 2:8 | יתר | οἱ ] |
| | | ὑπολελειμμένοι |
| Ha 2:15 | משקה | ὁ ]] τ[ῷ] |
| | | ποτίζων ]] [ποτίζοντ]ε̣ι |
| Ha 2:18 | יצר | ὁ ] |
| | | πλάσας ] [π]λάσ̣α̣ς |
| Ha 2:19 | ל/אבן | καὶ ]]] > |
| | | τῷ ] |
| | | λίθῳ ] (vocalization) |

RECONSTRUCTIONS (2×)

| | | |
|---|---|---|
| Na 2:10 | כסף | τὸ |
| | | ἀργύριον |
| Ha 1:6 | ארץ | τῆς |
| | | γῆς |

## 1.5 *R adds article against MT=LXX (5× + 5×)*

| | | |
|---|---|---|
| Mi 4:4 | צבאות | παντοκράτορος ]] [τῶ]ν δ[υνά]μ̣[εων] (phrase) |
| Za 1:3 | צבאות | --- ]] τῶν δυνάμ[εων] |
| Za 1:4 | צבאות | παντοκράτωρ ]] τῶν δυνάμεων |
| Za 3:7 | צבאות | παντοκράτωρ ]] τῶν δυ[νάμεων] |
| Za 8:20 | צבאות | παντοκράτωρ ]] τῶν δυνά[μεων] |

RECONSTRUCTIONS (5×)

| | | |
|---|---|---|
| Na 2:14 | צבאות | παντοκράτωρ ]]] [τῶν δυνάμεων] |
| Za 1:3 | צבאות | παντοκράτωρ ]] [τῶν δ]υνάμεων |
| Za 1:3 | צבאות | --- ]] [τῶν δυ]νάμεων |
| Za 1:14 | צבאות | παντοκράτωρ ]] [τῶν δυν]ά[μεων] |
| Za 2:12 | צבאות | παντοκράτωρ (8) ]]] [τῶν δυνάμεων] |

### 1.6 *Conclusions*

As a rule, R (more than the LXX) follows MT with regard to the article, like the revision of α′ for which see K. Hyvärinen, *Die Übersetzung von Aquila*, Coniectanea Biblica (Lund 1977) 31–6. In 34 instances R follows the LXX in this matter (1.1); it also adds the article with MT against the LXX (1.2 [2×]), and it omits the article with MT against the LXX (1.3 [2×+6×]). At the same time, it follows the LXX in adding the article against MT in certain conditions (1.4 [10×+2×]), and it also adds the article against MT≐LXX (5×+5×). (However, the latter evidence involves only one phrase.) Because of these statistics, the reconstructions recorded in 1.1 (27×) and 1.3 (6×) are relatively reliable.

## 2. Lamed *inf.*

### 2.1 Lamed *inf. rendered by τοῦ: R=LXX (4×+2×)*

| | | |
|---|---|---|
| Jo 3:10 | ל/עשות | τοῦ ] τ[οῦ]<br>ποιῆσαι |
| Jo 4:2 | ל/ברח | τοῦ ]<br>φυγεῖν ] φυγεῖ[ν] |
| Mi 5:1 | ל/היות | τοῦ (2) ]<br>εἶναι ] [εἶ]ναι |
| Mi 5:1 | ל/היות | τοῦ (2) ]<br>εἶναι ] ε[ἶ]ναι |

RECONSTRUCTIONS (2×)

| | | |
|---|---|---|
| Jo 3:4 | ל/בוא | τοῦ<br>εἰσελθεῖν ]] [πορεύεσθ]αι |
| Ha 1:8 | ל/אכול | εἰς ]]] ><br>τὸ ]]] [τοῦ] (diff. case)<br>φαγεῖν ] [φ]αγεῖν |

### 2.2 Lamed *inf.: R adds τοῦ against LXX (2×)*

| | | |
|---|---|---|
| Ha 3:14 | ל/הפיצ/ני | --- ]] τοῦ<br>διανοίξουσι ]] σκο[ρπίσ]αι<br>--- ]] ἡμᾶς |
| Za 2:4 | ל/עשות | (1:21) ]] [το]ῦ<br>ποιῆσαι |

### 2.3 Lamed *inf.: R omits τοῦ against LXX (2×+1×)*

| | | |
|---|---|---|
| Jo 2:5 | ל/הביט | τοῦ ]] ><br>ἐπιβλέψαι ] ἐπιβλέψα[ι] |
| Ha 2:1 | ל/ראות | τοῦ ]] ><br>ἰδεῖν ] ἰδ[εῖν] |

RECONSTRUCTION (1×)

| | | |
|---|---|---|
| Ha 2:18 | ל/עשות | τοῦ ]]] ><br>ποιῆσαι ] [π]οιῆσαι |

### 2.3.1 Lamed *inf.: R=LXX omits (0×+2×)*

RECONSTRUCTIONS (2×)

| | | |
|---|---|---|
| Jo 2:1 | ל/בלע | καταπιεῖν ] [κ]αταπιεῖν |
| Ha 1:17 | ל/הרג | ἀποκτέννειν ] [ἀποκτέννει]ν |

### 2.4 *Conclusions*

R follows the LXX in employing the Greek article for the *lamed* of the Hebrew inf. (2.1 [4 × ]). It even adds the article against the LXX (2.2 [2 × ]), but also omits the article against the LXX (2.3 [2 × ]). Although R is not consistent, there is more evidence for the use of the article in this construction than for its omission.

## 3. *Construct words*

### 3.1 *Construct words: R=LXX has Greek art. before nom. regens (7 × + 1 × )*

In the distinction between groups 3.1 and 3.2 no different syntactical conditions have been recognized, although there are more proper nouns and undetermined nouns among the nomina recta in 3.2.

| | | |
|---|---|---|
| Mi 4:4 | פי | τὸ ] |
| | | στόμα ] |
| | יהוה | κυρίου ]] 𐤉𐤄[𐤅𐤄] |
| Mi 5:2 | בני | τοὺς (3) ] το[ὺς] |
| | | υἱοὺς |
| | ישׂראל | Ισραηλ |
| Mi 5:3 | ב/גאון | καὶ (4) ] |
| | | ἐν ] |
| | | τῇ ] |
| | | δόξῃ ]] ἐπάρσει |
| | שׁם | τοῦ ]] > |
| | | ὀνόματος ] |
| | יהוה | κυρίου ]] 𐤉𐤄𐤅𐤄 |
| Na 3:16 | מ/כוכבי | ὑπὲρ ]] ὡς |
| | | τὰ ]] τοὺς |
| | | ἄστρα ]] ἀστέρας |
| | ה/שמים | τοῦ ] τ[οῦ] |
| | | οὐρανοῦ |
| Ha 1:6 | ל/מרחבי | ἐπὶ ]] εἰ[ς] |
| | | τὰ ] τὰ |
| | | πλάτη ] πλά[τη] |
| | ארץ | τῆς |
| | | γῆς |
| Ha 2:17 | ישבי | τῶν ] |
| | | κατοικούντων ]] ἐνοι[κ]ούντων |
| | ב/ה | αὐτήν ]] ἐν [αὐτ]ῇ |
| Za 8:23 | לשׁנות | τῶν ] |
| | | γλωσσῶν |
| | ה/גוים | τῶν |
| | | ἐθνῶν ] [ἐθ]νῶν |

RECONSTRUCTION (1 × )

| | | |
|---|---|---|
| Ha 1:8 | מ/זאבי | ὑπὲρ |
| | | τοὺς (calc. of space) |
| | | λύκους |
| | ערב | τῆς ]]] > |
| | | Ἀραβίας ]] [ἑσπέ]ρας |

### 3.2 *Construct words: R=LXX omits Greek art. before nom. regens as in MT (9 × + 4 × )*

| | | |
|---|---|---|
| Mi 1:1 | ב/ימי | ἐν ] |
| | | ἡμέραις ] ἡμ[έραις] |
| | יותם | Ιωαθαμ ]]] [ιωθαμ] |

| | | |
|---|---|---|
| Mi 1:5 | ו/ב/חטאות | καὶ ] |
| | | διὰ ]]] [δι'] |
| | | ἁμαρτίαν ] [ἁμ]αρτίαν |
| | בית | οἴκου |
| | ישׂראל | Ισραηλ |
| Mi 4:8 | בת | θυγάτηρ ] |
| | ציון | Σιων ]]] [σειων] |
| Mi 5:1 | ב/אלפי | ἐν (2) ] |
| | | χιλιάσιν ] χ[ιλιάσιν] |
| | יהודה | Ιουδα ] [ιο]υδα |
| Mi 5:1 | מ/ימי | ἐξ (2) ]] ἀφ' |
| | | ἡμερῶν ] ἡμ[ερῶν] |
| | עולם | αἰῶνος |
| Mi 5:3 | ב/עז | ἐν (4) ] |
| | | ἰσχύι ] ἰ[σ]χύι |
| | יהוה | κυρίου ]] [𐤉𐤄𐤅]𐤄 |
| Mi 5:3 | אפסי | ἄκρων (4) ]] περάτων |
| | ארץ | τῆς ] |
| | | γῆς ] |
| Ha 3:11 | ברק | ἀστραπῆς ] ἀσ[τραπῆς] |
| | חנית/ך | ὅπλων ]]] [σιβύνης] |
| | | σου |
| Ha 3:14 | ראשׁ | κεφαλὰς ]] κεφαλὴν |
| | פרז/ו (K) פרז/יו (Q) | δυναστῶν ]] ἀτει[χίσ]των |
| | | --- ]] αὐτοῦ |

RECONSTRUCTIONS (4 ×)

| | | |
|---|---|---|
| Mi 4:10 | בת | θύγατερ ] [θύ]γατερ |
| | ציון | Σιων ]]] σ[ειων] |
| Na 2:7 | שׁערי | πύλαι ] [Πύλ]α[ι] |
| | ה/נהרות | τῶν ] |
| | | ποταμῶν ] |
| Zp 1:2 | מ/על | ἀπὸ ]]] [ἐπάνωθεν] |
| | פני | προσώπου ] [π]ροσώπου |
| | ה/אדמה | τῆς ] |
| | | γῆς ] γ[ῆς] |
| Zp 1:3 | מ/על | ἀπὸ |
| | פני | προσώπου ] [προσώπ]ọυ |
| | ה/אדמה | τῆς ] |
| | | γῆς ] |

## 3.3 *Construct words: R adds article before nom. regens (1 ×)*

| | | |
|---|---|---|
| Mi 4:7 | ב/הר | ἐν ] |
| | | --- ]] τῷ |
| | | ὄρει ] |
| | ציון | Σιων ]] σει[ων] |

## 3.4 *Construct words: R (= MT) omits article before nom. regens (1 × + 13 ×)*

| | | |
|---|---|---|
| Mi 5:3 | ב/גאון | καὶ (4) ] |
| | | ἐν ] |
| | | τῇ ] |
| | | δόξῃ ]] ἐπάρσει |
| | שׁם | τοῦ ]] > |
| | | ὀνόματος ] |
| | יהוה | κυρίου ]] 𐤉𐤄𐤅𐤄 |

RECONSTRUCTIONS (13 ×)—See remark in 3.5

| | | |
|---|---|---|
| Jo 2:1 | ב/מעי | ἐν |
| | | τῇ ]]] > |
| | | κοιλίᾳ |
| | ה/דג | τοῦ |
| | | κήτους ] [κήτου]ς̣ |
| Jo 2:2 | מ/מעי | ἐκ |
| | | τῆς ]]] > |
| | | κοιλίας |
| | ה/דגה | τοῦ |
| | | κήτους |
| Jo 3:5 | אנשי | οἱ ]]] > |
| | | ἄνδρες |
| | נינוה | Νινευη |
| Mi 1:3 | במותי (K) במתי (Q) | τὰ ]]] > |
| | | ὕψη |
| | ארץ | τῆς ]]] > |
| | | γῆς |
| Mi 1:5 | פשע | ἡ ]]] > |
| | | ἀσέβεια ]] ἀσέβια |
| | יעקב | τοῦ ]] > |
| | | Ιακωβ ] |
| Mi 1:5 | במות | ἡ ]]] > |
| | | ἁμαρτία ]]] > |
| | | οἴκου ]]] [ὕψη] |
| | יהודה | Ιουδα |
| Mi 4:5 | ב/שם אלה/יו | τὴν ]]] [ἐν ὀνόματι] |
| | | ὁδὸν ]] [θε]οῦ |
| | | αὐτοῦ ]] αὐτῶν |
| Mi 5:6 | שארית | τὸ (7) ]]] > |
| | | ὑπόλειμμα ]] [κατά]λοιπον |
| | יעקב | τοῦ ]] > |
| | | Ιακωβ ] ιακωβ |
| Ha 1:14 | כ/דגי | ὡς |
| | | τοὺς ]]] > |
| | | ἰχθύας |
| | ה/ים | τῆς ] [τ]ῆς |
| | | θαλάσσης ] θαλά[σσης] |
| Zp 1:3 | (ו)דגי | οἱ ]]] > |
| | | ἰχθύες |
| | ה/ים | τῆς |
| | | θαλάσσης |
| Za 2:11 | יושבת | οἱ (7) ]]] > |
| | | κατοικοῦντες ]] [κ]ατοικ[οῦσα] |
| | בת | θυγατέρα ] θ[υ]γ̣α[τέρα] |
| | בבל | Βαβυλῶνος |
| Za 3:5 | ו/מלאך | καὶ |
| | | ὁ ]]] > |
| | | ἄγγελος ] [ἄ]γγελος |
| | יהוה | κυρίου ]] 𐤉𐤄[𐤅𐤄] |
| Za 3:6 | מלאך | ὁ ]]] > |
| | | ἄγγελος ] [ἄ]γγελος |
| | יהוה | κυρίου ]] 𐤉[𐤄𐤅𐤄] |

## 3.5 *Conclusions*

As a rule, R leaves out the article before nouns in the construct state, usually following the LXX (3.2 [9 × + 4 × ]), and also once against the LXX (3.4). In other instances R retains the article of the LXX (3.1 [7 × + 1 × ]), and once it adds the article against the LXX (3.3). It thus seems that R would rather leave out the article in this construction in which the

Hebrew has no article, even though at times R follows the LXX in the other direction. This tendency is not sufficiently clear, so that calc. of space must guide our decisions. When no decision is possible, the article is omitted.

## 4. *Pronominal suffix*

### 4.1 *Pronominal suffix: R = LXX has article before noun, sometimes with different nouns (23× + 37×)*

| | | |
|---|---|---|
| Jo 2:4 | ו/גל/יך | καὶ ]<br>τὰ ]<br>κύματά ]<br>σου ] σο[υ] |
| Jo 2:6 | ל/ראש/י | ἡ ]] τὴν<br>κεφαλή ]] κεφαλήν<br>μου ] |
| Jo 3:8 | מ/דרכ/ו | ἀπὸ ]] ἐκ<br>τῆς ]<br>ὁδοῦ ] ὁδο[ῦ]<br>αὐτοῦ ] [α]ὐ̣[τοῦ] |
| Jo 3:10 | מ/דרכ/ם | ἀπὸ ]<br>τῶν ]] τῆ̣ς<br>ὁδῶν ]] [ὁδο]ῦ<br>αὐτῶν ] αὐτ[ῶν] |
| Jo 4:2 | דבר/י | οἱ ]] ὁ<br>λόγοι ]] λόγος<br>μου ] |
| Mi 1:6 | ו/יסד/יה | καὶ ]<br>τὰ ]<br>θεμέλια ]<br>αὐτῆς ] |
| Mi 4:3 | ו/חנית/יהם | καὶ ]<br>τὰ ]] τὰς<br>δόρατα ]] σιβύ[νας]<br>αὐτῶν ] [α]ὐτῶν |
| Mi 5:4 | ב/ארמנת/ינו | ἐπὶ (5) ]<br>τὴν ]] τὰς<br>χώραν ]] βάρ̣[εις]<br>ἡμῶν |
| Mi 5:5 | ב/ארצ/נו | ἐπὶ (6) ]] εἰς<br>τὴν ] τ̣[ὴν]<br>γῆν<br>ἡμῶν |
| Mi 5:5 | ב/גבול/נו | ἐπὶ (6) ]] εἰς<br>τὰ ]<br>ὅρια ]<br>ἡμῶν |
| Na 2:6 | ב/הלכות/ם (K) ב/הליכת/ם (Q) | ἐν<br>τῇ ]] ταῖς<br>πορείᾳ ]] πορεία[ι]ς<br>αὐτῶν ] αὐ̣τῶ̣ν |
| Na 3:10 | עלל/יה | τὰ ] τ[ὰ]<br>νήπια<br>αὐτῆς |
| Na 3:12 | מבצר/יך | τὰ ] (after [πά]ντα)<br>ὀχυρώματά<br>σου |
| Na 3:13 | בריח/יך | τοὺς ] τ[ο]ὺς<br>μοχλούς ] μοχ[λούς]<br>σου |

| | | |
|---|---|---|
| Ha 1:16 | ל/מכמרת/ו | τῷ ]] τῇ |
| | | ἀμφιβλήστρῳ ]] σα[γήνῃ] |
| | | αὐτοῦ ] [αὐτ]οῦ |
| Ha 2:7 | מזעזע/יך | οἵ ] |
| | | ἐπίβουλοί ]] σαλεύοντές |
| | | σου ]] σε |
| Ha 2:16 | כבוד/ך | τὴν ] ṭὴν |
| | | δόξαν ] |
| | | σου ] σ̣[ο]υ |
| Ha 2:18 | יצר/ו | τὸ ] |
| | | πλάσμα ] |
| | | αὐτοῦ ] αὐ̣τοῦ |
| Ha 3:9 | קשת/ך | τὸ ] |
| | | τόξον ] τό[ξον] |
| | | σου |
| Zp 3:7 | עלילות/ם | ἡ ]] τὰ (after πάντα) |
| | | ἐπιφυλλὶς ]] ἐπιτ[ηδεύματα] |
| | | αὐτῶν |
| Za 3:5 | ראש/ו | τὴν ] τ[ὴν] |
| | | κεφαλὴν |
| | | αὐτοῦ |
| Za 3:5 | ראש/ו | τὴν ] |
| | | κεφαλὴν ] κ[εφαλ]ὴν |
| | | αὐτοῦ ] |
| Za 3:7 | ב/דרכ/י | ἐν |
| | | ταῖς ] |
| | | ὁδοῖς ] |
| | | μου ] |

RECONSTRUCTIONS (37 ×)

| | | |
|---|---|---|
| Jo 2:2 | אלה/יו | τὸν |
| | | θεὸν |
| | | αὐτοῦ ] [αὐτο]ῦ |
| Jo 4:2 | אדמת/י | τῇ ]]] [τῆς] |
| | | γῇ ]]] [γῆς] |
| | | μου |
| Mi 1:3 | מ/מקומ/ו | ἐκ |
| | | τοῦ |
| | | τόπου |
| | | αὐτοῦ |
| Mi 1:6 | אבנ/יה | τοὺς |
| | | λίθους |
| | | αὐτῆς |
| Mi 1:7 | פסיל/יה | τὰ (after [πάντα]) |
| | | γλυπτὰ ] |
| | | αὐτῆς ] |
| Mi 1:7 | אתננ/יה | τὰ (after [πάντα]) |
| | | μισθώματα ] [μισθώ]ματα |
| | | αὐτῆς ] |
| Mi 1:7 | עצב/יה | τὰ (after [πάντα]) |
| | | εἴδωλα ] [εἴ]δωλα |
| | | αὐτῆς ] [α]ὐτῆς |
| Mi 2:8 | עמ/י | ὁ |
| | | λαός |
| | | μου |
| Mi 3:5 | פי/הם | τὸ |
| | | στόμα |
| | | αὐτῶν ] [αὐτ]ῶν |
| Mi 4:3 | חרבת/יהם | τὰς (calc. of space) |
| | | ῥομφαίας ]] μαχα[ίρας] |
| | | αὐτῶν ] [αὐτῶ]ν |

| | | |
|---|---|---|
| Mi 4:9 | יועצ/ך | ἡ ]]] [ὁ]<br>βουλή ]]] [σύμβουλός]<br>σου ] |
| Mi 5:1 | ו/מוצאת/יו | καὶ (2)<br>αἱ<br>ἔξοδοι ]<br>αὐτοῦ ] |
| Mi 5:2 | אח/יו | τῶν (3)<br>ἀδελφῶν<br>αὐτῶν ]] αὐτοῦ |
| Mi 5:4 | ב/ארצ/נו | ἐπὶ (5) ]]] [εἰ]ς̣<br>τὴν<br>γῆν<br>ὑμῶν ]]] [ἡμῶ]ν |
| Na 2:13 | ו/מענת/יו | καὶ<br>τὸ ]]] [τὴν]<br>κατοικητήριον ]] [μά]ν̣δραν<br>αὐτοῦ |
| Na 2:14 | ו/כפיר/יך | καὶ<br>τοὺς<br>λέοντάς ] [λέον]τά[ς]<br>σου ] σ[ου] |
| Na 3:9 | עצמה [עצמ/ה] | ἡ<br>ἰσχὺς ]<br>αὐτῆς ] αὐ[τ]ῆς |
| Na 3:10 | נכבד/יה | τὰ ]]] [τοὺς]<br>ἔνδοξα ]]] [ἐνδόξους]<br>αὐτῆς ] [αὐ]τῆς |
| Na 3:10 | גדול/יה | οἱ (after [πάντες])<br>μεγιστᾶνες] [μεγιστᾶ]νες<br>αὐτῆς ] αὐ[τ]ῆ̣[ς] |
| Na 3:13 | עמ/ך | ὁ<br>λαός<br>σου |
| Na 3:14 | מבצר/יך | τῶν ]]] [τὰ]<br>ὀχυρωμάτων ]]] [ὀχυρώματά]<br>σου |
| Ha 1:5 | ב/ימ/יכם | ἐν<br>ταῖς<br>ἡμέραις ] [ἡμέρ]αις<br>ὑμῶν ] |
| Ha 1:7 | משפט/ו | τὸ<br>κρίμα ] [κρί]μα<br>αὐτοῦ ] |
| Ha 1:7 | ו/שׂאת/ו | καὶ<br>τὸ<br>λῆμμα<br>αὐτοῦ |
| Ha 1:8 | סוס/יו | οἱ<br>ἵπποι<br>αὐτοῦ ] [αὐ]τοῦ |
| Ha 1:15 | ב/מכמרת/ו | ἐν<br>ταῖς ]]] [τῇ]<br>σαγήναις ]] σαγήνῃ<br>αὐτοῦ ] |
| Ha 1:16 | ל/חרמ/ו | τῇ ]]] [τῷ̣]<br>σαγήνῃ ]] [ἀμφιβλή]στρῳ̣<br>αὐτοῦ ] |
| Ha 2:1 | על<br>משמרת/י | ἐπὶ<br>τῆς<br>φυλακῆς<br>μου ] |

| | | |
|---|---|---|
| Ha 2:1 | תוכחת/י | τὸν |
| | | ἔλεγχόν |
| | | μου |
| Ha 2:15 | מעור/יהם | τὰ ]]] [τὴν] (calc. of space) |
| | | σπήλαια ]] [ἀσχημοσ]ύνην |
| | | αὐτῶν ] αὐ[τῶ]ν |
| Zp 1:4 | יד/י | τὴν ] [τὴ]ν̣ |
| | | χεῖρά ] |
| | | μου ] |
| Zp 1:17 | דמ/ם | τὸ |
| | | αἷμα |
| | | αὐτῶν ] [αὐτῶ]ν |
| Zp 1:18 | כספ/ם | τὸ |
| | | ἀργύριον |
| | | αὐτῶν |
| Zp 1:18 | זהב/ם | τὸ |
| | | χρυσίον ] [χρυσίο]ν |
| | | αὐτῶν ] α[ὐτῶν] |
| Za 1:4 | כ/אבת/יכם | καθὼς ] κα̣[θὼς] |
| | | οἱ |
| | | πατέρες ] [πατέρ]ες |
| | | ὑμῶν ] |
| Za 3:4 | עונ/ך | τὰς ]]] [τὴν] |
| | | ἀνομίας ]]] [ἀνομίαν] |
| | | σου |
| Za 3:7 | את חצר/י | τὴν ] τ[ὰς] |
| | | αὐλήν ]]] [αὐλάς] |
| | | μου |

## 4.2 *Pronominal suffix: R=LXX omits article (12×)*

| | | |
|---|---|---|
| Jo 2:5 | מ/נגד | ἐξ ]] ἐ̣ξ̣ ἐναντία̣ς |
| | עינ/יך | ὀφθαλμῶν ] ὀφθ̣αλμῶν |
| | | σου ] |
| Jo 3:8 | ב/כפ/יהם | ἐν ] |
| | | χερσὶν ] χερσὶ̣ν̣ |
| | | αὐτῶν ] α̣ὐ̣τ̣ῶ̣ν̣ |
| Jo 3:9 | מ/חרון | ἐξ ]] ἀπὸ |
| | | ὀργῆς ]]] [θυμοῦ] |
| | אפ/ו | θυμοῦ ]] [ὀργ]ῆς |
| | | αὐτοῦ ] α̣[ὐτοῦ] |
| Mi 4:4 | תחת | ὑποκάτω ] ὑπ̣οκάτω |
| | גפנ/ו | ἀμπέλου ] |
| | | αὐτοῦ ] αὐ[τοῦ] |
| | ו/תחת | καὶ ἕκαστος ὑποκάτω ]]] [καὶ ὑποκάτω] |
| | תאנת/ו | συκῆς ] [σ]υκῆς |
| | | αὐτοῦ ] αυ̣[τ]οῦ |
| Mi 4:5 | ב/שם | ἐν ὀνόματι |
| | יהוה | κυρίου ]] 𐤉𐤄[𐤅𐤄] |
| | אלה/ינו | θεοῦ ] |
| | | ἡμῶν ] ἡ̣μ[ῶ]ν̣ |
| Ha 1:16 | חלק/ו | μερίδα ]] ἄρτος |
| | | αὐτοῦ |
| Ha 2:4 | ב/אמונת/ו | ἐκ ]] ἐν |
| | | πίστεώς ]] πίστει |
| | | μου ]] αὐτοῦ |
| Ha 3:11 | ברק | ἀστραπῆς ] ἀσ[τραπῆς] |
| | חנית/ך | ὅπλων ]]] [σιβύνης] |
| | | σου |
| Ha 3:13 | עמ/ך | λαοῦ ] λαο[ῦ] |
| | | σου |
| Ha 3:14 | ב/מט/יו | ἐν ] |
| | | ἐκστάσει ]] ῥάβδοις |
| | | --- ]] αὐτοῦ |

| | | |
|---|---|---|
| Ha 3:14 | פרז/ו (K) פרז/יו (Q) | δυναστῶν ]] ἀτει[χίσ]των |
| | | --- ]] αὐτοῦ |
| Za 9:1 | מנחת/ו | θυσία ]] κατάπαυ[σις] (vocalization) |
| | | αὐτοῦ |

## 4.3 *Pronominal suffix: R omits article (against LXX) (9 × + 1 × )*

| | | |
|---|---|---|
| Jo 2:5 | היכל | τὸν ]] > |
| | | ναὸν ] |
| | קדש/ך | τὸν ]] > |
| | | ἅγιόν ] ἅ[γ]ιόν |
| | | σου ] |
| Mi 4:5 | ב/שם אלה/יו | τὴν ]]] [ἐν ὀνόματι] |
| | | ὁδὸν ]] [θε]οῦ |
| | | αὐτοῦ ]] αὐτῶν |
| Mi 5:3 | אלה/יו | τοῦ (4) ]] > |
| | | θεοῦ ] |
| | | αὐτῶν ]]] [αὐτοῦ] |
| Na 2:6 | אדיר/יו | οἱ ]] > |
| | | μεγιστᾶνες ]] δυναστῶν |
| | | αὐτῶν ]] αὐτοῦ |
| Ha 1:17 | חרמ/ו | τὸ ]] > |
| | | ἀμφίβληστρον ]] μάχαιραν |
| | | αὐτοῦ ] |
| Ha 2:4 | נפש/ו | ἡ ]] > |
| | | ψυχή |
| | | μου ]] αὐτοῦ |
| Ha 2:5 | נפש/ו | τὴν ]] > |
| | | ψυχὴν ] ψυχὴ[ν] |
| | | αὐτοῦ |
| Ha 2:15 | רע/הו | τὸν ]] > |
| | | πλησίον ] πλ[ησίον] |
| | | αὐτοῦ |
| Zp 1:17 | ו/לחמ/ם | καὶ ] [κ]α[ὶ] |
| | | τὰς ]] > |
| | | σάρκας ]]] π[τώμ]α[τ]α |
| | | αὐτῶν |

RECONSTRUCTION (1 ×)

| | | |
|---|---|---|
| Zp 2:10 | תחת | ἀντὶ |
| | גאונ/ם | τῆς ]]] > |
| | | ὕβρεως |
| | | αὐτῶν ] αὐτῶν |

## 4.4 *Pronominal suffix: R adds article (against LXX) (2 × + 4 × )*

| | | |
|---|---|---|
| Ha 1:9 | פנ/יהם | --- ]] τοῦ |
| | | προσώποις ]] προσώπου |
| | | αὐτῶν ] |
| Ha 3:14 | עליצת/ם | --- ]] τὸ |
| | | χαλινοὺς ]] γαυρίαμα |
| | | αὐτῶν ] |

RECONSTRUCTIONS (4 ×)

| | | |
|---|---|---|
| Jo 2:3 | קול/י | --- ]]] [τῆς] |
| | | φωνῆς |
| | | μου |

| | | |
|---|---|---|
| Na 2:8 | על | ἐν ]]] [ἐπὶ] |
| | לבב/הן | --- ]]] [τὴν] |
| | | καρδίαις ]]] [καρδίαν] |
| | | αὐτῶν |
| Na 2:14 | רכב/ה | --- ]]] [τὸ] |
| | | πλῆθός ]]] [ἅρμα] |
| | | σου ]]] [αὐτῆς] |
| Zp 2:9 | עמ/י | --- ]]] [τοῦ] |
| | | λαοῦ ] |
| | | μου ] [μ]ο[ῦ] |

### 4.5 *Conclusions*

In most instances R retains the article of the LXX before combinations of nouns with pronominal suffixes (4.1 [23×]), while it even adds the article against the LXX (4.4 [2×+4×]). In 9 instances, however, R omits the article under these conditions (4.3), and in another 12 instances it leaves out the article with the LXX (4.2). Therefore, in most instances the article is retained in the reconstruction of these constructions (4.1 [37×]).

## 5. *Article before proper nouns*

### 5.1 *Article before proper nouns: R=LXX (1×+3×)*

In the following instances the article is added after the prepositions -ל and -ב (Za 9:1 [reconstructed] is an exception):

| | | |
|---|---|---|
| Mi 5:1 | ב/ישראל | ἐν (2) ] |
| | | τῷ ] |
| | | Ισραηλ ] ι[σραηλ] |
| | | RECONSTRUCTIONS (3×) |
| Za 1:14 | ל/ירושלם | τὴν (calc. of space) |
| | | Ιερουσαλημ |
| Za 1:14 | ו/ל/ציון | καὶ |
| | | τὴν (calc. of space) |
| | | Σιων ]] σε̣[ιων] |
| Za 9:1 | ישראל | τοῦ |
| | | Ισραηλ ] |

### 5.2 *Article before proper nouns: R omits article of LXX (3×)*

| | | |
|---|---|---|
| Mi 1:5 | יעקב[2] | τοῦ ]] > |
| | | Ιακωβ ] |
| Mi 5:5 | נמרד | τοῦ (6) ]] > |
| | | Νεβρωδ ] |
| Mi 5:6 | יעקב | τοῦ (7) ]] > |
| | | Ιακωβ ] ιακωβ̣ |

Note that all these are construct combinations. See further 5.4.

#### 5.2.1 *R=LXX omits article (6×)*

In the following instances the article is omitted after the prepostions על and -ב or in the construct case.

| | | |
|---|---|---|
| Mi 1:1 | מלכי | *βασιλέων* ]] *βασιλέως* |
| | יהודה | *Ιουδα* ] |
| Mi 4:7 | ב/הר | *ἐν* ] |
| | | --- ]] *τῷ* |
| | | *ὄρει* ] |
| | ציון | *Σιων* ]] *σει[ων]* |
| Mi 4:10 | בת | *θύγατερ* ] *[θύ]γατερ* |
| | ציון | *Σιων* ]] *σ[ειων]* |
| Zp 1:4 | על | *ἐπὶ*] |
| | יהודה | *Ιουδαν* ] *ιου[δαν]* |
| Zp 1:4 | כל | *πάντας* ] *[πάντ]ας* |
| | יושבי | *τοὺς* |
| | | *κατοικοῦντας* ] |
| | ירושלם | *Ιερουσαλημ* ]] *ἐν ιερ[ουσαλημ]* |
| Za 9:1 | ו/דמשק | *καὶ*] |
| | | *Δαμασκοῦ*] |

## 5.3 *Conclusions*

In three instances R omits LXX's article before proper nouns [5.2], in six cases it omits the article with the LXX (5.2.1), but in other instances it retains the article of the LXX (1× + 3× [5.1]). In accordance with the majority rule, the article is omitted also in the following instances (note that in these cases the conditions for retaining the article [5.1] are not met):

RECONSTRUCTIONS (3×)

In the following cases the article is omitted against the evidence of the LXX:

| | | |
|---|---|---|
| Mi 5:5 | מ/אשור | *ἐκ* (6) ]] *[ἐξ]* |
| | | *τοῦ* ]]] > (calc. of space) |
| | | *Ασσουρ* ] |
| Na 3:9 | פוט | *τῆς* ]]] > |
| | | *φυγῆς* ]] *φουδ* (calc. of space) |
| Ha 2:17 | לבנון | *τοῦ* ]]] > (calc. of space) |
| | | *Λιβάνου* |

In many additional places (16) the non-representation of the article before the proper noun in the LXX is reconstructed also for R:

Jo 3:5 [*ἄνδρες νινευη*]; 4:2 [*εἰς θαρσις*]; Mi 1:1 [*περὶ σαμαροίας*]; 1:1 [*κ*]*αὶ* [*ιερουσ*]*αλημ*; 1:5 [*οἴκου ισραηλ*]; 1:5 [*ἀσέβιαν ιακωβ*]; 1:5 [*ὕψη ιουδα*]; 4:8 *θυγάτηρ* [*σειων*]; 4:8 [*τῇ θυγατρὶ ιερουσ*]*αλημ*; 5:1 (2) *ἐν χ*[*ιλιάσιν ιο*]*υδα*; 5:2 (3) *το*[*ὺς υἱοὺς ισραηλ*]; Zp 1:1 [*βασιλέως ιουδα*]; Za 1:12 *π*[*όλεις ιουδα*]; 2:11 [*εἰς σειων*]; 2:11 (7) *θ*[*υ*]*γα*[*τέρα βαβυλῶνος*]; 8:19 [*τῷ ο*]*ἴκῳ* [*ιουδα*].

## 5.4 *Article before κύριος/𐤉𐤄𐤅𐤄*

### 5.4.1 *General practice (18×)*

Since MT does not have an article before יהוה, neither *κύριος* of the LXX nor 𐤉𐤄𐤅𐤄 of R is preceded by an article: Jo 3:3 4:2; Mi 1:1,3 4:4,7 5:3(4),3(4); Ha 2:16; Zp 1:3; Za 1:2,3,4 3:5,6,7 9:1,1. Accordingly יהוה is normally reconstructed as 𐤉𐤄𐤅𐤄 without the article.

### 5.4.2 *Article before κύριος/𐤉𐤄𐤅𐤄: R (= LXX) has article (2× + 2×)*

| | | |
|---|---|---|
| Ha 2:20 | ו/יהוה | *ὁ δὲ κύριος* ]] *καὶ ὁ* 𐤉𐤄𐤅𐤄 |

| | | |
|---|---|---|
| Za 9:1 | ל/יהוה | *κύριος* ]] *τῷ* 𐤉𐤄𐤅𐤄 |

RECONSTRUCTIONS (2 × )

| | | |
|---|---|---|
| Zp 1:5 | ל/יהוה | *κατὰ τοῦ* ]]] [*τῷ*]<br>*κυρίου* ]]] [𐤉𐤄𐤅𐤄] |
| Zp 1:17 | ל/יהוה | *τῷ*<br>*κυρίῳ* ]] 𐤉𐤄𐤅[𐤄] |

Note that in three of these cases the Greek article represents -ל.

### 5.4.3 *Article before κύριος*/𐤉𐤄𐤅𐤄: *R omits (1 × )*

| | | |
|---|---|---|
| Zp 2:10 | יהוה | *τὸν* ]] > (different construction)<br>*κύριον* ]] [𐤉𐤄]𐤅𐤄 |

## 6. את

### 6.1 את—*Greek article: R = LXX (7 × + 12 × )*

| | | |
|---|---|---|
| Jo 2:1 | את יונה | *τὸν* ]<br>*Ιωναν* ] |
| Jo 3:10 | את מעש/יהם | *τὰ* ] *τ̣ὰ*<br>*ἔργα* ]<br>*αὐτῶν* ] *αὐτ̣[ῶν]* |
| Mi 5:5 | את ארץ<br>אשור | *τὸν* (6) ]] *τὴν γῆν*<br>*Ασσουρ* ] |
| Zp 1:4 | את שם | *καὶ* ]] ><br>*τὰ* ]] *τὸ*<br>*ὀνόματα* ]] *ὄνομα* |
| Zp 1:5 | ו/את<br>ה/משתחוים | *καὶ* ]] ><br>*τοὺς* ] *τ[ο]ὺς*<br>*προσκυνοῦντας* ] *προσκ̣[υνοῦν]τας* |
| Za 1:13 | את<br>ה/מלאך | *τῷ* ] *τῷ̣*<br>*ἀγγέλῳ̣* |
| Za 3:7 | את חצר/י | *τὴν* ]]] *τ[ὰς]*<br>*αὐλήν* ]]] *αὐλάς*<br>*μου* |

RECONSTRUCTIONS (12 × )

| | | |
|---|---|---|
| Jo 1:16 | את יהוה | *τὸν*<br>*κύριον* ]] 𐤉𐤄[𐤅𐤄] |
| Mi 4:7 | את ה/צלעה | *τὴν*<br>*συντετριμμένην* ] [*ἐκτεθλιμμένη*]*ν̣* |
| Mi 5:5 | ו/את ארץ | *καὶ* (6)<br>*τὴν*<br>*γῆν* ] |
| | נמרד | *τοῦ* ]] ><br>*Νεβρωδ* ] |
| Ha 1:6 | את ה/כשדים | *τοὺς Χαλδαίους* |
| Ha 2:14 | את כבוד | *τὴν*<br>*δόξαν* |
| | יהוה | *κυρίου* ]] 𐤉𐤄𐤅𐤄 |
| Ha 3:13 | את משיח/ך | *τοὺς* ]]] [*τοῦ*]<br>*χριστούς* ]]] [*χριστοῦ*]<br>*σου* ] |
| Zp 1:4 | את שאר (את שם) | *τὰ* ]]] [*τὸ*]<br>*ὀνόματα* ]] *ὑπ*[*όλειμμα*] |
| Zp 1:13 | את יינ/ם | *τὸν*<br>*οἶνον* ]<br>*αὐτῶν* ] |

| | | |
|---|---|---|
| Za 2:2 | את יהודה | (19) *τὸν Ιουδαν* |
| | את ישׂראל | *καὶ* ]]] > |
| | | *τὸν Ισραηλ* |
| | ו/ירושלם | --- ]]] [*καὶ τὴν*] *ιερου*[*σαλημ*] |
| Za 3:1 | את | --- ]]] [*τὸν*] |
| | יהושע | *'Ιησοῦν* |
| Za 3:7 | את משמרת/י | *τὰ* ]]] [*τὴν*] |
| | | *προστάγματά* ]] [*φυλα*]*κήν* |
| | | *μου* ] |
| Za 3:7 | את בית/י | *τὸν* |
| | | *οἶκόν* ] |
| | | *μου* ] |

6.2 *Conclusions*

As a rule, את is represented by the Greek article, which is also required by the Hebrew article or pronominal suffix often following (cf. 1.6 and 4.5).

## 7. *Tenses of the verb*

### 7.0 קטל *translated by historic present, when R=LXX (2× +4× )*

| | | |
|---|---|---|
| Za 2:12 | כה | *τάδε* (8) ] [*τάδ*]*ε* |
| | אמר | *λέγει* ] *λέγε*[*ι*] |
| Za 3:7 | כה | *τάδε* ] |
| | אמר | *λέγει* ] |
| | יהוה | *κύριος* ]] [Paleo-Hebrew tetragrammaton] |
| | צבאות | *παντοκράτωρ* ]] *τῶν δυ*[*νάμεων*] |

RECONSTRUCTIONS (4×)

The same phrase: Mi 3:5; Za 1:4,14; 8:20.

### 7.1 קטל *translated by past (usually aorist), when R=LXX (19× )*

| | | |
|---|---|---|
| Jo 2:4 | עברו | *διῆλθον* ] *διῆλ*[*θον*] |
| Jo 2:5 | אמרתי | *εἶπα* ] *εἶπα̣* |
| Jo 2:5 | נגרשתי | *ἀπῶσμαι* ] *ἀ̣πῶ*[*σμαι*] |
| Jo 2:7 | ירדתי | *κατέβην* ] |
| Jo 3:10 | דבר | *ἐλάλησε* ]] *ἐλ*[*άλ*]*ησεν* |
| Jo 3:10 | עשׂה | *ἐποίησεν* ] |
| Jo 4:2 | קדמתי | *προέφθασα* ] [*προ*]*έφθα*[*σα*] |
| Mi 4:9 | אבד | *ἀπώλετο* ] *ἀπώ*[*λετο*] |
| Na 2:8 | גלתה | *ἀπεκαλύφθη* ] *ἀπεκ*[*α*]*λ̣ύφθ*[*η*] |
| Na 3:16 | הרבית | *ἐπλήθυνας* ] *ἐπλ*[*ήθυνας*] |
| Ha 1:15 | העלה | *ἀνέσπασε* ]] *ἀνέσπασεν* |
| Ha 2:8 | שׁלות | *ἐσκύλευσας* ] *ἐσ*[*κ*]*ύλευσας* |
| Ha 2:18 | פסל/ו | *ἔγλυψεν* ] [*ἔγλυψε*]*ν* |
| | | *αὐτὸ* ] |
| Ha 2:18 | בטח | *πέποιθεν* ] |
| Ha 3:10 | נתן | *ἔδωκεν* ] [*ἔδω*]*κεν* |
| Zp 1:17 | חטאו | *ἐξήμαρτον* ] *ἐ̣*[*ξήμα*]*ρ̣τ̣ο̣*[*ν*] |
| Zp 2:10 | חרפו | *ὠνείδισαν* ] *ὠνείδι*[*σαν*] |
| Za 1:2 | קצף | *ὠργίσθη* ] [*ὠργίσθ*]*η* |
| Za 8:23 | שׁמענו | *ἀκηκόαμεν* ] [*ἀ*]*κ̣ηκόαμεν* |

#### 7.1.1 *Idem, when R differs from LXX (13× +5× )*

| | | |
|---|---|---|
| Jo 3:10 | שׁבו | *ἀπέστρεψαν* ]] *ἐπέστρεψαν* |
| Mi 4:6 | הרעתי | *ἀπωσάμην* ]] *ἐκά*[*κωσα*] |
| Na 2:7 | נפתחו | *διηνοίχθησαν* ]] *ἠνοίχθησαν* |
| Na 2:8 | העלתה | *ἀνέβαινε* ]] [...]*η* |

| | | |
|---|---|---|
| Na 3:7 | שׂדדה | δειλαία ]] [τεταλαι]πώρηκε[ν] |
| Ha 2:16 | שׂבעת | πλησμονὴν ]] ἐνεπλήσ[θης] |
| Ha 2:18 | הועיל | ὠφελεῖ ]] ὠφέλησεν (tense) |
| Ha 3:10 | ראו/ך | ὄψονταί ]] εἴδοσ[άν] (tense) σε |
| Ha 3:14 | נקבת | διέκοψας ]] διέτρη[σα]ς |
| Za 1:3 | אמר | λέγει ]] εἶπεν (tense) |
| Za 1:4 | קראו | ἐνεκάλεσαν ]] ἐκάλουν (aspect) |
| Za 2:12 | שׁלח/ני | ἀπέσταλκέ (8) ]] ἀ[πέ]σṭẹịλέν (tense) με |
| Za 9:2 | חכמה | ἐφρόνησαν ]] [ἐ]φρόνησεν |

RECONSTRUCTIONS (5 ×)

| | | |
|---|---|---|
| Jo 2:6 | אפפו/ני | περιεχύθη ]]] π[εριεχύθησάν] μοι ]] με |
| Mi 1:1 | היה~ | ---]]] [ἐγένετο] |
| Na 3:10 | הלכה | πορεύσεται ]]] [ἐπορεύθη] (tense) |
| Na 3:13 | אכלה | καταφάγεται ]]] [ἔφαγεν] (tense) |
| Ha 3:10 | עבר | πορείας ]]] [παρῆλθεν] |

## 7.2 קטל *translated by future, when R=LXX (3×)*

| | | |
|---|---|---|
| Mi 5:2 | ילדה | τέξεται (3) ] |

(Cf. יתנ/ם—δώ[σει] in parallel stich.)

| | | |
|---|---|---|
| Na 3:10 | ידו | βαλοῦσι ]] βαλοῦ[σιν] |

(Cf. ירטשׁו—[ἐδαφιοῦσιν] in parallel stich.)

| | | |
|---|---|---|
| Na 3:13 | נפתחו | ἀνοιχθήσονται ] ἀ̣νο[ι]χθ[ήσονται] |

(Similarly in LXX: אכלה—καταφάγεται.)

### 7.2.1 *Idem, when R differs from LXX (1×)*

| | | |
|---|---|---|
| Ha 1:11 | חלף | μεταβαλεῖ ] διελεύσεται |

(LXX translates all verbs in this verse with futures, for which cf. v. 10—R is not preserved for other words in this verse.)

## 7.3 וְקטל *translated by future, when R=LXX (14×)*

| | | |
|---|---|---|
| Mi 1:3 | ו/ירד | καὶ καταβήσεται ] καṭαβήσεται |
| Mi 1:6 | ו/שׂמתי | καὶ ] κα[ὶ] θήσομαι ] [θ]ήσομαι |
| Mi 1:6 | ו/הגרתי | καὶ ] κατασπάσω ] |
| Mi 3:6 | ו/באה | καὶ δύσεται ] [δ]ύσεται |
| Mi 5:3 | ו/עמד | καὶ (4) ] στήσεται ] [στ]ήσεται |
| Mi 5:3 | ו/רעה [ו/ראה ו/רעה ו/] | καὶ (4) ]] > ὄψεται ]] > καὶ ] ποιμανεῖ ] πο[ι]μανεῖ |
| Mi 5:4 | ו/היה | καὶ (5) ] ἔσται ] ἔσ[ται] |
| Mi 5:5 | ו/רעו | καὶ (6) ποιμανοῦσι ]] [ποιμανοῦ]σιν |
| Na 2:14 | ו/הבערתי | καὶ ἐκκαύσω ] [ἐκκα]ύσω |

| | | |
|---|---|---|
| Ha 2:7 | ו/היית | καὶ ] |
| | | ἔσῃ ] |
| Zp 1:13 | ו/נטעו | καὶ |
| | | καταφυτεύσουσιν ] [καταφυτεύ]σουσιν |
| Zp 1:17 | ו/הלכו | καὶ ] |
| | | πορεύσονται ] πορεύσον[τα]ι |
| Za 3:7 | ו/נתתי | καὶ ] |
| | | δώσω ] [δώσ]ω |
| Za 9:4 | ו/הכה | καὶ ] |
| | | πατάξει ] π[ατάξει] |

## 7.3.1 *Idem, when R differs from LXX (11× + 4×)*

| | | |
|---|---|---|
| Jo 3:9 | ו/שב | καὶ |
| | | ἀποστρέψει ]] [ἐπιστ]ρέψ[ει] |
| Mi 3:6 | ו/חשכה | καὶ ] [κ]αὶ |
| | | σκοτία ]] σκοτασθ[ήσεται] |
| Mi 4:3 | ו/כתתו | καὶ ] |
| | | κατακόψουσι ]] συνκόψου[σιν] |
| Mi 4:7 | ו/שׂמתי | καὶ |
| | | θήσομαι ]] θήσω |
| Mi 5:3 | ו/ישבו | ὑπάρξουσι (4) ]] καὶ ἐπιστραφήσονται |
| Mi 5:4 | ו/הקמנו | καὶ (5) |
| | | ἐπεγερθήσονται ]] ἐπεγεροῦμεν |
| Na 2:6 | ו/הכן | καὶ ] |
| | | ἑτοιμάσουσι ]] ἑτοιμάσε[ι] |
| Na 3:6 | ו/שׂמתי/ך | καὶ ] [κα]ὶ |
| | | θήσομαί ]] θήσω |
| | | σε |
| Ha 1:8 | ו/פשו | καὶ ] |
| | | ἐξιππάσονται ] ὁρμή[σουσιν] |
| Zp 1:4 | ו/הכרתי | καὶ ] [κ]α[ὶ] |
| | | ἐξαρῶ ]] ἐ[ξ]ολ[εθρεύ]σω |
| Za 2:16 | ו/בחר | καὶ (12) |
| | | αἱρετιεῖ ]] [ἐκλέ]ξεται |

RECONSTRUCTIONS (4×)

| | | |
|---|---|---|
| Mi 1:4 | ו/נמסו | καὶ |
| | | σαλευθήσεται ]]] [τακή]σον[ται] |
| Mi 4:4 | ו/ישבו | καὶ |
| | | ἀναπαύσεται ]]] [καθίσ]ονται |
| Mi 4:8 | ו/באה | καὶ |
| | | εἰσελεύσεται ]]] [ἐλεύσετα]ι |
| Za 8:21 | ו/הלכו | καὶ |
| | | συνελεύσονται ]]] [ἐλεύ]σονται |

## 7.4 וְקטל *translated by past by R and LXX (0× + 1×)*

RECONSTRUCTION (1×)

| | | |
|---|---|---|
| Mi 3:5 | ו/קדשו | --- ]]] [καὶ] |
| | | ἤγειραν ]]] [ἡγίασαν] |

(Cf. וקראו—*καὶ κηρύσσοντας* in parallel stich in the LXX.)

## 7.5 יקטל *translated by ind. fut., when R=LXX (19×)*

| | | |
|---|---|---|
| Jo 2:5 | אוסיף | προσθήσω ] [προσ]θήσω |
| Mi 4:6 | אספה | συνάξω ] συνά[ξω] |
| Mi 5:2 | יתנ/ם | δώσει (3) ] δώ[σει] |
| | | αὐτοὺς |
| Na 2:6 | יכשלו | ἀσθενήσουσιν ] [ἀσ]θενήσουσιν |
| Na 3:7 | אבקשׁ | ζητήσω ] |

| | | |
|---|---|---|
| Na 3:15 | תכרית/ך | ἐξολεθρεύσει ] [ἐξολ]εθρεύσει σε ] |
| Ha 1:8 | יעפו | καὶ πετασθήσονται ] [πετα]σθήσονται |
| Ha 1:9 | יבוא | ἥξει ] |
| Ha 1:16 | יזבח | θύσει ] |
| Ha 1:17 | יחמול | φείσεται ] |
| Ha 2:1 | אעמדה | στήσομαι ] στήσ[ομαι] |
| Ha 2:4 | יחיה | ζήσεται ] ζήσετ[αι] |
| Ha 2:7 | יקומו | ἀναστήσονται ] |
| Ha 2:14 | תמלא | ἐμπλησθήσεται ] [πλησ]θήσεται |
| Ha 2:17 | יכס/ך | καλύψει ] [καλύ]ψει σε ] |
| Ha 3:9 | תבקע | ῥαγήσεται ] |
| Ha 3:14 | יסערו | σεισθήσονται ] σεισθ[ή]σονται |
| Za 8:23 | נלכה | πορευσόμεθα ] [πο]ρευσόμεθα |
| Za 9:4 | יורש/נה | κληρονομήσει ] [κληρονο]μήσει αὐτὴν ] |

## 7.5.1 *Idem, when R differs from LXX (9× + 10×)*

| | | |
|---|---|---|
| Mi 1:4 | יתבקעו | τακήσονται ]] [ῥα]γήσον[τα]ι |
| Mi 5:3 | יגדל | μεγαλυνθήσεται (4) ]] μεγαλ[υνθή]σονται |
| Na 2:6 | יזכר | μνησθήσονται ]] μνησθήσεται |
| Ha 1:10 | יתקלס | ἐντρυφήσει ]] [ἐν]παίξει |
| Ha 1:17 | יריק | ἀμφιβαλεῖ ]] [ἐκκεν]ώσει |
| Ha 2:3 | יכזב | εἰς κενόν ]] [δ]ιαψεύσεται |
| Ha 2:16 | תסוב | ἐκύκλωσεν ]] κυκλώσει (tense) |
| Ha 3:9 | תעור | ἐντενεῖς ]] ἐξεγ[ερ]εῖς |
| Za 3:7 | תשמר | διαφυλάξῃς ]] φ[υλ]άξεις |

RECONSTRUCTIONS (10×)

| | | |
|---|---|---|
| Jo 3:9 | ישוב | --- ]] ἐπι[σ]τ[ρέψει] |
| Mi 1:7 | אשים | θήσομαι ]]] θήσ[ω] |
| Mi 1:7 | ישובו | συνέστρεψεν ]]] [ἐπιστρέψουσ]ιν (tense) |
| Mi 3:5 | יתן | ἐδόθη ]]] [δώσει] (tense) |
| Mi 4:6 | אקבצה | εἰσδέξομαι ]]] [ἀθροίσω] |
| Ha 1:8 | יבאו | --- ]]] [ἐλεύσονται] |
| Ha 2:19 | יורה | φαντασία ]] φω[τιεῖ] |
| Ha 3:11 | יהלכו | --- ]] [πορεύ]σοντα[ι] |
| Ha 3:12 | תדוש | κατάξεις ]] ἀλ[ο]ή[σεις] |
| Za 2:8 | תשב | κατοικηθήσεται (4) ]] τι[θήσεις] |

## 7.6 יקטל *translated by ind. of past or present tense by both R and LXX (5×)*

| | | |
|---|---|---|
| Jo 2:4 | ו/נהר | καὶ ποταμοί ]] [καὶ ποταμ]ὸς |
| | יסבב/ני | με ]] > |
| | | ἐκύκλωσαν ]] περιεκύκλωσ[έ]ν |
| | | {..~με} ]] μ[ε] |

(All the preceding verbs in the LXX describe past action: קראת ויענני—ἐβόησα...καὶ εἰσήκουσέ μου; שמע ותשליכני—ἤκουσας...ἀπέρριψάς με)

| | | |
|---|---|---|
| Jo 2:6 | אפפו/ני | περιεχύθη ]]] π[εριεχύθησάν] |
| | | μοι ]] με |
| | מים | ὕδωρ ]] ὕδατα |
| | עד | ἕως ] ἕως |
| | נפש | ψυχῆς, ] |
| | תהום | ἄβυσσος ] |
| | יסבב/ני | ἐκύκλωσέ ]] ἐκύκλω[σέν] |
| | | με |

(Tense of אפפוני carried over to translation of יסבבני.)

| | | |
|---|---|---|
| Mi 2:7 | ייטיבו | εἰσι καλοὶ ]] [ἠγ]ἀθυναν |

(Cf. context: דברי ייטיבו עם הישר הולך.)

| | | |
|---|---|---|
| Mi 2:8 | יקומם | ἀντέστη ]] [ἀντέ]στησαν |
| Mi 2:8 | תפשטון | ἐξέδειραν ]] ἐξεδύσ[ατε] |

(Cf. ואתמול in context.)

### 7.6.1 *Idem, when R differs from LXX (1×)*

| | | |
|---|---|---|
| Ha 3:10 | יחילו | καὶ ]]] ><br>ὠδινήσουσι ]] [ὠδίνησ]αν |

(In this context, R rendered the sequence ראוך...יחילו with two verbs in the aorist and the LXX with two verbs in the future tense.)

## 7.7 יקטל *translated after conjunctions or negations by aorist subj. by R=LXX (5×)*

| | | |
|---|---|---|
| Jo 3:9 | ו/לא | καὶ ] [κα]ὶ<br>οὐ ]<br>μὴ ] |
| | נאבד | ἀπολώμεθα ] ἀπολ[ώμε]θα |
| Mi 4:3 | ו/לא {...עוד} | καὶ ]<br>οὐκέτι μὴ ]] οὐ μὴ |
| | ילמדון | μάθωσι ]] μάθωσιν |
| | עוד | {...} ]] ἔτι |
| Mi 5:4 | ו/כי | καὶ (5) ]<br>ὅταν ]] ὅτι |
| | ידרך | ἐπιβῇ ] |
| Mi 5:5 | ו/כי | καὶ (6)<br>ὅταν ]]] [ὅτι] |
| | ידרך | ἐπιβῇ ] |
| Na 3:12 | אם | ἐὰν |
| | ינועו | σαλευθῶσι ]] σαλευθ[ῶσιν] |

### 7.7.1 *Idem, when R differs from LXX (5× + 2×)*

| | | |
|---|---|---|
| Mi 5:4 | יבוא | ἐπέλθῃ (5) ]] ἔλθῃ |
| Mi 5:5 | יבוא | ἐπέλθῃ (6) ]] ἔλθῃ |
| Ha 1:5 | יספר | τις ἐκδιηγῆται ]]] [ἐκδιηγ]ηθῇ |
| Za 3:7 | תלך | πορεύῃ ]] πορευθῇς |
| Za 8:20 | יבאו | ἥξουσι ]] [ἔλ]θωσιν |

RECONSTRUCTIONS (2×)

| | | |
|---|---|---|
| Ha 2:2 | ירוץ | διώκῃ ]]] [τρέχ]ῃ |
| Za 8:23 | יחזיקו | ἐπιλάβωνται ] [ἐπιλάβω]νται |

## 7.8 ויקטל *translated by past by both R and LXX (11× + 3×)*

| | | |
|---|---|---|
| Jo 1:16 | ו/ייראו | καὶ<br>ἐφοβήθησαν ] [ἐ]φοβή[θη]σαν |
| Jo 2:4 | ו/תשליכ/ני | --- ]]] [καὶ]<br>ἀπέρριψάς ]] [ἀ]πέρρειψάς<br>με ] μ[ε] |
| Jo 3:10 | ו/ירא | καὶ ]<br>εἶδεν ] [εἶ]δε[ν] |
| Jo 4:2 | ו/יתפלל | καὶ ]<br>προσηύξατο ]] π[ροσ]εύξατο |
| Ha 1:15 | ו/יאספ/הו | καὶ ]<br>συνήγαγεν ] συνήγα[γεν]<br>αὐτὸν |

| | | |
|---|---|---|
| Za 3:1 | ו/ירא/ני | καὶ ]<br>ἔδειξέ ]] ἔ[δειξέν]<br>μοι |
| Za 3:2 | ו/יאמר | καὶ ] [κ]αὶ<br>εἶπε ]] εἶπεν |
| Za 3:4 | ו/יאמר | καὶ ] [κ]αὶ<br>εἶπε ]] εἶπεν |
| Za 3:5 | ו/ישׂימו | καὶ ]<br>ἐπέθηκαν ] ἐπέθηκ[αν] |
| Za 3:6 | ו/יעד | καὶ<br>διεμαρτύρατο ]]] [ἐ]μαρτύρα[το] |
| Za 9:3 | ו/תבן | καὶ<br>ᾠκοδόμησε ]] [ᾠκοδό]μησεν |

RECONSTRUCTIONS (3 × )

| | | |
|---|---|---|
| Jo 3:8 | ו/יתכסו | καὶ ]<br>περιεβάλοντο ] πε[ριεβάλοντο] |
| Jo 3:8 | ו/יקראו | καὶ ] κα[ὶ]<br>ἀνεβόησαν |
| Jo 4:1 | ו/ירע אל | καὶ ] κ[αὶ]<br>ἐλυπήθη ] [ἐ]λ[υπήθη] |

### 7.8.1 *Idem, when R differs from LXX (5 × + 1 × )*

| | | |
|---|---|---|
| Jo 1:16 | ו/יזבחו | καὶ ]<br>ἔθυσαν ]] ἐθυσίασαν |
| Jo 3:8 | ו/ישבו | καὶ ] καὶ<br>ἀπέστρεψαν ]] ἐπέστ[ρεψ]εν |
| Jo 3:10 | ו/ינחם | καὶ<br>μετενόησεν ]] [παρ]εκλήθη <ι> |
| Jo 4:1 | ו/יחר ל/ו | καὶ ]<br>συνεχύθη ]] ἠθ[ύμησεν] |
| Za 9:3 | ו/תצבר | καὶ<br>ἐθησαύρισεν ]] ἐβούνισεν |

RECONSTRUCTION (1 × )

| | | |
|---|---|---|
| Za 3:5 | ו/ילבש/הו | καὶ ] κ[αὶ]<br>περιέβαλον ]]] [ἐνέδυσαν]<br>αὐτὸν |

### 7.9 ויקטל *translated by future by both R and LXX (5 × )*

In the following instances, R and the LXX read וְיקטל, sometimes against MT (the vocalization recorded is that of MT).

| | | |
|---|---|---|
| Ha 1:10 | וַ/יצבר | καὶ<br>βαλεῖ ] [β]αλεῖ |
| Ha 1:15 | וְ/יגיל | καὶ (16) ]<br>χαρήσεται ]] χαρεῖται |
| Ha 1:16 | וִ/יקטר | καὶ ]<br>θυμιάσει ] |
| Ha 2:1 | וַ/אֲצפה | καὶ ἀποσκοπεύσω ] |
| Za 1:3 | וְ/אשׁוב | καὶ<br>ἐπιστραφήσομαι ] [ἐπιστραφ]ήσομαι |

### 7.9.1 *Idem, when R differs from LXX (6 × + 1 × )*

| | | |
|---|---|---|
| Ha 1:10 | וַ/ילכד/ה | καὶ<br>κρατήσει ]] συνλήμψετ[αι]<br>αὐτοῦ ]]] [αὐτό] |

| | | |
|---|---|---|
| Ha 1:11 | וַ/יעבר | καὶ<br>διελεύσεται ]] παρ[ελεύσεται] |
| Ha 2:1 | וְ/אתיצבה | καὶ ]<br>ἐπιβήσομαι ]] στῃ[λώσομαι] |
| Ha 2:3 | וְ/יפח | καὶ ]<br>ἀνατελεῖ ]] ἐνφανήσετ[άι] |
| Ha 2:5 | וַ/יקבץ | καὶ ]<br>εἰσδέξεται ]] ἀθροί[σει] |
| Ha 2:6 | וְ/יאמר | καὶ ] κα̣[ὶ]<br>ἐροῦσιν ]] [ἐρ]εῖ |

RECONSTRUCTION (1 ×)

| | | |
|---|---|---|
| Ha 2:5 | וַ/יאסף | καὶ<br>ἐπισυνάξει ]]] [συνάξει] |

See further Za 9:5.

## 7.10 *Conclusions*

As a rule, R has a fixed system of equivalents for the Hebrew tenses which more or less follows that of the LXX but which at times adheres to that system more closely than the LXX: קטל = past (7.1 [19 ×, 13 × + 5 ×]), and rarely future (7.2 [3 ×, 1 ×]), וְקטל = future (7.3 [14 ×, 12 × + 4 ×]) and once past (7.4 [reconstr.]); יקטל = ind. fut. (7.5 [19 ×, 9 × + 10 ×]) and rarely ind. of a past tense (7.6 [5 ×]), but also aor. subj. after conjunctions (7.7 [5 ×, 5 × + 2 ×]; וַיקטל is rendered mainly by past tenses (7.8 [11 × + 3 ×, 5 × + 1 ×]), and less frequently by the future tense (7.9 [5 ×, 6 × + 1 ×]), the latter on the basis of a different vocalization (וְיקטל). For Aquila's system of equivalents for the verbal tenses, see Hyvärinen, op. cit., 62–8.

## 7.11 *The use of verbs with neuter plural nouns*

The classical rule that the neuter plural noun governs a verb in the singular is followed by R in two instances:

| | | |
|---|---|---|
| Ha 1:9 | כל/ה | συντέλεια ]] [π]άντα |
| | ל/חמס | εἰς ἀσεβεῖς ]] εἰς ἀδικίαν |
| | יבוא | ἥξει ] |
| Ha 2:6 | אלה | ταῦτα ] ταῦτ̣α |
| | כל/ם | πάντα ] πάν[τα] |
| | … | … |
| | ישׂאו | λήμψονται ]] λήψε[ται] |

In one case this rule is abandoned, as often in the LXX:

| | | |
|---|---|---|
| Mi 1:4 | ו/נמסו | καὶ<br>σαλευθήσεται ]] [τακή]σον̣[ται] |
| | ה/הרים | τὰ ὄρη ] |

In the following doubtful case, calc. of space have guided our decision:

| | | |
|---|---|---|
| Jo 2:6 | אפפו/ני | περιεχύθη ]]] π[εριεχύθησάν]<br>μοι ]] με |
| | מים | ὕδωρ ]] ὕδατα |

In three cases, it should be observed, the specific form of R follows the Hebrew.

## 8. *The verb: simplex and composita*

### 8.1 *Simplex in R for compositum in LXX (5× + 11×)*

| | | |
|---|---|---|
| Mi 5:4 | יבוא | ἐπέλθῃ (5) ]] ἔλθῃ |
| Mi 5:5 | יבוא | ἐπέλθῃ (6) ]] ἔλθῃ |
| Na 2:7 | נפתחו | διηνοίχθησαν ]] ἠνοίχθησαν |
| Za 1:4 | קראו | ἐνεκάλεσαν ]] ἐκάλουν |
| Za 3:7 | תשמר | διαφυλάξῃς ]] φ[υλ]άξεις |

RECONSTRUCTIONS (11×)

| | | |
|---|---|---|
| Jo 3:5 | ו/יאמינו | καὶ<br>ἐνεπίστευσαν ]]] [ἐπίσ]τευσα[ν] |
| Mi 4:8 | ו/באה | καὶ<br>εἰσελεύσεται ]]] [ἐλεύσετα]ι |
| Na 2:5 | ירוצצו | διατρέχουσαι ]]] [δραμοῦν]ται |
| Na 3:13 | אכלה | καταφάγεται ]]] [ἔφαγεν] (calc. of space) |
| Na 3:14 | החזיקי | κατακράτησον ]]] [κράτησον] |
| Na 3:15 | תאכל/ך | καταφάγεταί σε ]]] [φάγεταί σε] (2×) (calc. of space) |
| Ha 1:6 | מקים | ἐξεγείρω ]]] [ἐγείρω] |
| Ha 2:5 | ו/יאסף | καὶ<br>ἐπισυνάξει ]]] [συνάξει] |
| Ha 2:14 | תמלא | ἐκπλησθήσεται ]]] [πλησ]θήσεται |
| Za 3:6 | ו/יעד | καὶ<br>διεμαρτύρατο ]]] [ἐ]μαρτύρα[το] |
| Za 8:21 | ו/הלכו | καὶ<br>συνελεύσονται ]]] [ἐλεύ]σονται (calc. of space) |

### 8.2 *Compositum in R for simplex of LXX (2× + 1×)*

| | | |
|---|---|---|
| Jo 2:4 | {...}<br>יסבב/ני | με ]] ><br>ἐκύκλωσαν ]] περιεκύκλωσ[έ]ν<br>{.. ~με} ]] μ[ε] |
| Na 2:8 | מתפפת | φθεγγόμεναι ]] ἀποφθεγγ[ο]μέν[ων] |

RECONSTRUCTION (1×)

| | | |
|---|---|---|
| Na 3:15 | התכבדי | καὶ ]]] ><br>βαρυνθήσῃ ]]] [καταβαρύν]θητι (for reconstr. see context) |

### 8.3 *Different preverbs (5× + 1×)*

| | | |
|---|---|---|
| Jo 3:8 | ו/ישבו | καὶ ] καὶ<br>ἀπέστρεψαν ]] ἐπέστ[ρεψ]εν |
| Jo 3:10 | שבו | ἀπέστρεψαν ]] ἐπέστρεψαν |
| Mi 4:3 | ו/כתתו | καὶ ]<br>κατακόψουσι ]] συνκόψου[σιν] |
| Ha 1:11 | ו/יעבר | καὶ<br>διελεύσεται ]] παρ[ελεύσεται] |
| Za 1:4 | שובו | ἀποστρέψατε ]] [ἐ]πι[στρέψατε] |

RECONSTRUCTION (1×)

| | | |
|---|---|---|
| Jo 3:9 | ו/שב | καὶ<br>ἀποστρέψει ]] [ἐπιστ]ρέψ[ει] |

(Note that this as well as three of the aforementioned cases refer to the rendering of שוב by ἐπιστρέφω. For further reconstructions of שוב as ἐπιστρέφω, see Mi 1:7; 2:8; Za 1:3.)

### 8.4 *Same preverb, different verb (and number) (4×)*

| | | |
|---|---|---|
| Mi 2:8 | תפשטון | ἐξέδειραν ]] ἐξεδύσ[ατε] |
| Ha 3:13 | ערות | ἐξήγειρας ]] [ἐξε]κένωσα[s] |
| Ha 3:14 | נקבת | διέκοψας ]] διέτρη[σα]s |

| | | |
|---|---|---|
| Zp 1:4 | ו/הכרתי | *καὶ* ] [*κ*]*α*[*ὶ*]<br>*ἐξαρῶ* ]] *ἐ*[*ξ*]*ολ*[*εθρεύ*]*σω* |

## 8.5 *Conclusions*

R adheres to a system of fixed equivalents (see 11) in which there is less room for composita than in the LXX. Hence, such verbs as בא, שוב and קרא are preferably rendered by simplex forms rather than by compounds. As a consequence, R has a certain preference for the simplex forms of the verb: 8.1 (5× + 11×) compared with 8.2 (2× + 1×). When space allows, this tendency is followed in the reconstruction.

# 9. *Synonymous parts of speech*

In an attempt to understand R's translation technique, we list here all words of the LXX which have been replaced by 'synonymous' parts of speech in R. The notion of synonymity should not be taken in the same sense as in the study of literature. Rather, the use of the term here implies that on a translational level the old and new translation options are synonymous, while the words themselves need not be. This category should be viewed together with section 10 which records the revisional efforts of R. In a way, such revisional work may be reflected in this category as well, so that R's revisional activity can be considered as more extensive than indicated there. First, there are cases in which R replaced a word with a seemingly synonymous word, but to him the new word seemed actually more appropriate than the old one. Second, there are also listed here instances of changes made for the sake of consistency such as the replacement of *ὅταν* and *διότι* with *ὅτι* (Hebrew כי). Likewise, in such a case as Na 2:6 ימהרו was probably rendered with *ταχύνω* rather than *σπεύδω* (LXX) because of the frequent rendering of the adjective מַהֵר with *ταχύς*. A noun like היכל in Na 2:7 was probably rendered with *ναός* rather than *βασίλεια* (LXX) because the stem of the latter may have been reserved for the root מלך.

## 9.1 *Synonymous verbs*

### 9.1.1 *Different verbs (stems) (13× + 4×)*

| | | |
|---|---|---|
| Jo 1:16 | ו/יזבחו | *καὶ* ]<br>*ἔθυσαν* ]] *ἐθυσίασαν* |
| Jo 3:4 | ל/בוא | *τοῦ*<br>*εἰσελθεῖν* ]] [*πορεύεσθ*]*αι* |
| Jo 3:9 | ו/נחם | *εἰ* ]]] [*καὶ*]<br>*μετανοήσει* ]] *π̣α̣ρ*[*ακληθήσετα*]*ι* |
| Jo 3:10 | ו/ינחם | *καὶ*<br>*μετενόησεν* ]] [*παρ*]*ε̣κ̣λήθη* <*ι*> |
| Na 2:6 | ימהרו | *σπεύσουσιν* ]] *ταχυνοῦσιν* |
| Na 2:7 | נמוג | *διέπεσε* ]] [*ἐσα*]*λεύθη* |
| Ha 1:10 | יתקלס | *ἐντρυφήσει* ]] [*ἐν*]*παίξει* |
| Ha 1:10 | ו/ילכד/ה | *καὶ*<br>*κρατήσει* ]] *συνλήμψετ*[*αι*]<br>*αὐτοῦ* ]]] [*αὐτό*] |
| Ha 1:15 | יגר/הו | *καὶ* ]<br>*εἵλκυσεν* ]] *ἔσυρεν*<br>*αὐτὸν* |
| Za 2:2 | זרו | *διασκορπίσαντα* (1:19) ]] *λικμή*[*σαντα*] |
| Za 2:16 | ו/בחר | *καὶ* (12)<br>*αἱρετιεῖ* ]] [*ἐκλέ*]*ξεται* |
| Za 8:20 | יבאו | *ἥξουσι* ]] [*ἔλ*]*θωσιν* |

| | | |
|---|---|---|
| Za 9:3 | ו/תצבר | καὶ ] |
| | | ἐθησαύρισεν ]] ἐβούνισεν |

RECONSTRUCTIONS (4 ×)

| | | |
|---|---|---|
| Na 2:5 | ירוצצו | διατρέχουσαι ]]] [δραμοῦν]ται |
| Na 3:14 | באי | ἔμβηθι ]]] [ἐλθὲ] |
| Ha 2:3 | חכה | ὑπόμεινον ]]] [προσδέχου] |
| Za 3:5 | ו/ילבש/הו | καὶ ] κ[αὶ] |
| | | περιέβαλον ]]] [ἐνέδυσαν] |
| | | αὐτὸν |

## 9.1.2 *Synonymous verbs—different form (4 ×)*

| | | |
|---|---|---|
| Mi 4:7 | ו/שׂמתי | καὶ |
| | | θήσομαι ]] θήσω |
| Na 3:6 | ו/שׂמתי/ך | καὶ ] [κα]ὶ |
| | | θήσομαί ]] θήσω |
| | | σε |
| Za 2:12 | שׁלח/ני | ἀπέσταλκέ (8) ]] ἀ[πέ]ọṭẹịλέν |
| | | με |
| Za 3:7 | תלך | πορεύῃ ]] πορευθῇς |

## 9.2 *Synonymous nouns and adjectives (33 × + 9 ×)*

| | | |
|---|---|---|
| Jo 3:9 | אפ/ו | θυμοῦ ]] [ὀργ]ῆς |
| | | αὐτοῦ ] ạ[ὐτοῦ] |
| Mi 2:8 | אדר | τὴν ]]] > |
| | | δορὰν ]] [περιβ]όλαιον |
| | | αὐτοῦ ]] > |
| Mi 4:3 | חרבת/יהם | τὰς |
| | | ῥομφαίας ]] μαχα[ίρας] |
| | | αὐτῶν ] [αὐτῶ]ν |
| Mi 4:3 | ו/חניתת/יהם | καὶ ] |
| | | τὰ ]] τὰς |
| | | δόρατα ]] σιβύ[νας] |
| | | αὐτῶν ] [α]ὐτῶν |
| Mi 5:3 | ב/גאון | καὶ (4) ] |
| | | ἐν ] |
| | | τῇ ] |
| | | δόξῃ ]] ἐπάρσει |
| Mi 5:3 | אפסי | ἄκρων (4) ]] περάτων |
| Mi 5:6 | שׁארית | τὸ (7) ]]] > |
| | | ὑπόλειμμα ]] [κατά]λοιπον |
| Mi 5:6 | עשׂב | ἄγρωστιν (7) ]] χό[ρτον] |
| Na 2:6 | אדיר/יו | οἱ ]] > |
| | | μεγιστᾶνες ]] δυναστῶν |
| | | αὐτῶν ]] αὐτοῦ |
| Na 2:7 | ו/ה/היכל | καὶ ] |
| | | τὰ ]] ὁ |
| | | βασίλεια ]] να[ὸς] |
| Na 2:8 | ו/הצב | καὶ ] |
| | | ἡ ] |
| | | ὑπόστασις ]] λαμπήνη |
| Na 2:8 | ו/אמהת/יה | καὶ ] |
| | | αἱ ] |
| | | δοῦλαι ]] ἁβραὶ |
| | | αὐτῆς ] |
| Na 2:13 | ו/מענת/יו | καὶ |
| | | τὸ ]]] [τὴν] |
| | | κατοικητήριον ]] [μά]ṿδραν |
| | | αὐτοῦ |
| Na 3:10 | ל/גלה | εἰς ] |
| | | μετοικεσίαν ]] ἀποι[κίαν] |

| | | |
|---|---|---|
| Na 3:15 | כ/ארבה | ὡς ] |
| | | βροῦχος ]] ἀκρίς |
| Na 3:16 | מ/כוכבי | ὑπὲρ ]] ὡς |
| | | τὰ ]] τοὺς |
| | | ἄστρα ]] ἀστέρας (form only) |
| Ha 1:7 | אים | φοβερὸς ]] θάμβος |
| Ha 1:10 | משחק | παίγνια ]] γ[έλως] |
| Ha 2:17 | חמס | ἀσέβεια ]] ἀδικία |
| Ha 2:17 | ו/חמס | καὶ ] καὶ |
| | | ἀσεβείας ]] ἀδικίαν |
| Ha 2:19 | תפוש | ἔλασμα ]] σεσαγμένον |
| Ha 2:19 | זהב | χρυσίου ]] χρυ[σο]ῦν |
| Ha 2:19 | ו/כסף | καὶ |
| | | ἀργυρίου ]] [ἀργυ]ροῦν |
| Ha 3:9 | מטות | σκῆπτρα ]] ῥάβδ[ο]υς |
| Ha 3:12 | ב/זעם | ἐν ] |
| | | ἀπειλῇ ]] ἐμ[βριμήσει] |
| Ha 3:14 | ב/מסתר | λάθρᾳ ]] κρυφῇ |
| Zp 1:15 | ו/מצוקה | καὶ |
| | | ἀνάγκης ]] [στ]ενοχωρίας |
| Zp 1:15 | שאה | ἀωρίας ]] ἀπορίας |
| Zp 1:15 | ו/אפלה | καὶ ] |
| | | γνόφου ]] σκοτίας |
| Zp 1:15 | ו/ערפל | καὶ ] [κα]ὶ |
| | | ὁμίχλης ]] [γ]νόφου |
| Zp 1:16 | שופר | σάλπιγγος ]] [κ]ε[ρ]ατί[νης] (cf. Barth. 60–63) |
| Zp 2:9 | ו/יתר | καὶ ] |
| | | οἱ ] [ο]ἱ |
| | | κατάλοιποι ]] ἐπίλοι[ποι] |
| Za 9:3 | חוצות | ὁδῶν ]] ἐξόδων |

RECONSTRUCTIONS (9 ×)

For all these, see notes on the reconstruction.

| | | |
|---|---|---|
| Jo 3:9 | מ/חרון | ἐξ ]] ἀπὸ |
| | | ὀργῆς ]]] [θυμοῦ] |
| Mi 1:2 | מ/היכל | ἐξ ]]] [ἐκ] |
| | | οἴκου ]]] [ναοῦ] |
| Mi 4:3 | חרב | ῥομφαίαν ]] μ[άχαιραν] |
| Mi 4:9 | יועצ/ך | ἡ ]]] [ὁ] |
| | | βουλή ]]] [σύμβουλός] |
| | | σου ] |
| Na 3:15 | כ/ילק | ὡς |
| | | ἀκρίς ]]] [βροῦχος] |
| Ha 2:15 | הוי | ὦ ]]] [οὐαὶ] |
| Ha 2:17 | בהמות | θηρίων ]]] [κτηνῶν] |
| Ha 3:11 | חנית/ך | ὅπλων ]]] [σιβύνης] |
| | | σου |
| Zp 1:17 | ו/לחמ/ם | καὶ ] [κ]α[ὶ] |
| | | τὰς ]] > |
| | | σάρκας ]]] π[τώμ]α[τ]α |
| | | αὐτῶν |

9.3 *Synonymous prepositions, conjunctions and particles (see also F10.2)*

**מן**, -**מ**—R is not consistent in the rendering of this preposition. Usually it follows the LXX in the choice of either ἐκ (5 ×) or ἀπό (6 ×), διά (Ha 2:17), κατένα[ντι] (for **ממול** [Mi 2:8]) and ἀπέναντι (**מקדם** [Jo 4:5])—textual differences between MT and R = LXX are excluded from this list. At the same time, R replaces ἀπό of the LXX with ἐκ (Jo 3:8) and ἐξ of the LXX with ἀπό (Jo 3:9; Mi 5:1[2]). In addition, R rendered the comparative **מן** once with ὑπ[έρ] (Na 3:8), and the local מן once with -θεν: מרחוק—πώρρ[ωθεν] (Ha 1:8 [LXX: μακρόθεν]). In the reconstruction of this preposition the LXX is usually followed.

-ב—Quite consistently rendered by R with ἐν (27 ×), but also with εἰς (5 ×), 3 instances of which follow the LXX (Jo 3:4; Na 3:14; Za 9:4 [reconstructed, but secured by the next word]) and two instances of which replace ἐπί of the LXX (Mi 5:5[6],5[6]), with ἐπί (Mi 5:4[5] and Na 3:10 [reconstructed, but secured by the next word]), both of which follow the LXX and twice with διά (=LXX, Mi 1:5,5).

-ל—For the *lamed* of the inf. see F2. The preposition is rendered by both the LXX and R with εἰς (12 ×), with the dative of nouns (4 ×) or pronouns (6 ×). Once R replaces ἐπί of the LXX with εἰ[ς] (Ha 1:6), and once the dative of the pronoun in the LXX with εἰς (Za 2:9[5]). לכן is rendered by διὰ τοῦτο by both the LXX and R (3 ×).

-כ—R usually follows the LXX in its translation of ὡς (9 ×) or καθώς (2 ×), but once καθώς of the LXX is replaced with ὡ[ς] (Na 2:8), while the reverse change takes place in Ha 3:14 (MT: כמו).

כי—Usually R changes διότι of the LXX to ὅτι (Mi 1:3,7; 4:4; 5:3[4]; Ha 1:5,6,16; 2:3,8,17; Zp 2:10; Za 9:1), in three cases, ὅταν to ὅτι (Mi 5:4[5],4[5],5[6]), and in four instances retains ὅτι of the LXX (Jo 3:10; Mi 4:5; Ha 2:18,18). In the following instances ὅτι is reconstructed for διότι of the LXX: Jo 4:2; Ha 2:3; Za 2:10[6],12[8],17[13]; 8:23; 9:2 and in Mi 5:5[6] for ὅταν.

עד—Always ἕως + gen.: Jo 2:6; Mi 1:7; 4:7; 5:3[4]; Ha 3:13, as in the LXX (except for Mi 1:7). It is reconstructed likewise in Mi 4:3,8; 5:2[3]; Zp 2:9; Za 8:20.

| | | |
|---|---|---|
| Mi 1:8 | על | ἕνεκεν ]] διὰ |
| | זאת | τούτου ] τ[οῦτ]ο (cf. Barth. 84–85) |
| Ha 1:8 | מ/רחוק | μακρόθεν ]] πώρρ[ωθεν] |
| Ha 1:15 | על כן | ἕνεκεν τούτου (16) ]] διὰ τοῦτο (cf. Barth. 84–85) |
| Ha 1:16 | על כן | ἕνεκεν τούτου ]] διὰ τοῦτο |
| Ha 2:19 | אין | οὐκ ]] οὐ [μή] |
| | | ἔστιν ] ἔ[σ]τιν |
| Za 2:9 | ל/ה | αὐτῇ (5) ]] εἰς [αὐτήν] |

### 10. *Approximations to the Hebrew text/language*

In this category we record renderings of R which presumably reflect approximations to the Hebrew text.

It is important to keep in mind here the caveat mentioned in the preface that the analysis of R's techniques is based on the assumption that R had before him the text of the LXX as reconstructed in Ziegler's edition. Furthermore, one should remember that the recognition of an approximation to the Hebrew text is subjective.

10.1 *Lex. meaning of the Hebr.: adjectives, nouns, verbs (43 × + 15 ×)*

| | | |
|---|---|---|
| Jo 1:14 | נקיא | δίκαιον ]] ἀθῷ[ον] (righteous ]] guiltless) |
| Jo 2:6 | חבוש | ἔδυ ]] περιέσχ[ε]ν (R reflects different reading: חבש) |
| Jo 3:8 | איש | ἕκαστος ]] ἀ[νὴρ] (also Mi 4:4; see Barth. 48–54) |
| Jo 4:1 | ו/יחר ל/ו | καὶ ] |
| | | συνεχύθη ]] ἠθ[ύμησεν] |
| Mi 1:2 | ו/מלא/ה | καὶ πάντες οἱ ]] καὶ τὸ π[λή]ρωμα |
| | | ἐν ]] > |
| | | αὐτῇ ]] α[ὐτῆς] (and all on it ]] and its fulness) |
| Mi 1:4 | יתבקעו (will burst open) | τακήσονται ]] [ῥα]γήσον[τα]ι (will melt ]] will be broken) |

| | | |
|---|---|---|
| Mi 1:6 | ל/גי | εἰς ] |
| | | --- ]] τὴν |
| | | χάος ]] φάραγγα (abyss ]] ravine) |
| Mi 4:4 | איש | ἕκαστος ]] ἀνὴρ |
| Mi 4:4 | צבאות | παντοκράτορος ]] [τῶ]ν δ[υνά]μ[εων] (Almighty ]] (of hosts; also Za 1:3,4,14; 3:7; 8:20) |
| Mi 4:6 | הרעתי | ἀπωσάμην ]] ἐκά[κωσα] (I thrust away ]] I did wickedly) |
| Mi 5:4 | ב/ארמנת/ינו | ἐπὶ (5) ] |
| | | τὴν ]] τὰς |
| | | χώραν ]] βάρεις] (territory ]] large buildings) |
| | | ἡμῶν |
| Mi 5:4 | נסיכי | δήγματα (5) ]] ἄρχοντας (bites; etymology **נשך** ]] princes) |
| Na 2:6 | ה/סכך | τὰς ]] [τ]ὸ |
| | | προφυλακὰς ]] ἐπικάλυμμα (guards ]] cover) |
| | | αὐτῶν ]] > |
| Na 2:9 | מפנה | ὁ ]]] > |
| | | ἐπιβλέπων ]] [ἐπισ]τρέφω[ν] |
| Na 3:8 | ה/תיטבי | --- ? ]] μὴ |
| | | ἑτοίμασαι ]] ἀγαθύνεις |
| Na 3:8 | מ/נא | μερίδα ]] ὑπ[ὲρ νω] (LXX: root **מנה**) |
| | אמון | Αμων |
| Na 3:8 | חיל | ἀρχὴ ]] ἰσχὺς |
| Na 3:9 | פוט | τῆς ]]] > |
| | | φυγῆς ]] φουδ (LXX poss.: **פלט**) |
| Ha 1:8 | ו/קלו | καὶ ] |
| | | ἐξαλοῦνται ]] κουφ[ότεροι] (will leap out ]] are lighter) |
| Ha 1:8 | ו/פשו | καὶ ] |
| | | ἐξιππάσονται ]] ὁρμή[σουσιν] |
| Ha 1:9 | קדימ/ה | ἐξ ἐναντίας ]] καύσων (different etymology) |
| Ha 1:11 | חלף | μεταβαλεῖ ]] διελεύσεται |
| Ha 1:17 | יריק | ἀμφιβαλεῖ ]] [ἐκκεν]ώσει (will throw around ]] will empty) |
| Ha 2:1 | ו/אתיצבה | καὶ ] |
| | | ἐπιβήσομαι ]] στη[λώσομαι] (I will mount on ]] I will stand like a στήλη; cf. Barth. 59–60) |
| Ha 2:3 | ו/יפח | καὶ ] |
| | | ἀνατελεῖ ]] ἐνφανήσετ[αι] (will rise ]] will appear) |
| Ha 2:3 | יתמהמה | ὑστερήσῃ ]] στραγ[γεύσηται] (will be late ]] will tarry) |
| Ha 2:5 | ו/יקבץ | καὶ ] |
| | | εἰσδέξεται ]] ἀθροί[σει] (will admit ]] will assemble) |
| Ha 2:6 | עבטיט | στιβαρῶς ]] πάχος πηλοῦ (taken by R as two words: **עב טיט**) |
| Ha 2:7 | מזעזע/יך | οἱ ] |
| | | ἐπίβουλοί ]] σαλεύοντές (advisers ]] those who shake) |
| | | σου ]] σε |
| Ha 2:15 | מעור/יהם | τὰ ]]] [τὴν] |
| | | σπήλαια ]] [ἀσχημοσ]ύνην (caverns ]] privy parts) |
| | | αὐτῶν ] αὐ[τῶ]ν (different etymology) |
| Ha 2:20 | הס | εὐλαβείσθω ]] σιώπησον (be cautious ]] be quiet) |
| Ha 3:12 | תדוש | κατάξεις ]] ἀλ[ο]ή[σεις] (will break ]] will thresh) |
| Ha 3:13 | סלה | διάψαλμα ]] σελε (transliteration) |
| Ha 3:14 | ב/מט/יו | ἐν ] |
| | | ἐκστάσει ]] ῥάβδοις (stretching out ]] staffs) |
| | | --- ]] αὐτοῦ |
| Ha 3:14 | פרז/ו (K) פרז/יו (Q) | δυναστῶν ]] ἀτει[χίσ]των (leaders ]] unwalled ones; cf. Za 2:8) |
| | | --- ]] αὐτοῦ |
| Ha 3:14 | עליצת/ם | --- ]] τὸ |
| | | χαλινοὺς ]] γαυρίαμα (bridles ]] exultation) |
| | | αὐτῶν ] |
| Ha 3:15 | דרכת | ἐπεβίβασας ]] ἐνέτει[νες] |
| Zp 1:2 | אסף | ἐκλείψει ]] [συ]ναγωγῇ |
| | אסף | ἐκλιπέτω ]] συν[αγ''] (different etymology) |
| Zp 1:4 | ו/הכרתי | καὶ ] [κ]α[ὶ] |
| | | ἐξαρῶ ]] ἐ[ξ]ολ[εθρεύ]σω |

| Zp 3:6 | מ/בלי איש | παρὰ<br>τὸ<br>μηδένα ]] [μὴ] ---<br>ὑπάρχειν ]] [ὑπάρ]χ[ε]ιν<br>{...μηδένα} ]] ἄνδ[ρα] |
|---|---|---|
| Za 3:4 | מחלצות | ποδήρη ]] μετε[κδύμα]τα (robe that falls over the feet ]] changes of clothing) |
| Za 3:7 | מהלכים | ἀναστρεφομένους ]] ἐνπ[ερι]π[ατοῦντας] (see note on reconstruction) |
| Za 9:4 | הנה | διὰ τοῦτο ]] ἰδοὺ |

RECONSTRUCTIONS (15 ×)

| Mi 1:2 | ל/עד | εἰς ]<br>μαρτύριον ]]] μάρτυ[ρα] |
|---|---|---|
| Mi 1:7 | זונה (twice) | πορνείας ]]] [πόρνης] |
| Mi 3:5 | ו/קדשו | --- ]]] [καὶ]<br>ἤγειραν ]]] [ἡγίασαν] |
| Mi 4:4 | ו/ישבו | καὶ<br>ἀναπαύσεται ]]] [καθίσ]ονται |
| Mi 4:5 | ב/שם אלה/יו | τὴν ]]] [ἐν ὀνόματι]<br>ὁδὸν ]] [θε]οῦ<br>αὐτοῦ ]] αὐτῶν |
| Mi 4:6 | אקבצה | εἰσδέξομαι ]]] [ἀθροίσω] |
| Mi 4:9 | יועצ/ך | ἡ ]]] [ὁ]<br>βουλή ]]] [σύμβουλός]<br>σου ] |
| Na 2:14 | צבאות | παντοκράτωρ ]]] [τῶν δυνάμεων] |
| Na 3:14 | שאבי | ἐπίσπασαι ]]] [ὕδρευσα]ι |
| Ha 1:7 | ו/נורא | καὶ<br>ἐπιφανής ]]] [φοβερὸς] (LXX: etymology ראה) |
| Ha 2:2 | ירוץ | διώκῃ ]]] [τρέχ]ῃ |
| Ha 3:9 | סלה | διάψαλμα ]]] [σελε] |
| Za 2:12 | צבאות | παντοκράτωρ (8) ]]] [τῶν δυνάμεων] |
| Za 2:17 | הס | εὐλαβείσθω ]]] [σιώπησον] |
| Za 2:17 | מ/מעון | ἐκ ]<br>--- ]]] [τοῦ]<br>νεφελῶν ]]] [κατοικητηρίου] |

## 10.2 *Lex. meaning of the Hebr.: prepositions and particles (9 × + 14 ×) (see also F9.3)*

**גם**—*καί* of the LXX is replaced by *καί γε* (see Barth. 31–47) in the following instances: Na 3:10,10,11,11; Ha 2:16 (reconstructed: Zp 1:18,18). *καί* of the LXX for **וגם** of MT is replaced by *καί γε* in Za 3:7,7; 9:2. For the space between *καί* and *γε*, see Za 9:2.

| Jo 3:9 | ו/נחם | εἰ ]]] [καὶ]<br>μετανοήσει ]] παρ[ακληθήσετα]ι |
|---|---|---|
| Mi 1:7 | ו/עד | καὶ ]<br>ἐκ ]] ἕως |
| Mi 4:7 | ו/עד | καὶ ἕως εἰς ] [καὶ ἕ]ως<br>τὸν αἰῶνα ] τοῦ αἰῶνος |
| Ha 2:4 | הנה | ἐὰν ]] ἰδ[οὺ] |
| Ha 2:6 | ל/ו | {...τὰ} ὄντα αὐτοῦ ]] αὐτῷ |
| Ha 2:7 | ה/לוא | ὅτι ]] οὐχὶ |
| Ha 2:17 | ישבי | τῶν ]<br>κατοικούντων ]] ἐνοι[κ]ούντων |
|  | ב/ה | αὐτήν ]] ἐν [αὐτ]ῇ |
| Ha 2:19 | ב/קרב/ו | ἐν ]<br>--- ]] μέσῳ<br>αὐτῷ ]] αὐτοῦ |
| Zp 1:6 | מ/אחרי | ἀπὸ ]] [ἀπὸ] ὄπισθε[ν] |

RECONSTRUCTIONS (14×)

| | | |
|---|---|---|
| Jo 4:2 | על | ἐν ]]] [ἐπὶ] |
| Mi 3:5 | על | εἰς ]]] [ἐπὶ] |
| Mi 4:3 | עד | ἕως εἰς ] [ἕως] |
| | רחוק | μακράν ] [μα]κράν |
| Mi 5:6 | אשר | ὅπως (7) ]]] [ὃς] |
| | לא | μὴ ]]] [οὐκ] |
| Na 2:8 | על | ἐν ]]] [ἐπὶ] |
| Na 3:12 | על | εἰς ]]] [ἐπὶ] |
| Na 3:12 | עם | {.. ~ ἔχουσαι} ]]] [σὺν] |
| | בכורים | σκοποὺς ]]] σκοπ[οῖς] |
| | {...} | ἔχουσαι ]] > |
| Na 3:13 | ב/קרב/ך | ἐν ] [ἐ]ν |
| | | --- ]]] [μέσῳ] |
| | | σοί ]]] [σου] |
| Ha 1:6 | משכנות | σκηνώματά |
| | לא | οὐκ |
| | ל/ו | αὐτοῦ ]]] [αὐτῷ] |
| Ha 1:10 | משחק | παίγνια ]]] γ[έλως] |
| | ל/ו | αὐτοῦ [αὐτῷ] |
| Ha 2:1 | על | ἐν ]]] [ἐπὶ] |
| Ha 2:19 | הנה | τοῦτο ]]] [ἰδοὺ] |
| Zp 1:5 | ל/יהוה | κατὰ τοῦ ]]] [τῷ] |
| | | κυρίου ]]] [𐤉𐤄𐤅𐤄] |
| Zp 3:6 | מ/אין | μηδὲ ]]] [διὰ τοῦ μὴ εἶναι] |

## 10.3 *Exact representation of elements of the Hebrew* (15× + 9×)

This paragraph lists examples in which R seeks to correct imprecise renderings in the LXX by matching a part of speech in Hebrew with the corresponding part of speech in Greek: verbs are rendered with verbs, prepositions with prepositions, etc.

| | | |
|---|---|---|
| Jo 2:7 | ב/עד/י | κάτοχοι ]] κατ' ἐμοῦ (holding down ]] against me) |
| Jo 2:7 | ל/עולם | αἰώνιοι ]] εἰς [αἰῶνα] |
| Mi 1:2 | ו/מלא/ה | καὶ πάντες οἱ ]] καὶ τὸ π[λή]ρωμα |
| | | ἐν ]]] > |
| | | αὐτῇ ]] α[ὐτῆς] |
| Mi 2:7 | ייטיבו | εἰσι καλοὶ ]] [ἠγ]ά̣θυναν |
| Na 3:7 | שדדה | δειλαία ]] [τεταλαι]πώρηκε[ν] (verb) |
| Na 3:10 | ב/שבי | αἰχμάλωτος ]] [ἐν αἰχ]μαλω[σί]ᾳ (captive ]] in captivity) |
| Ha 1:8 | ו/פרש/יו | καὶ |
| | | --- ]]] [οἱ] |
| | | ὁρμήσουσι ]] [ἱπ]π̣εις |
| | | --- ]] αὐτοῦ |
| Ha 2:2 | ו/יענ/ני | καὶ ] |
| | | ἀπεκρίθη ] |
| | | πρός με ]] μοι |
| Ha 2:13 | ב/די | ἱκανοὶ ]] [ἐν ἱκανό]τητ[ι] (sufficient ]] in sufficiency) |
| Ha 2:19 | הוא[1] | καὶ ]] > |
| | | αὐτό ]] αὐτὸς |
| | | ἐστι ]] > |
| Ha 2:19 | יורה | φαντασία ]] φω[τιεῖ] (appearance ]] will give light) |
| Ha 2:19 | תפוש | ἔλασμα ]] σεσαγμένον (metal plate ]] packed; abstract noun versus passive participle) |
| Ha 3:14 | ל/הפיצ/ני | --- ]] τοῦ |
| | | διανοίξουσι ]] σκο[ρπίσ]αι (they open ]] to scatter) |
| | | --- ]] ἡμᾶς |
| Zp 3:6 | יושב | κατοικεῖν ]] [κατοι]κοῦντα |
| Za 1:4 | אל/יהם | αὐτοῖς ]] πρὸς α[ὐτοὺς] |

RECONSTRUCTIONS (9 ×)

| | | |
|---|---|---|
| Jo 3:8 | ב/חזקה | *ἐκτενῶς* ]]] [*ἐν ἰσχύι*] |
| Mi 3:5 | ו/קראו | *καὶ* |
| | | *κηρύσσοντας* ]]] [*ἐκήρυξαν*] |
| Mi 3:5 | ו/אשר | *καὶ* |
| | | --- ]]] [*ὃς*] |
| Na 3:10 | ב/זקים | *χειροπέδαις* ]]] [*ἐν χειροπέδαις*] |
| Ha 1:7 | הוא | *ἐστιν* ]]] [*αὐτός*] |
| Ha 2:13 | ב/די | --- ]]] [*ἐν ἱκανότητι*] |
| | ריק | *πολλὰ* ]]] [*κενὸν*] |
| Ha 3:10 | עבר | *πορείας* ]]] [*παρῆλθεν*] |
| Ha 3:13 | ל/ישע | *τοῦ σῶσαι* ]]] [*εἰς σωτηρίαν*] |
| Za 9:2 | תגבל | *ἐν* ]]] > |
| | ב/ה | *τοῖς* ]]] > |
| | | *ὁρίοις* ]]] [*ὁρίζει*] |
| | | *αὐτῆς* ]] [*αὐ*]*τήν* |

## 10.4 *Form*

### 10.4.1 *Number (in nouns, pronouns and verbs) (19 × + 22 × )*

| | | |
|---|---|---|
| Jo 2:4 | ו/נהר | *καὶ ποταμοί* ]] [*καὶ ποταμ*]*ὸς* |
| Jo 2:6 | מים | *ὕδωρ* ]] *ὕδατα* |
| Jo 3:10 | מ/דרכ/ם | *ἀπὸ* ] |
| | | *τῶν* ]] *τῆ̣ς* |
| | | *ὁδῶν* ]] [*ὁδο*]*ῦ* |
| | | *αὐτῶν* ] *αὐτ*[*ῶν*] |
| | ה/רעה | *τῶν* ]] [*τ*]*ῆ̣ς* |
| | | *πονηρῶν* ]] *πονηρ*[*ᾶς*] |
| Mi 1:7 | ישובו | *συνέστρεψεν* ]] [*ἐπιστρέψουσ*]*ιν* |
| Mi 4:4 | ו/ישבו | *καὶ* |
| | | *ἀναπαύσεται* ]]] [*καθίσ*]*ονται* |
| Mi 5:2 | אח/יו | *τῶν* (3) |
| | | *ἀδελφῶν* |
| | | *αὐτῶν* ]] *αὐτοῦ* |
| Na 2:6 | יזכר | *καὶ* ]] > |
| | | *μνησθήσονται* ]] *μνησθήσεται* |
| Na 2:6 | אדיר/יו | *οἱ* ]] > |
| | | *μεγιστᾶνες* ]] *δυναστῶν* |
| | | *αὐτῶν* ]] *αὐτοῦ* |
| Na 2:6 | ו/הכן | *καὶ* |
| | | *ἑτοιμάσουσι* ]] *ἑτοιμάσε*[*ι*] |
| Na 3:10 | ב/ראש | *ἐπ'* ]]] [*ἐπὶ*] |
| | | *ἀρχὰς* ]] [*κεφαλ*]*ὴν* |
| Ha 1:15 | ב/מכמרת/ו | *ἐν* |
| | | *ταῖς* ]]] [*τῇ*] |
| | | *σαγήναις* ]] *σαγήνῃ* |
| | | *αὐτοῦ* ] |
| Ha 1:16 | ו/מאכל/ו | *καὶ* |
| | | *τὰ* ]] *τὸ* |
| | | *βρώματα* ]] *β*[*ρ*]*ῶμα* |
| | | *αὐτοῦ* ] |
| Ha 2:6 | ישאו | *λήμψονται* ]] *λήψε*[*ται*] (see 7.11) |
| Ha 2:7 | ל/משסות | *εἰς* ] |
| | | *διαρπαγὴν* ]] *διαρπαγὰς* |
| Ha 3:13 | ראש | *κεφαλὰς* ]] [*κεφαλὴ*]*ν* |
| Ha 3:14 | ראש | *κεφαλὰς* ]] *κεφαλὴν* |
| Zp 1:4 | את שם | *καὶ* ]] > |
| | | *τὰ* ]] *τὸ* |
| | | *ὀνόματα* ]] *ὄνομα* |
| Zp 3:7 | עלילות/ם | *ἡ* ]] *τὰ* |
| | | *ἐπιφυλλὶς* ]] *ἐπιτ*[*ηδεύματα*] |
| | | *αὐτῶν* |

| | | |
|---|---|---|
| Za 9:2 | חכמה | *ἐφρόνησαν* ]] [*ἐ*]*φρόνησεν* |

RECONSTRUCTIONS (22×)

| | | |
|---|---|---|
| Jo 2:4 | מצולה | *βάθη* ]]] *βάθ*[*ος*] |
| Jo 2:4 | ימים | *θαλάσσης* ]]] [*θαλασσῶν*] |
| Jo 2:6 | אפפו/ני | *περιεχύθη* ]]] *π*[*εριεχύθησάν*] |
| | | *μοι* ]] *με* (see 7.11) |
| Jo 4:2 | זה | *οὗτοι* ]]] [*οὗτος*] |
| Mi 1:6 | ל/מטעי | *εἰς* ] *εἰ*[*s*] |
| | | *φυτείαν* ]]] [*φυτείας*] |
| Mi 1:7 | מ/אתנן | *ἐκ* ]] *ἐγ* |
| | | *μισθωμάτων* ]]] *μισ*[*θώματος*] |
| Mi 1:7 | אתנן | *μισθωμάτων* ]]] *μι*[*σθώματος*] |
| Mi 2:7 | ה/ישר | *καὶ ὀρθοὶ* ]]] [*τοῦ ὀρθοῦ*] |
| Mi 5:3 | אלה/יו | *τοῦ* (4) ]] > |
| | | *θεοῦ* ] *θεοῦ* |
| | | *αὐτῶν* ]]] [*αὐτοῦ*] |
| Na 1:14 | פסל | *τὰ γλυπτὰ* ]]] [*γλυπτὸν*] |
| Na 3:3 | חלל | *τραυματιῶν* ]]] [*τραυματίου*] |
| Na 3:7 | מנחמים | *παράκλησιν* ]]] *π*[*αρακαλοῦντάς*] |
| Na 3:10 | גורל | *κλήρους* ]]] [*κλῆρον*] |
| Na 3:11 | מ/אויב | *ἐξ ἐχθρῶν* ]]] [*ἐξ ἐχθροῦ*] |
| Ha 3:13 | את משיח/ך | *τοὺς* ]]] [*τοῦ*] |
| | | *χριστούς* ]]] [*χριστοῦ*] |
| | | *σου* ] |
| Zp 1:3 | עוף | *τὰ πετεινὰ* ]]] [*πετεινὸν*] |
| Zp 3:7 | השכימו | *ὄρθρισον* ]]] *ὀ*[*ρθρίσατε*] (cf. context) |
| Za 2:11 | המלטי | *ἀνασῴζεσθε* (7) ]]] [*ἀνασῴζου*] |
| Za 2:11 | יושבת | *οἱ* (7) ]]] > |
| | | *κατοικοῦντες* ]] [*κ*]*ατοικ*[*οῦσα*] |
| Za 3:4 | עונ/ך | *τὰς* ]]] [*τὴν*] |
| | | *ἀνομίας* ]]] [*ἀνομίαν*] |
| | | *σου* |
| Za 3:7 | את חצר/י | *τὴν* ]]] *τ*[*ὰς*] |
| | | *αὐλήν* ]]] [*αὐλάς*] |
| | | *μου* |
| Za 9:3 | מצור | *ὀχυρώματα* ]]] *ὀχύ*[*ρωμα*] |

## 10.4.2 *Case endings (7× + 1×)*

| | | |
|---|---|---|
| Jo 2:7 | ה/ארץ | --- ]] *ἡ* |
| | | *εἰς γῆν* ]]] [*γῆ*] |
| Na 2:8 | כ/קול | *καθὼς* ]] *ὡ*[*s*] |
| | | --- ]]] [*φωνὴ*] |
| | יונים | *περιστεραὶ* ]] [*περιστ*]*ερῶν* |
| | מתפפת | *φθεγγόμεναι* ]] *ἀποφθεγγ*[*ο*]*μέν*[*ων*] |
| Ha 2:2 | ה/לחות | *πυξίον* ]]] [*πυξίω*]*ν* |
| Ha 3:9 | נהרות | *ποταμῶν* ]] [*ποτα*]*μοί* |
| | תבקע | *ῥαγήσεται* ] |
| | ארץ | *γῆ* ] *γῆ* |
| Ha 3:14 | ל/אכל | *ἔσθων* ]] [*ἐσ*]*θίων* |
| | עני | *πτωχὸς* ]] *πτωχὸν* |
| Za 9:1 | ו/כל | *καὶ* ] |
| | | *πάσας* ]] *πασῶν* |
| | שבטי | *φυλὰς* ]]] *φ*[*υλῶν*] |
| | ישראל | *τοῦ* |
| | | *Ισραηλ* ] |
| Za 9:2 | ו/גם | *καὶ* ]] *καί γε* |
| | חמת | *Εμαθ* ] |
| | תגבל | *ἐν* ]]] > |
| | | *τοῖς* ]]] > |
| | | *ὁρίοις* ]]] [*ὁρίζει*] |
| | ב/ה | *αὐτῆς* ]] [*αὐ*]*τήν* |

RECONSTRUCTION (1 ×)

| | | |
|---|---|---|
| Ha 2:13 | ב/די<br>אש | ἱκανοὶ ]] [ἐν ἱκανό]τητ[ι]<br>ἐν ]]] ><br>πυρί ]]] [πυρός] |

### 10.4.3 *Person: nouns, pronouns, verbs (5× + 2×)*

| | | |
|---|---|---|
| Mi 2:7 | הולך | πεπόρευνται ]] [πορευομ]ένου |
| Mi 2:8 | תפשטון | ἐξέδειραν ]] ἐξεδύσ[ατε] |
| Mi 5:4 | ו/הקמנו | καὶ (5)<br>ἐπεγερθήσονται ]] ἐπεγεροῦμεν |
| Ha 2:7 | נשכ/יך | δάκνοντες ]<br>αὐτόν ]] σε |
| Za 3:4 | את/ך | αὐτόν ]] σε |

RECONSTRUCTIONS (2 ×)

| | | |
|---|---|---|
| Mi 1:8 | אספדה<br>ו/איליה | κόψεται ]]] [κόψομαι]<br>καὶ<br>θρηνήσει ]]] [θρηνήσω] |
| Na 3:7 | ל/ך | αὐτῇ ]]] [σοι] |

### 10.4.4 *Tenses (1× + 1×)*

As shown in 7.10, R has a fixed system of equivalents for the Hebrew tenses which more or less follows that of the LXX, but which at times adheres to that system more closely than the LXX. In addition to the material listed in 7, note the timeless representation of אין for which cf. Barth. 65–68.

| | | |
|---|---|---|
| Mi 4:4 | ו/אין | καὶ ] [κα]ὶ<br>οὐκ ἔσται ]] οὐκ ἐστιν |

RECONSTRUCTION (1 ×)

| | | |
|---|---|---|
| Mi 4:9 | אין | οὐκ<br>ἦν ]]] [ἐστιν] |

### 10.5 *Addition of element(s) (3×)*

Excluded are additions in R which presumably involve a different Hebrew *Vorlage*, listed in 14.1.

| | | |
|---|---|---|
| Ha 1:15 | ב/חרמ/ו | ἐν<br>--- ]]] [τῷ]<br>ἀμφιβλήστρῳ ] [ἀμ]φιβλήστρῳ<br>--- ]] αὐτοῦ |
| Ha 3:14 | פרז/ו (K) פרז/יו (Q) | δυναστῶν ]] ἀτει[χίσ]των<br>--- ]] αὐτοῦ |
| Za 8:21 | נלכה<br>הלוך | πορευθῶμεν ] [πορευθῶ]μεν<br>--- ]] πο[ρευόμενοι] |

### 10.6 *Omission of element(s) (12× + 6×)*

Excluded are omissions by R which presumably involve a different Hebrew *Vorlage*, listed in 14.1.

| | | |
|---|---|---|
| Jo 2:7 | ירדתי | κατέβην ] |
| | + + + | εἰς ]] > |
| | ה/ארץ | --- ]] ἡ |
| | | γῆν ]]] [γῆ,] |
| | + + + | ἧς ]]] > |
| | ברח/יה | οἱ ]]] > |
| | | μοχλοὶ ] [μοχλο]ὶ |
| | | αὐτῆς ] |

(Note the different reconstruction of the LXX in vv. 6–7 necessitating the addition of εἰς.)

| | | |
|---|---|---|
| Jo 3:3 | מהלך | ὡσεὶ ]]] > |
| | | πορείας ] π̣ορείας |
| Jo 3:4 | מהלך | ὡσεὶ ]]] > |
| | | πορείαν ] [πο]ρε[ί]α̣[ν] |
| Mi 1:1 | אשר | ὑπὲρ ]] > |
| | | ὧν ]] ὅ[ν] |
| | חזה | εἶδε |
| | על | περὶ |
| Mi 2:8 | אדר | τὴν ]]] > |
| | | δορὰν ]] [περιβ]όλαιον |
| | | αὐτοῦ ]] > |
| Mi 4:7 | ו/עד | καὶ ἕως ] [ἕ]ως |
| | | εἰς ]] > |
| Mi 5:1 | ל/היות | τοῦ (2) ] |
| | | εἶναι ] ε[ἶ]ν̣αι |
| | + + + | εἰς ]] > |
| | מושל | ἄρχοντα ]] ἄρχ[ο]ντα |
| Na 2:6 | ה/סכך | τὰς ]] [τ]ὸ̣ |
| | | προφυλακὰς ]] ἐπικάλυμμα |
| | | αὐτῶν ]] > |
| Na 3:8 | + + + | ἅρμοσαι ]] > |
| | ה/תיטבי | χορδήν, ]] μὴ |
| | | ἑτοίμασαι ]] ἀγαθύνεις |
| | מ/נא (root מנה) | μερίδα, ]] ὑπ[ὲρ νω] |
| | אמון | Αμων |
| Ha 1:5 | + + + | ὃ ]] > |
| | לא | οὐ ] |
| | | μὴ |
| | תאמינו | πιστεύσητε |
| | כי | ὅτι |
| | יספר | τις ἐκδιηγῆται ] [ἐκδιηγ]ηθῇ |
| Ha 2:6 | חידות | εἰς ]] > |
| | | διήγησιν ]] διήγησις |
| Ha 2:19 | הוא[1] | καὶ ]] > |
| | | αὐτό ]] αὐτὸς |
| | | ἐστι ]] > |

### RECONSTRUCTIONS (6 ×)

| | | |
|---|---|---|
| Mi 3:6 | ל/כם | ὑμῖν ]]] [ὑμεῖν] |
| | | ἔσται ]]] > |
| Mi 3:6 | ל/כם | ὑμῖν ]] [ὑμ]εῖν |
| | | ἔσται ]]] > |
| Mi 5:1 | ו/אתה | καὶ (2) ] |
| | | σύ ] |
| | בית לחם | Βηθλεεμ οἶκος ]] οἶκο[ς ʺʺʺ] |
| | אפרתה | τοῦ ]]] > |
| | | Εφραθα ] [ε]φραθα |
| | צעיר | ὀλιγοστὸς ] ὀλι[γ]οστὸς |
| | + + + | εἶ ]] > |

| | | |
|---|---|---|
| Na 3:13 | הנה | ἰδοὺ |
| | עמ/ך | ὁ |
| | | λαός |
| | | σου |
| | נשים | ὡς ]]] > |
| | | γυναῖκες |
| Ha 2:13 | אש | ἐν πυρί ]]] [πυρός] |
| Za 8:23 | כי | διότι ]]] [ὅτι] |
| | שמענו | ἀκηκόαμεν ] [ἀ]κ̣ηκόαμεν |
| | + + + | ὅτι ]] > |
| | אלהים | ὁ ]] > |
| | | θεὸς ] |
| | עמ/כם | μεθ' ] |
| | | ὑμῶν |
| | + + + | ἐστιν ]]] > |

(Note that the resulting text of R creates a sequence which is grammatically impossible in Greek.)

## 10.6.1 *Omission of elements possibly involving different Hebrew text (0× + 11×)*

This category continues 10.6, the only difference being that here the LXX possibly reflects a different Hebrew text.

RECONSTRUCTIONS (11×)

| | | |
|---|---|---|
| Mi 1:1 | ו/ירושלם | καὶ ] [κ]αὶ |
| | | περὶ ]]] > |
| | | Ιερουσαλημ ] [ιερουσ]αλημ |
| Mi 1:7 | עצב/יה | τὰ |
| | | εἴδωλα ] [εἴ]δωλα |
| | | αὐτῆς ] [α]ὐτῆς |
| | אשים | θήσομαι ]]] θήσ̣[ω] |
| | שממה | εἰς ]]] > |
| | | ἀφανισμόν |
| Mi 2:7 | עם | μετ' ] μ[ετὰ] |
| | | αὐτοῦ ]]] > |
| Mi 4:4 | + + + | ἕκαστος ]]] > |
| Mi 4:4 | + + + ? | ταῦτα ]]] > |
| Na 3:10 | ב/ראש | ἐπ' ]]] [ἐπὶ] |
| | | ἀρχὰς ]] [κεφαλ]ὴν |
| | כל | πασῶν ] πασῶ[ν] |
| | חוצות | τῶν ]]] > |
| | | ὁδῶν |
| | | αὐτῆς ]]] > |
| Na 3:10 | ו/על | καὶ ἐπὶ |
| | + + + | πάντα ]]] > |
| | נכבד/יה | τὰ ]]] [τοὺς] |
| | | ἔνδοξα ]]] [ἐνδόξους] |
| | | αὐτῆς ] [αὐ]τῆς |
| Ha 1:5 | + + + | ὃ ]]] > |
| Ha 1:7 | משפט/ו | τὸ |
| | | κρίμα ] [κρί]μα |
| | | αὐτοῦ ] |
| | + + + | ἔσται ]]] > |
| Ha 1:14 | כ/רמש | ὡς |
| | | τὰ ]]] > |
| | | ἑρπετὰ |
| | + + + | τὰ ]]] > |
| | לא | οὐκ |
| | {..~ב/ו} | ἔχοντα ] [ἔχον]τα |
| | משל | ἡγούμενον ] |
| | ב/ו | {...} |
| Ha 2:19 | הנה | τοῦτο ]]] [ἰδοὺ] |
| | | δέ ]]] > |

### 10.7 *Stylistic transpositions of the LXX (7× + 1×)*

| | | |
|---|---|---|
| Jo 2:4 | {...} | *με* ]] > |
| | יסבב/ני | *ἐκύκλωσαν* ]] *περιεκύκλωσ[έ]ν* |
| | | {.. ~ *με*} ]] *μ[ε]* |
| Jo 3:3 | שלשת | {.. ~ *τριῶν*} ] *τριῶ[ν]* |
| | ימים | *ἡμερῶν* |
| | | *τριῶν* ]]] > |
| Mi 1:1 | {אשר ~ ..} | *καὶ* ]] > |
| | {היה ~ ..} | *ἐγένετο* ]] > |
| | דבר | *λόγος* ] |
| | יהוה | *κυρίου* ]] [𐤉𐤄𐤅]𐤄 |
| | ~ אשר | --- ]] [*ὃς*] |
| | ~ היה | --- ]] [*ἐγένετο*] |
| Mi 4:3 | ו/לא {..עוד} | *καὶ* ] |
| | | *οὐκέτι μὴ* ]] *οὐ μὴ* |
| | ילמדון | *μάθωσι* ]] *μάθωσιν* |
| | עוד | {...} ]] *ἔτι* |
| Na 3:12 | עם | {.. ~ *ἔχουσαι*} ]]] [*σὺν*] |
| | בכורים | *σκοποὺς* ]]] *σκοπ[οῖς]* |
| | | {...} *ἔχουσαι* ]] > |
| Ha 2:20 | ו/יהוה | *ὁ δὲ κύριος* ]] *καὶ ὁ* 𐤉𐤄𐤅𐤄 |
| Zp 3:6 | מ/בלי איש | *παρὰ* |
| | | *τὸ* |
| | | *μηδένα* ]] [*μὴ*] --- |
| | | *ὑπάρχειν* ] [*ὑπάρ*]*χ*[*ε*]*ιν* |
| | | {.. ~ *μηδένα*} ]] *ἄνδ̣[ρα]* |

RECONSTRUCTION (1×)

| | | |
|---|---|---|
| Jo 3:7 | {...} | *μηδὲ* ]]] > |
| | ו/מים | *ὕδωρ* ]]] [*καὶ ὕδ″*] |
| | אל | {.. ~ *μηδὲ*} ]]] [*μὴ*] |

## 11. *Consistency and inconsistency*

### 11.1 *Consistency*

The literal, even pedantic character of R is obvious in most of the preceding sections, especially in 10. This type of literal translation coincides with the tendency to represent consistently every Hebrew word with a corresponding Greek equivalent. The preserved text is too small for an extensive examination of R's consistency. However, evidence of this tendency can be collected from the preceding paragraphs as well as from an examination of R's lexical choices.

Some examples of R's consistency in lexical choices are provided here:

(1) **כי** All occurrences of **כי** are rendered with *ὅτι*, see 9.3. In the lacunae, renderings of **כי** are reconstructed accordingly.

(2) **אל** Apart from one exception (Mi 4:3), **אל** is rendered by *πρός*:

| | | |
|---|---|---|
| Jo 2:5 | אל | *πρὸς* ] *πρὸ[ς]* |
| Jo 3:2 | אל/יך | *πρὸς* ] [*π*]*ρ*[*ὸ*]*ς* |
| | | *σέ* ] *σέ* |
| Jo 3:8 | אל | *πρὸς* ] [*πρ*]*ὸς* |
| Jo 4:2 | אל | *πρὸς* ] |
| Mi 4:3 | אל | *ἐπ'* ]] [*ἐ*]*φ'* |
| Za 1:3 | אל/יכם | *πρὸς* ] |
| | | *ὑμᾶς* ] |
| Za 1:4 | אל/יהם | *αὐτοῖς* ]] *πρὸς α*[*ὐτοὺς*] |

| | | |
|---|---|---|
| Za 1:14 | אל/י | *πρός* ] |
| | | *με* |
| Za 2:8 | אל | *πρὸς* (4) ] [*π*]*ρὸς* |
| Za 3:4 | אל | *πρὸς* ] *πρ*[*ὸς*] |

(3) יהוה See the data in 5.4.

## 11.2 *Inconsistency*

As a rule, R is a consistent and literal translator (reviser). However, like all other revisers, R is often not consistent. This can be observed in some of the data adduced above. Note 2.2 as compared with 2.3, 3.1 compared with 3.2, 4.1 compared with 4.2, and 5.2 compared with 5.3.

Further examples of inconsistent renderings are provided here.

(1) מים is rendered with both *ὕδωρ* and *ὕδατα*. See note on the reconstruction of Jo 3:7.

(2) הלוא is rendered with both *οὐ* and *οὐχί*. See ibid. on Mi 1:5.

(3) Different forms of *τίθημι* for שׂים (*θήσω* and *θήσομαι*) are recorded ibid. on Mi 1:7.

(4) Different renderings of קרא (almost all = LXX), reflecting their respective contexts:

| | | |
|---|---|---|
| Jo 3:2 | ו/קרא | *καὶ* ] [*κ*]*ạὶ* |
| | | *κήρυξον* ] *κήρυ̣*[*ξ*]*ον* |
| Jo 3:5 | ו/יקראו | *καὶ* |
| | | *ἐκήρυξαν* ] *ἐ̣κήρ*[*υξαν*] |
| Jo 3:8 | ו/יקראו | *καὶ* ] *κα̣*[*ὶ*] |
| | | *ἀνεβόησαν* |
| Za 1:4 | {...אל} קראו | *ἐνεκάλεσαν* ]] *ἐκάλουν* |
| Za 1:14 | קרא | *ἀνάκραγε* ] [*ἀνάκρα*]*γε* |

(5) In one verse R used two different Greek roots for derivatives of one Hebrew root: Ha 1:10 משׂחק —*γ*[*έλως*] (LXX: *παίγνια*) and ישׂחק —*ἐνπαι̣*[*ξεται*] (LXX: *ἐμπαίξεται*), probably because the translation of the verse began with [*ἐν*]*παίξει* (LXX: *ἐντρυφήσει*, MT: יתקלס).

## 11.3 *Non-stereotyped renderings*

The following examples represent relatively free renderings in R, such as addition or omission of the article, prepositions, pronouns, particles, and other non-stereotyped renderings (noun/verb, *waw* rendered by *δέ*), singular/plural forms, etc. Due to the nature of the Greek language, some of these cannot be avoided in the translation.

A large group of examples appears in 0.2 (shared translation technique of the LXX and R in significant details) and these examples are not repeated here. Additional examples follow.

In most of these instances R follows the LXX, so that we note once again that R may be following that translation in some of its non-stereotyped renderings. By the same token he would probably have used some different equivalents if his translation had been made independently of the LXX.

| | | |
|---|---|---|
| Jo 3:8 | אלהים | *τὸν* ] (art.) |
| | | *θεὸν* ] *θ̣*[*εὸν*] |
| Jo 4:1 | ו/יחר ל/ו | *καὶ* ] |
| | | *συνεχύθη* ]] *ἠθ̣*[*ύμησεν*] |
| Mi 1:5 | ו/ב/חטאות | *καὶ* ] |
| | | *διὰ* ]]] [*δι'*] (prep.) |
| | | *ἁμαρτίαν* ] [*ἁμ*]*αρτίαν* |

| | | |
|---|---|---|
| Mi 4:5 | ו/אנחנו | *ἡμεῖς* ] |
| | | *δὲ* ] *δ̣ὲ* |
| Mi 4:9 | חיל | *ὠδῖνες* ] *[ὠδῖ]νες* (pl.) |
| Na 2:10 | זהב | *τὸ* ] |
| | | *χρυσίον* ] *χ[ρυσίον]* |
| Zp 1:4 | יושבי | *τοὺς* |
| | | *κατοικοῦντας* ] |
| | ירושלם | *Ιερουσαλημ* ]] *ἐν ιερ[ουσαλημ]* |

## 12. *Orthographic and (morpho)phonological peculiarities*

This section describes the orthographic and (morpho)phonological peculiarities of R, documented by references to H. St. J. Thackeray, *A Grammar of the Old Testament in Greek* (Cambridge 1909) as well as to M. Dunand, *Papyrus grecs bibliques (Papyrus F. Inv. 266)* (Le Caire 1966). Extensive background material is available in F. T. Gignac, *A Grammar of the Greek Papyri of the Roman and Byzantine Periods*, I–II (Milano, 1976; 1982). When the full evidence, positive and negative, is provided, this is indicated in the headings. R's orthographic practices are rather consistent.

For the correct understanding of this paragraph it should be realized that Ziegler's edition does not exactly represent the orthography of the MSS (see the section on "Orthographika" on pp. 109–119).

### 12.1 *ι = ει (12× + 4×) (Thackeray 85–7)*

*ει* for *ι* occurs especially in certain morphophonemic conditions such as *ὑμεῖν*, *γειν-*, *ῥειψ-* (cf. Gignac I, 189–191), for which no negative examples (*ὑμῖν*, *ἡμῖν*, *γιν-*, *ῥιψ-*) are available:

| | | |
|---|---|---|
| Jo 2:4 | ו/תשליכ/ני | --- ]]] *[καὶ]* |
| | | *ἀπέρριψάς* ]] *[ἀ]π̣έ̣ρρειψάς* |
| | | *με* ] *μ[ε]* |
| Mi 1:2 | ב/כם | *ἐν* ] |
| | | *ὑμῖν* ]] *ὑμεῖν* |
| Mi 3:6 | ל/כם | *ὑμῖν* ]] *[ὑμ]εῖν* |
| Ha 2:2 | קורא | *ὁ* ]] > |
| | | *ἀναγινώσκων* ]] *ἀναγεινώσκων* |
| Ha 2:15 | משקה | *ὁ* ]] *τ[ῷ]* |
| | | *ποτίζων* ]] *[ποτίζοντ]ε̣ι* |
| Za 1:4 | תהיו | *γίνεσθε* ]] *γείνε[σθε]* |
| Za 3:5 | בגדים | *ἱμάτια* ]] *εἱμάτια* |

A second group concerns transliterated Hebrew words:

| | | |
|---|---|---|
| Mi 1:1 | ה/מרשתי | *τὸν* |
| | | *Μωρασθι* ]] *μωρασθει* |
| Mi 4:7 | ציון | *Σιων* ]] *σει[ων]* |
| Zp 1:4 | ה/כמרים | *τῶν* ] *τῶ[ν]* |
| | | *ἱερέων* ]] *[χωμα]ρειμ* |
| Za 1:14 | ו/ל/ציון | *καὶ* |
| | | *τὴν* |
| | | *Σιων* ]] *σε[ιων]* |
| Za 9:2 | ו/צידון | *καὶ* ] |
| | | *Σιδών* ]] *σειδ̣[ών]* |

RECONSTRUCTIONS (4×)

| | | |
|---|---|---|
| Mi 3:6 | ל/כם | *ὑμῖν* ]]] *[ὑμεῖν]* |
| Mi 4:8 | ציון | *Σιων* ]]] *[σειων]* |
| Mi 4:10 | ציון | *Σιων* ]]] *σ[ειων]* |

| | | |
|---|---|---|
| Za 2:11 | ציון | Σιων (7) ]]] [σειων] |

Note also the reverse phenomenon:

| | | |
|---|---|---|
| Mi 1:5 | פשע | ἡ ]]] ><br>ἀσέβεια ]] ἀσέβια |

### 12.2 ει = οι *(1 × + 2 ×)*

| | | |
|---|---|---|
| Mi 1:5 | שמרון | Σαμάρεια ]] [σα]μάροια |

RECONSTRUCTIONS (2 ×)

| | | |
|---|---|---|
| Mi 1:1 | שמרון | Σαμαρείας ]]] [σαμαροίας] |
| Mi 1:6 | שמרון | Σαμάρειαν ]]] σα[μάροιαν] |

### 12.3 *Preverbs and prefixes with final nasal (9 × + 1 ×) (Thackeray 132–4; Gignac I, 155–77) (full evidence)*

| | | |
|---|---|---|
| Mi 1:7 | ישרפו | ἐμπρήσουσιν ]] ἐνπρήσου[σιν] |
| Mi 2:8 | ו/אתמול | καὶ ]<br>ἔμπροσθεν ]] ἔνπροσθ[εν] |
| Mi 4:3 | ו/כתתו | καὶ ]<br>κατακόψουσι ]] συνκόψου[σιν] |
| Ha 1:10 | ישחק | ἐμπαίξεται ]] ἐνπαί[ξεται] |
| Ha 1:10 | ו/ילכד/ה | καὶ<br>κρατήσει ]] συνλήμψετ[αι]<br>αὐτοῦ ]]] [αὐτό] |
| Ha 2:3 | ו/יפח | καὶ ]<br>ἀνατελεῖ ]] ἐνφανήσετ[αι] |
| Ha 2:5 | ישבע | ἐμπιπλάμενος ]] ἐνπιπλάμ[ενος] |
| Za 1:4 | ה/ראשנים | οἱ ]<br>ἔμπροσθεν ]] ἔνπροσθεν |
| Za 3:7 | מהלכים | ἀναστρεφομένους ]] ἐνπ[ερι]π[ατοῦντας] |

RECONSTRUCTION (1 ×)

| | | |
|---|---|---|
| Ha 1:10 | יתקלס | ἐντρυφήσει ]] [ἐν]παίξει |

Note however

| | | |
|---|---|---|
| Ha 3:12 | ב/זעם | ἐν ἀπειλῇ ]] ἐν ἐμ[βριμήσει] |

### 12.4 ἐκ *before nasals (3 ×) (Thackeray 101–2; Dunand 15; Gignac I, 172–6)*

| | | |
|---|---|---|
| Mi 1:7 | מ/אתנן | ἐκ ]] ἐγ<br>μισθωμάτων ]]] μισ[θώματος] |
| Ha 2:7 | ו/יקצו | καὶ ]<br>ἐκνήψουσιν ]] ἐγνή[ψουσ]ιν |
| Ha 2:19 | הקיצה | ἔκνηψον ]] ἔγνηψον |

### 12.5 γγ = νγ *(2 ×) (Thackeray 130–4; Gignac I, 171) (full evidence)*

| | | |
|---|---|---|
| Zp 1:14 | קרוב | ἐγγὺς ]] ἐνγὺς |
| Zp 1:14 | קרוב | ἐγγὺς ]] ἐνγὺς |

Note also φάραγγα (Mi 1:6), ἀποφθεγγ[ο]μέν[ων] (Na 2:8), στραγ[γεύσηται] (Ha 2:3), φέγγος (Ha 3:11), [ἄ]γγελος (Za 3:5,6).

### 12.6 διά = δι' *(1× + 2×) (Thackeray 136–7; Gignac I, 315–21) (full evidence)*

Elision is the regular practice of R with ἀπό, ἐπί, κατά, μετά and διά (see 12.8 for ἐπί). This paragraph refers only to διά.

| | | |
|---|---|---|
| Ha 2:17 | מ/דמי | διὰ ]] δι'<br>αἵματα ] |

RECONSTRUCTIONS (2×)

| | | |
|---|---|---|
| Mi 1:5 | ב/פשע | διὰ ]]] [δι']<br>ἀσέβειαν ]]] [ἀσέβιαν] |
| Mi 1:5 | ו/ב/חטאות | καὶ ]<br>διὰ ]]] [δι']<br>ἁμαρτίαν ] [ἁμ]αρτίαν |

### 12.7 τ = θ *(1×) (Thackeray 124–9; Gignac I, 136–8)*

| | | |
|---|---|---|
| Mi 4:3 | ישאו | ἀντάρῃ ]] ἀνθάρῃ |

### 12.8 ἐπ' = ἐφ' *(2×) (Thackeray 124–7; Gignac I, 133–8) (full evidence)*

| | | |
|---|---|---|
| Mi 4:3 | אל | ἐπ' ]] [ἐ]φ'<br>ἔθνος ] |

This instance reflects the irregular insertion of the aspirate before ἔθνος (= ἕθνος), also known from other sources (cf. W. Schulze, *Kleine Schriften* [Göttingen 1933] 517ff.) In all other instances R uses ἐπ' before the smooth breathing (Jo 2:4; Mi 4:7; 5:4(5); Ha 2:18) and ἐφ' before the rough breathing (Ha 2:6).

| | | |
|---|---|---|
| Ha 2:6 | על/יו (על/ו) | τὸν κλοιὸν αὐτοῦ ]] ἐφ' ἑατὸν |

### 12.9 λαμβάνω *(2×) (Thackeray 108–11; Ziegler 114; Gignac II, 269) (full evidence)*

| | | |
|---|---|---|
| Ha 1:10 | ו/ילכד/ה | καὶ<br>κρατήσει ]] συνλήμψετ[αι]<br>αὐτοῦ ]]] [αὐτό] |
| Ha 2:6 | ישאו | λήμψονται ]] λήψε[ται] |

### 12.10 α = ε *(1× + 1×) (Thackeray 73–4; Gignac I, 278–86)*

| | | |
|---|---|---|
| Za 2:3 | ארבעה | τέσσαρας (1:20) ]] [τέσσα]ρες |

RECONSTRUCTION (1×)

| | | |
|---|---|---|
| Za 2:10 | כ/ארבע | ἐκ (6) ]]] [ὡς]<br>τῶν ]]] [τοὺς]<br>τεσσάρων ]]] [τέσσαρες] |

### 12.11 ο = ω *(1×) (Thackeray 89–91; Gignac I, 275–7)*

| | | |
|---|---|---|
| Ha 1:8 | מ/רחוק | μακρόθεν ]] πώρρ[ωθεν] |

### 12.12 *Sibilants (1×) (Thackeray 108; Gignac I, 120–4)*

| | | |
|---|---|---|
| Mi 4:3 | ו/חנית/יהם | καὶ ]<br>τὰ ]] τὰς<br>δόρατα ]] σιβύ[νας]<br>αὐτῶν ] [α]ὐτῶν |

Reconstructed also in Na 3:11.

12.13 *ν movable (Thackeray 134–5; Gignac I, 114–16) (full evidence)*

R used the *ν* movable, as is usual, before vowels (Jo 3:8,9,10; 4:5,5; Mi 4:3; 5:2(3); Na 2:6,6; Ha 2:7,18,18,19; Zp 1:13; Za 9:3), but also before consonants:

| | | |
|---|---|---|
| Jo 2:4 | יסבב/ני | *με ἐκύκλωσαν* ]] *περιεκύκλωσ[έ]ν μ[ε]* |
| Jo 2:6 | חבוש | *ἕδυ* ]] *περιέσχ[ε]ν (τὴν)* |
| Jo 3:10 | דבר | *ἐλάλησε* ]] *ἐλ[άλ]ησεν (τ[οῦ])* |
| Jo 3:10 | עשה | *ἐποίησεν* ] (4:1 *κ[αὶ]*) |
| Mi 5:5 | ו/רעו | *καὶ* (6) |
| | | *ποιμανοῦσι* ]] *[ποιμανοῦ]σιν (τὴν)* |
| Ha 1:15 | העלה | *ἀνέσπασε* ]] *ἀνέσπασεν (καὶ)* |
| Ha 2:18 | הועיל | *ὠφελεῖ* ]] *ὠφέλησεν (γλυπτόν)* |
| Za 2:2 | מה | *τί ἐστι* (1:19) ] *[τί ἐστι]ν (ταῦṭ[α])* |
| Za 3:4 | ו/יאמר | *καὶ* ] *κα[ὶ]* |
| | | *εἶπε* ]]] *[εἶπεν] [πρ]ὸς* |
| Za 8:20 | יבאו | *ἥξουσι* ]] *[ἔλ]θωσιν (λαοὶ)* |
| Za 9:2 | חכמה | *ἐφρόνησαν* ] *[ἐ]φρόνησεν (σφόδρα)* |
| Za 9:3 | ו/תבן | *καὶ* |
| | | *ᾠκοδόμησε* ]] *[ᾠκοδό]μησεν (τύρος)* |

Accordingly, the *ν* movable is reconstructed also before consonants: (Jo 2:6 *ἐκύκλῳ[σέν με]*; 3:4 *[ἐκήρυξεν καὶ]*; 4:1 *ἠθ̣[ύμησεν]* (2 *καὶ*); Mi 1:1 *[εἶδεν περὶ]*; 1:7 *σ[υνήγαγεν] καὶ*; 4:3 *συνκόψου[σιν τὰς]*; Na 2:9 *φεύ[γουσιν στ]ῆ̣[τε]*; 3:7 *[τεταλαι]πώρηκε[ν νινευη]*; 3:10 *βαλοῦ[σιν κλῆρον]*; 3:12 *σαλευθ[ῶσιν καὶ]*; Ha 2:5 *[ἐπλάτυνεν] καθὼς*; 2:8 *σκυλεύ[σουσίν σε]*; Zp 1:13 *[κατοικήσουσιν καὶ]*; 1:13 *[πίωσιν τὸν]*; Za 1:14 *[εἶπεν] πρός*; 2:2 *[εἶπεν πρός]*; 2:3 *[ἔδειξέν μοι]*; 2:4 *[εἶπεν λέγων]*; 2:8 *[εἶπεν πρὸς]*; 3:1 *ἔ[δειξέν μοι]*; 3:5 *[ἔστηκεν* (6) *καὶ]*.

12.14 *αυ = α (1×) (Thackeray 79; Gignac I, 226–7) (full evidence)*

| | | |
|---|---|---|
| Ha 2:6 | עלי/ו (על/ו) | *τὸν κλοιὸν αὐτοῦ* ]] *ἐφ' ἑατὸν* |

12.15 *Augment (Thackeray 198–200; Gignac II, 240–1) (full evidence)*

| | | |
|---|---|---|
| Jo 4:2 | ו/יתפלל | *καὶ* ] |
| | | *προσηύξατο* ]] *π̣[ροσ]εύ̣ξαṭο* |

## III. Textual Relations (13–15)

The following analysis of the textual relationship between R, the LXX and MT differs basically from the preceding paragraphs in that it does not discuss the inner-Greek relation between the two translations LXX and R, but rather their respective Hebrew *Vorlagen vis-à-vis* MT. The analysis involves the reconstruction of elements in these *Vorlagen* which is necessarily subjective. The outcome shows the Hebrew *Vorlage* of R to be much closer to MT than to that of the LXX, so that R's revisional labour must have included the approximating of the 'LXX' to a forerunner of MT, which however was not identical with it. Most recognized differences between these two Hebrew texts consist of minor details.

This is mainly reflected in 14.1 (R = MT against LXX [59 + 35]), and probably also in 15.1 (LXX = MT against R [16 + 3]), and even in 15.3 (R differs from both LXX and MT [6]), which all indicate that R's *Vorlage* was similar to, rather than identical with MT. For each of these groups similar examples of agreements at the level of *vocalization* have been added. However, these are less convincing since they merely represent exegetical traditions at the time of translation. In fact, R shares more agreements in vocalization with the LXX (against MT) than with MT (against the LXX). This indicates that these renderings have not been corrected. The statistics are as follows:

| | |
|---|---|
| R=LXX against MT (13.1): | 14+1 (reconstruction) |
| Idem, in vocalization (13.2): | 21 |
| R=MT against LXX (14.1): | 59+35 |
| Idem, in vocalization (14.2): | 15+5 |
| LXX=MT against R (15.1): | 16+3 |
| Idem, in vocalization (15.2): | 2 |
| R differs from both LXX and MT (15.3): | 6 |
| Indecisive (15.4): | 1 |

The proximity between R and MT is clearly reflected in the following analysis. In all these cases this proximity is explained in terms of R's revision of the LXX towards a *different* Hebrew text (similar to MT). However, in some cases in which the text of the LXX does not reflect a variant Hebrew reading as indicated below, the proximity between R and the MT was thus created at the inner-Greek (translational) level. If that were the case these examples should actually be transferred to 10, but our basic contention of the closeness between R and the MT would not be affected by such an internal shift.

In most of the examples, reconstructed Hebrew readings are either added in parenthesis or are clear from the notation (minuses, transpositions).

## 13.1 *R=LXX against MT (14× + 1×)*

The reconstructed *Vorlage* common to R and the LXX is recorded in parenthesis after the text of the MT in the left column.

| | | |
|---|---|---|
| Jo 2:3 | מ/צרה (ב/צרה) | *ἐν* |
| | | *θλίψει* ] [*θλίψ*]*ει* |
| Mi 1:5 | ו/ב/חטאות (ו/ב/חטאת) | *καὶ* ] |
| | | *διὰ* ]]] [*δι'*] |
| | | *ἁμαρτίαν* ] [*ἁμ*]*αρτίαν* |
| Mi 1:6 | ל/מטעי (ו/ל/מטעי) | *καὶ* ] |
| | | *εἰς* ] *εἰ*[*s*] |
| | | *φυτείαν* ]]] [*φυτείας*] |
| Mi 3:5 | + + + | *ἐπ'* |
| | (על/יו) | *αὐτὸν* ] [*αὐτ*]*ọν* |
| Mi 4:3 | ישׂאו (ישׂא) | *ἀντάρῃ* ]] *ἀνθάρῃ* |
| Mi 5:3 | ב/גאון (ו/ב/גאון) | *καὶ* (4) ] |
| | | *ἐν* ] |
| | | *τῇ* ] |
| | | *δόξῃ* ]] *ἐπάρσει* |
| Na 2:6 | ימהרו (ו/ימהרו) | *καὶ* ] [*κ*]*αὶ* |
| | | *σπεύσουσιν* ]] *ταχυνοῦσιν* |
| Na 2:13 | ו/מענת/יו (ו/מענת/ו) | *καὶ* |
| | | *τὸ* ]]] [*τὴν*] |
| | | *κατοικητήριον* ]] [*μά*]*ṿδραν* |
| | | *αὐτοῦ* |
| Ha 1:15 | יגר/הו (ו/יגר/הו) | *καὶ* ] |
| | | *εἵλκυσεν* ]] *ἔσυρεν* |
| | | *αὐτὸν* |
| Ha 2:5 | ו/לא (לא) | *οὐκ* ] |
| Ha 2:6 | על/יו ~ (משל) | *παραβολὴν* ] |
| | ~ משל (על/יו) | *κατ'* ] *κ*[*ατ'*] |
| | | *αὐτοῦ* ] [*αὐτ*]*οῦ* |

| | | |
|---|---|---|
| Ha 2:17 | (יחית/ך) יחית/ן | *ποτήσει*] [*ποτήσ*]*ει* |
| | | *σε* ] |
| Ha 2:18 | (על יצר/ו) יצר/ו | *ἐπὶ* ] |
| | | *τὸ* ] |
| | | *πλάσμα* ] |
| | | *αὐτοῦ* ] *αụ̓τοῦ* |
| Ha 3:9 | (תעיר) תעור | *ἐντενεῖς* ]] *ἐξεγ*[*ερ*]*ẹι̣̂ς* |

RECONSTRUCTION (1 ×)

| | | |
|---|---|---|
| Ha 1:8 | (ו/יעפו) יעפו | *καὶ* |
| | | *πετασθήσονται* ] [*πετα*]*σθήσονται* (calc. of space) |

## 13.2 *R = LXX against MT in vocalization (21 ×)*

The left column records the vocalization of MT, while the reconstructed reading of R = LXX is recorded in the right column.

| | | |
|---|---|---|
| Jo 4:2 | עַד | *ἔτι* ] (עֹד) |
| Mi 1:7 | יֻכַּתּוּ | *κατακόψουσι* ]] *κατακ*[*όψουσιν* (passive/active) |
| Mi 1:7 | יִשָּׂרְפוּ | *ἐμπρήσουσιν* ]] *ἐνπρήσου*[*σιν*] (יִשְׂרְפוּ) |
| Mi 4:8 | מִגְדַּל | *πύργος* |
| | עדר | *ποιμνίου* |
| | עֹפֶל | *αὐχμώδης* ] [*αὐχ*]*μώδης* (עָפֵל = אָפֵל?) |
| Mi 5:5 | בַּחֶרֶב | *ἐν* (6) ] |
| | | *ῥομφαίᾳ* ] *ῥ*[*ομφαίᾳ*] (בְּחֶרֶב) |
| Na 2:6 | חוֹמָתָהּ | *ἐπὶ* ] |
| | | *τὰ* ] |
| | | *τείχη* ] (*he* of direction; change of number) |
| Na 2:6 | וְהֻכַן | *καὶ* ] |
| | | *ἑτοιμάσουσι* ]] *ἑτοιμάσε*[*ι*] (both active forms) |
| Na 2:8 | וְהֻצַּב | *καὶ* ] |
| | | *ἡ* ] |
| | | *ὑπόστασις* ]] *λαμπήνη* (article + noun) |
| Na 2:8 | מְנַהֲגוֹת | *ἤγοντο* ]] *ἀγ*[*ό*]*μεν*[*α*]*ι̣* (passive form) |
| Na 2:10 | בֹּזּוּ | *διήρπαζον* ] [*διήρπαζ*]*ον* (בַּזּוּ?) |
| Na 3:8 | מִיָּם | *καὶ* ]] > |
| | | *ὕδωρ* ] *ὕδω*[*ρ*] (מַיִם) |
| Na 3:9 | עָצְמָה | *ἡ* |
| | | *ἰσχὺς* ] |
| | | *αὐτῆς* ] *αὐ*[*τ*]*ῆ̣ς* (עָצְמָהּ) |
| Na 3:14 | בַּטִּיט | *εἰς* ] |
| | | *πηλὸν* ] *πηλ*[*ὸν*] (בְּטִיט) |
| Ha 1:10 | וַיִּצְבֹּר | *καὶ* |
| | | *βαλεῖ* ] [*β*]*α̣λ̣ε̣ῖ̣* (וְיִצְבֹּר?) |
| Ha 1:10 | וַיִּלְכְּדָהּ | *καὶ* ] |
| | | *κρατήσει* ]] *συνλήμψετ*[*αι*] |
| | | *αὐτοῦ* ]]] [*αὐτό*] (וְיִלְכְּדָהּ?) |
| Ha 1:11 | וַיַּעֲבֹר | *καὶ* ] |
| | | *διελεύσεται* ]] *παρ*[*ελεύσεται*] (וְיַעֲבֹר?) |
| Ha 2:5 | כִּשְׁאוֹל | *καθὼς* ] |
| | | *ὁ* ] |
| | | *ᾅδης* ] (כַּשְּׁאוֹל) |
| Ha 2:5 | וַיִּקְבֹּץ | *καὶ* ] |
| | | *εἰσδέξεται* ]] *ἀθροι*[*σει*] (וְיִקְבֹּץ?) |
| Ha 2:6 | חִידוֹת | *εἰς* ]] > |
| | | *διήγησιν* ]] *διήγησις* (*חִידוּת?) |
| Ha 3:9 | תְּבַקַּע | *ῥαγήσεται* ] (תִּבָּקַע) |
| Ha 3:13 | עָרוֹת | *ἐξήγειρας* ]] [*ἐξε*]*κ̣ένωσα*[*s*] (verbal form, 2nd person sg.) |

## 14.1 *R=MT against LXX* (59× +35×)

The reconstructed *Vorlage* of the LXX (except for the minus signs and such obvious retroversions as לאמר and אלהים) is written in parenthesis after the reading of MT in the left column.

| | | |
|---|---|---|
| Jo 2:3 | + + + | *τὸν* ]]> |
| | + + + | *θεόν* ]] > |
| | + + + | *μου* ]] > |
| Jo 3:8 | + + + | *λέγοντες* ]] > |
| Jo 3:9 | ישׁוב | --- ]] *ἐπι̣[σ]τ[ρέψει]* |
| Mi 1:6 | (שׂדה) ה/שׂדה | --- ]] *τοῦ* |
| | | *ἀγροῦ* ] *ἀ[γρ]οῦ* |
| Mi 1:7 | (ו/מן?) ו/עד | *καὶ* ] |
| | | *ἐκ* ]] *ἕως* |
| Mi 1:7 | (ישׁוב) ישׁובו | *συνέστρεψεν* ]] *[ἐπιστρέψουσ]ιν* |
| Mi 2:7 | (?) הולך | *πεπόρευνται* ]] *[πορευομ]ένου* |
| Mi 4:4 | (ו/ישׁב?) ו/ישׁבו | *καὶ* |
| | | *ἀναπαύσεται* ]]] *[καθίσ]ονται* |
| Mi 4:5 | (ב/דרכ/ו?) ב/שׁם אלה/יו | *τὴν* ]]] *[ἐν ὀνόματι]* |
| | | *ὁδὸν* ]] *[θε]οῦ* |
| | | *αὐτοῦ* ]] *αὐτῶν* (R differs) |
| Mi 5:3 | (ו/ראה ו/רעה) ו/רעה | *καὶ* (4) ]] > |
| | | *ὄψεται* ]] > |
| | | *καὶ* ] |
| | | *ποιμανεῖ* ] *πο[ι]μανεῖ* |
| Mi 5:3 | + + + | *τὸ* (4) ]] > |
| | | *ποίμνιον* ]] > |
| | | *αὐτοῦ* ]] > |
| Mi 5:5 | את ארץ | *τὸν* (6) ]] *τὴν* |
| | | --- ]] *γῆν* |
| | אשׁור | *Ασσουρ* ] |
| Na 2:6 | + + + | *καὶ* ]] > |
| | + + + | *φεύξονται* ]] > |
| | + + + | *ἡμέρας* ]] > |
| Na 2:6 | (ו/כשׁלו) יכשׁלו | *καὶ* ]] > |
| | | *ἀσθενήσουσιν* ] *[ἀσ]θενήσουσιν* |
| Na 3:7 | (ירד) ידוד | *καταβήσεται* ]] *ἀποπ[ηδήσεται]* |
| Na 3:8 | (מים) מ/ים | *καὶ* ]] > |
| | | *ὕδωρ* ] *ὕδω[ρ]* |
| Ha 1:5 | + + + | *καί* ]] > |
| | + + + | *ἀφανίσθητε* ]] > |
| Ha 1:8 | (ו/פרשׁו) ו/פרשׁ/יו | *καὶ* |
| | | --- ]]] *[οἱ]* |
| | | *ὁρμήσουσι* ]] *[ἱπ]π̣εῖς* |
| | | --- ]] *αὐτοῦ* |
| Ha 1:15 | + + + | *ἡ* (16) ]] > |
| | | *καρδία* ]] > |
| | | *αὐτοῦ* ]] > |
| Ha 1:16 | (ל/מכמרת/ו?) ל/חרמ/ו | *τῇ* ]] *[τῷ]* |
| | | *σαγήνῃ* ]] *[ἀμφιβλή]στρῳ* |
| | | *αὐτοῦ* ] |
| Ha 1:16 | (ל/חרמ/ו?) ל/מכמרת/ו | *τῷ* ]] *τῇ* |
| | | *ἀμφιβλήστρῳ* ]] *σα[γήνῃ]* |
| | | *αὐτοῦ* ] *[αὐτ]οῦ* |
| Ha 1:17 | (על כן) ה/על כן | --- ]] *εἰ* |
| | | *διὰ τοῦτο* ] *διὰ τοῦ[το]* |
| Ha 2:3 | (ל/כזב) יכזב | *εἰς κενόν* ]] *[δ]ι̣αψεύσεται* |
| Ha 2:4 | (הן?) הנה | *ἐὰν* ]] *ἰδ[οὺ]* |
| Ha 2:4 | (נפשׁ/י) נפשׁ/ו | *ἡ* ]] > |
| | | *ψυχή* ] |
| | | *μου* ]] *αὐτοῦ* |

| | | |
|---|---|---|
| Ha 2:4 | ב/אמונת/ו (מ/אמונת/י) | ἐκ ]] ἐν |
| | | πίστεώς ]] πίστει |
| | | μου ]] αὐτοῦ |
| Ha 2:6 | ו/יאמר (ו/יאמרו) | καὶ ] κα[ὶ] |
| | | ἐροῦσιν ]] [ἐρ]εῖ |
| Ha 2:6 | + + + | ἑαυτῷ ]] > |
| Ha 2:6 | על/יו (על/ו) | τὸν κλοιὸν αὐτοῦ ]] ἐφ' ἑατὸν |
| Ha 2:13 | ב/די ריק (רבים?) | πολλὰ ]] [ἐν ἱκανότητι] κενὸν |
| Ha 2:14 | על ים (על/יהם) | αὐτούς ]] [ἐπὶ] θαλάσσ[ης] |
| Ha 2:16 | ו/קיקלון (ו/קו קלון?) | καὶ ] |
| | | συνήχθη ]] ἔμετος (two words) |
| | | ἀτιμία ]]] [ἀτιμίας] |
| Ha 2:18 | ו/מורה (מורה) | --- ]] [καὶ] |
| | | φαντασίαν ] [φα]ντασίαν |
| Ha 2:18 | על/יו | --- ]] ἐπ' αὐτὸ |
| Ha 2:19 | הוא[1] (ו/הוא) | καὶ ]] > |
| | | αὐτό ]] αὐτός |
| | | ἐστι ]] > |
| Ha 3:10 | הרים (עמים) | λαοί ]] ὄρη |
| Ha 3:13 | מ/בית ~ (רשע) | ἀνόμων ]] ἐξ οἴκου |
| | ~ רשע (מות?) | θάνατον ]] [ἀσ]ε̣β[οῦς] |
| Ha 3:13 | יסוד (אסר) | δεσμοὺς ]] θ̣εμελίους (R reflects MT, albeit as a plural noun) |
| Ha 3:14 | + + + | ἐν ]] > |
| | | αὐτῇ ]] > |
| Ha 3:15 | דרכת (ו/דרכת) | καὶ ]] > |
| | | ἐπεβίβασας ]] ἐνέτει[νες] |
| Zp 1:4 | את שאר (את שם) | τὰ ]]] [τὸ] |
| | | ὀνόματα ]] ὑπ̣[όλειμμα] |
| Zp 1:4 | את שם (ו/את שם) | καὶ ]] > |
| | | τὰ ]] τὸ |
| | | ὀνόματα ]] ὄνομα |
| Zp 1:4 | ה/כמרים | τῶν ] τῶ[ν] |
| | | ἱερέων ]] [χωμα]ρειμ |
| | עם | --- ]] μ[ετὰ] |
| | ה/כהנים | --- ]] [τῶν] |
| | | --- ]] [ἱ]ερέων |
| Zp 1:14 | + + + | ὅτι ]] > |
| Zp 2:10 | עם | --- ]] λαὸν |
| Zp 3:7 | תקחי (ו/תקחו) | καὶ ]]] > |
| | | δέξασθε ]] [δέ]ξαι |
| Zp 3:7 | אכן (הכן) | ἑτοιμάζου ]] διὰ τοῦτο |
| Zp 3:7 | כל | πᾶσα ]] πάντα |
| | עלילות/ם (עללות/ם) | ἡ ]] τὰ |
| | | ἐπιφυλλὶς ]] ἐπιτ[ηδεύματα] |
| | | αὐτῶν |
| Za 1:3 | נאם | --- ]]] [λέγει] |
| | יהוה | --- ]] 𐤉𐤄𐤅𐤄 |
| | צבאות | --- ]] τῶν δυνάμ[εων] |
| Za 1:3 | צבאות[3] | --- ]] [τῶν δυ]νάμεων |
| Za 2:2 | ו/ירושלם | --- (1:19) ]]] [καὶ] |
| | | --- ]]] [τὴν] |
| | | --- ]] ιερου[σαλημ] |
| Za 2:8 | פרזות (פרי?) | κατακάρπως (4) ]] [ἀτειχίσ]τας |
| Za 2:11 | יושבת (יושבי?) | οἱ (7) ]]] > |
| | | κατοικοῦντες ]] [κ]α̣τοικ[οῦσα] |
| Za 3:4 | מ/על/יך | --- ]] ἀπὸ |
| | | --- ]] σοῦ |
| Za 3:4 | את/ך (את/ו) | αὐτὸν ]] σε |
| Za 3:7 | את משמרת/י (את מצות/י) | τὰ ]]] [τὴν] |
| | | προστάγματά ]] [φυλα]κήν |
| | | μου ] |
| Za 8:20 | (רבים) + + + | πολλοὶ ]] > |
| Za 8:23 | עמ/כם (עמ/ך) | μετὰ ]] μεθ' |
| | | σοῦ ]] ὑμ[ῶν] |

| | | |
|---|---|---|
| Za 9:4 | הנה | *διὰ τοῦτο* ]] *ἰδοὺ* |

RECONSTRUCTIONS (35 ×)

| | | |
|---|---|---|
| Jo 2:7 | + + + | *ἧς* ]]] > |
| Jo 3:7 | (ו/ה/בקר) ה/בקר | *καὶ* ]]] > |
| | | *οἱ* |
| | | *βόες* |
| Jo 4:2 | אל | --- ]]] [*θεὸς*] |
| Mi 1:4 | (ו/נמגו?) ו/נמסו | *καὶ* |
| | | *σαλευθήσεται* ]]] [*τακή*]*σο*ṿ[*ται*] |
| Mi 1:4 | (אשׁ) ה/אשׁ | --- ]]] [*τοῦ*] |
| | | *πυρὸς* |
| Mi 1:4 | (ו/כ/מים) כ/מים | *καὶ* ]]] > |
| | | *ὡς* |
| | | *ὕδωρ* |
| Mi 1:5 | (--- בית?) במות | *ἡ* ]]] > |
| | | *ἁμαρτία* ]]] > |
| | | *οἴκου* ]]] [*ὕψη*] |
| Mi 1:7 | (ל/שׁממה) שׁממה | *εἰς* ]]] > |
| | | *ἀφανισμόν* |
| Mi 2:7 | (ו/ה/ישׁר) ה/ישׁר | *καὶ* ]]] [*τοῦ*] |
| | | *ὀρθοὶ* ]]] [*ὀρθοῦ*] |
| Mi 4:8 | (מ/בבל) + + + | *ἐκ Βαβυλῶνος* ]]] > |
| Mi 4:9 | (ו/עתה) עתה | *καὶ* ]]] > |
| | | *νῦν* |
| Mi 5:6 | (ב/גוים) + + + | *ἐν* (7) ]]] > |
| | | *τοῖς* ]]] > |
| | | *ἔθνεσιν* ]]] > |
| Mi 5:6 | + + + | *πίπτουσα* (7) ]]] > |
| Na 2:14 | (רב/כה) רכב/ה | --- ]]] [*τὸ*] |
| | | *πλῆθός* ]]] [*ἅρμα*] |
| | | *σου* ]]] [*αὐτῆς*] |
| Na 3:7 | (ל/ה?) ל/ך | *αὐτῇ* ]]] [*σοι*] |
| Na 3:9 | (ו/כושׁ) כושׁ | *καὶ* ]]] > |
| | | *Αἰθιοπία* |
| Na 3:15 | (ו/התכבדי) התכבדי | *καὶ* ]]] > |
| | | *βαρυνθήσῃ* ]]] [*καταβαρύν*]*θητι* |
| Ha 1:6 | + + + | *τοὺς* ]]] > |
| | | *μαχητάς* ]]] > |
| Ha 1:7 | + + + | *ἐξ*² ]]] > |
| | | *αὐτοῦ* ]]] > |
| Ha 1:8 | יבאו | --- ]]] [*ἐλεύσονται*] |
| Ha 1:10 | (ו/הוא?) הוא | *καὶ* ]]] > |
| | | *αὐτὸς* ] [*αὐ*]*τ̣ὸς* |
| Ha 2:19 | (ו/ל/אבן) ל/אבן | *καὶ* ]]] > |
| | | *τῷ̣* ] |
| | | *λίθῳ̣* ] |
| Ha 3:10 | (ו/יחילו) יחילו | *καὶ* ]]] > |
| | | *ὠδινήσουσι* ]] [*ὠδίνησ*]*αν* |
| Ha 3:12 | (ו/ב/אף) ב/אף | *καὶ* ]]] > |
| | | *ἐν* |
| | | *θυμῷ̣* |
| Zp 1:2 | כל | --- ]]] [*πάντα*] |
| Zp 1:4 | עם | --- ]]] *μ̣*[*ετὰ*] |
| Zp 1:5 | ו/את ה/משׁתחוים | *καὶ* ] *κ*[*α*]*ὶ* |
| | | --- ]]] [*τοὺς*] |
| | | --- ]]] [*προσκυνοῦντας*] |
| Za 1:2 | קצף | *ὀργὴν* |
| | (גדל) + + + | *μεγάλην* ]]] > (calc. of space) |
| Za 1:3 | נאם | --- ]]] [*λέγει*] |
| | יהוה | --- ]]] [𐤉𐤄𐤅𐤄] |
| Za 1:4 | (ו/אל) אל | *καὶ* ]] > |
| | | *μὴ* |

| | | |
|---|---|---|
| Za 1:13 | דברים (ו/דברים) | καὶ ]]] > |
| | | λόγους |
| Za 2:2 | + + + (אדני) | κύριε (1:19) ]]] > |
| Za 2:8 | + + + (ל/אמר) | λέγων ]]] > (calc. of space) |
| Za 3:5 | ו/אמר | καὶ ] |
| | | --- ]]] [εἶπα] |
| Za 8:19 | + + + | καὶ ]]] > |
| | + + + (ו/תשמחו) | εὐφρανθήσεσθε ]]] > |

## 14.2 *R=MT against LXX in vocalization (15× + 5×)*

The reconstructed reading of the LXX appears in the right column, that of MT=R in the left one.

| | | |
|---|---|---|
| Jo 2:6 | סוּף | ἐσχάτῃ (סֹוף) ]] [ἐσχά]τῃ, {d} ἕλος |
| Jo 3:3 | כִּדְבַר | καθὼς ]]] [κατ]ὰ |
| | | ἐλάλησε (כְּדַבֵּר) ]] τὸ ῥῆμα |
| Jo 4:2 | דְּבָרִי | οἱ ]] ὁ |
| | | λόγοι (דְּבָרַי) ]] λόγος |
| | | μου ] |
| Mi 1:6 | לַגַּי | εἰς ] |
| | | --- ]] τὴν |
| | | χάος (לְגַי) ]] φάραγγα |
| Mi 3:6 | וְחָשְׁכָה | καὶ ] [κ]αὶ |
| | | σκοτία (וַחֲשֵׁכָה) ]] σκοτασθ[ήσεται] |
| Na 3:14 | מַלְבֵּן | ὑπὲρ πλίνθον (-מִ + noun) ]] [π]λινθε[ί]ου |
| Ha 1:5 | יְסֻפָּר | τις ἐκδιηγῆται (יְסַפֵּר) ]] [ἐκδιηγ]ηθῇ |
| Ha 1:8 | עֶרֶב | τῆς ]]] > |
| | | Ἀραβίας (עֲרָב) ] [ἑσπέ]ρας |
| Ha 1:9 | כֻּלֹּה | συντέλεια (כָּלָה) ]] [π]άντα |
| Ha 1:9 | לְחָמָס | εἰς ] |
| | | ἀσεβεῖς (לְחֹמֵס) ]] ἀδικίαν |
| Ha 1:16 | שָׁמֵן | ἐλίπανε (שִׁמֵּן) ]] ἐλιπάνθη |
| Ha 2:16 | שָׂבַעְתָּ | πλησμονὴν (שָׂבְעַת) ]] ἐνεπλήσ[θης] |
| Ha 2:18 | יֹצְרוֹ | ἔπλασεν αὐτὸ (יְצָרוֹ) ]] ὁ πλάσας αὐτὸ |
| Ha 3:10 | זֶרֶם | σκορπίζων (זֹרֵם) ]] ἐντίνα[γ]μα |
| Za 9:1 | מְנֻחָתוֹ | θυσία (מִנְחָתוֹ) ]] κατάπαυ[σις] |
| | | αὐτοῦ |

RECONSTRUCTIONS (5×)

| | | |
|---|---|---|
| Jo 2:3 | שִׁוַּעְתִּי | κραυγῆς μου (שַׁוְעָתִי) ]]] [ἐπεκαλεσάμην] |
| Ha 1:15 | כֻּלֹּה | συντέλειαν (כָּלָה) ]]] [πάντα] |
| Ha 3:10 | עָבָר | πορείας ]]] [παρῆλθεν] (noun) |
| Ha 3:13 | את מְשִׁיחֶךָ | τοὺς ]]] [τοῦ] |
| | | χριστούς (מְשִׁיחַיךָ) ]]] [χριστοῦ] |
| | | σου ] |
| Za 3:7 | חֲצֵרָי | τὴν ]] τ[ὰς] |
| | | αὐλήν μου (חֲצֵרִי) ]]] [αὐλάς μου] |

## 15.1 *LXX=MT against R (16× + 3×)*

The reconstructed *Vorlage* of R is written in the right column.

| | | |
|---|---|---|
| Jo 3:8 | ו/ישבו | καὶ ] |
| | | ἀπέστρεψαν ]] ἐπέστ[ρεψ]εν (ו/ישב) |
| Jo 3:10 | ה/אלהים | ὁ ]] > (אלהים) |
| | | θεὸς ] |
| Mi 1:1 | מלכי | βασιλέων ]] βασιλέως (מלך) |
| Mi 5:3 | יגדל | μεγαλυνθήσεται (4) ]] μεγαλ[υνθή]σονται (יגדלו) |
| Na 2:9 | כ/ברכת | ὡς ]] > |
| | | κολυμβήθρα ] κολυμ[βήθρα] (ברכת) |

| | | |
|---|---|---|
| Na 3:11 | את | σὺ ]] > |
| Na 3:16 | מ/כוכבי | ὑπὲρ ]] ὡς (כ/כוכבי) |
| | | τὰ ]] τοὺς |
| | | ἄστρα ]] ἀστέρας |
| Ha 1:15 | ב/חרמ/ו | ἐν |
| | | --- ]]] [τῷ] |
| | | ἀμφιβλήστρῳ ] [ἀμ]φιβλήστρῳ |
| | | αὐτοῦ ]] > (ב/חרם) |
| Ha 1:16 | חלק/ו | μερίδα ]] ἄρτος (לחמ/ו) |
| | | αὐτοῦ |
| Ha 1:17 | חרמ/ו | τὸ ]] > |
| | | ἀμφίβληστρον ]] μάχαιραν (חרב/ו) |
| | | αὐτοῦ ] |
| Ha 2:6 | עד | ἕως ]] > |
| | מתי | τίνος ]] > |
| Ha 2:8 | אתה | σὺ ]] > |
| Ha 2:8 | ישלו/ך | --- ]] καὶ (ו/ישלו/ך = 1QpHab) |
| | | σκυλεύσουσί ]] σκυλεύ[σουσίν] |
| | | σε |
| Zp 1:5 | ו/את ה/משתחוים | καὶ ]] > (את ה/משתחוים) |
| | | τοὺς ] τ[ο]ὺς |
| | | προσκυνοῦντας ] προσκ[υνοῦν]τας |
| Za 2:8 | תשב | κατοικηθήσεται (4) ]] τι[θήσεις] (תשים) |
| Za 9:5 | תרא | --- ]] κ[α]ὶ (ו/תרא) |
| | | ὄψεται ] ὄ[ψεται] |

RECONSTRUCTIONS (3 ×)

| | | |
|---|---|---|
| Mi 4:5 | איש | ἕκαστος ]]] > |
| Za 8:19 | ל/ששון | εἰς ]]] > |
| | | χαρὰν ]]] > |
| Za 8:19 | ו/ל/שמחה | καὶ ]]] > (ל/שמחה) |
| | | εἰς |
| | | εὐφροσύνην ] [εὐφροσύνη]ν |

## 15.2 *LXX=MT against R in vocalization (2 × )*

| | | |
|---|---|---|
| Ha 2:4 | עֻפְּלָה | ὑποστείληται ]] σκοτία (עֲפֵלָה = אֲפֵלָה) |
| Ha 2:4 | יָשְׁרָה | εὐδοκεῖ ]] εὐθεῖα (יְשָׁרָה) |

## 15.3 *R differs from both LXX and MT (6 × )*

| | | |
|---|---|---|
| Mi 2:8 | יקומם | ἀντέστη ]] [ἀντέ]στησαν |

(R probably reflects יקומו, while the LXX possibly reflects יקום, although it could also reflect MT.)

| | | |
|---|---|---|
| Mi 2:8 | שובי | συντριμμὸν ]] ἐπι[στραφήσον]ται |

(R probably reflects ישובו and the LXX a noun שבר.)

| | | |
|---|---|---|
| Mi 5:3 | ו/ישבו | --- (4) ]] καὶ |
| | | ὑπάρξουσι ]] ἐπιστραφήσονται |

(R reflects MT, though with different vocalization; LXX may reflect יש.)

| | | |
|---|---|---|
| Mi 5:5 | ב/פתח/יה (ב/פחת/ה?) | ἐν (6) ] |
| | | τῇ ]] > |
| | | τάφρῳ ]] παραξ[ιφι''] |
| | | αὐτῆς ]]] > |

(LXX differs from MT, while R probably reflects a different vocalization of MT based on a noun פְּתִחָה.)

| | | |
|---|---|---|
| Ha 3:14 | ל/הפיצ/ני | διανοίξουσι ]] τοῦ σκο[ρπίσ]αι ἡμᾶς |

(R reflects MT with one difference [להפיצנו], while the *Vorlage* of the LXX is not clear.)

| | | |
|---|---|---|
| Zp 3:7 | מ/עינ/ה) מעונ/ה) | ἐξ ὀφθαλμῶν ]] [ἡ π]ηγὴ |
| | | αὐτῆς ] [αὐ]τῆς |

(R agrees with LXX in the consonantal reading [מעינה], but differs in the internal division: R reads מַעְיָנָהּ, while the LXX read מֵעֵינֶיהָ or מֵעֵינָהּ.)

## 15.4 *Indecisive (1 ×)*

| | | |
|---|---|---|
| Za 9:4 | אדני | κύριος ]] [illegible] |

(See note in D on Mi 1:2)

# 16. *Relation between R and MSS of the LXX and Hexaplaric sources*

## 16.1 *Data*

The following list records the agreements between R and individual readings of MSS of the LXX and of the Hexaplaric sources as recorded in Ziegler's edition. Sources are listed in the sequence of their appearance in the apparatus. All sources listed to the right of the square brackets agree with the reading of R against the other witnesses of the LXX. The + sign refers to minuscules additional to the majuscules mentioned. The Hexaplaric sources are referred to as α′, σ′, θ′, ϵ′ (Quinta), and anon.

Strong similarity (rather than identity) with other sources is indicated as ∼. The obelos is recorded as —̣. The following abbreviations are used for the versions: *E* for Aeth, *A* for Arm, *Co* for Coptic (as well as *Bo, Sa* and *Ach*), *Syr* for the Syro-Hexapla, *Syp* for the Syropalestinian version, *Ar* for Arab, and *La* for the Old Latin. (c) stands for the corrector, e.g., W(c). Some evidence relating to the Coptic versions is quoted from Barth.

| | | |
|---|---|---|
| Jo 2:4 | {...} | με ]] > |
| | יסבב/ני | ἐκύκλωσαν ]] περιεκύκλωσ[έ]ν |
| | | {.. ∼ με} ]] μ[ε] VLOC+ verss |
| Jo 2:5 | מ/נגד | ἐξ ] ἐ̣ξ̣ ἐναντίας ∼ σ′θ′ |
| Jo 2:5 | ל/הביט | τοῦ ]] > Cyr |
| | | ἐπιβλέψαι ] ἐπιβλέ̣ψα̣[ι] |
| Jo 2:5 | היכל | τὸν ]] > AQOC verss |
| | | ναὸν ] |
| Jo 2:5 | קדש/ך | τὸν ]] > 49 (c) 233' |
| | | ἅγιόν ] ἅ[γ]ιόν |
| | | σου ] |
| Jo 2:6 | נפש | ψυχῆς ] W'BSAQ*L+ *La A* |
| Jo 2:6 | סוף | ἐσχάτη ]] [ἐσχά]τ̣η, {d} ἕλος *Ach Sa* |
| | חבוש | ἔδυ ]] περιέσχ[ε]ν *Ach Sa* |
| | ל/ראש/י | ἡ ]] τὴν *Ach Sa* |
| | | κεφαλή ]] κεφαλήν *Ach Sa* |
| | | μου ] *Ach Sa* |
| Jo 3:3 | כ/דבר | καθὼς ]] [κατ]ὰ̣ ∼ BSVOLC+ Thph Luc |
| | | ἐλάλησε ]] τὸ ῥῆμα |
| Jo 3:3 | שלשת | {.. ∼ τριῶν} ] τριῶ[ν] OC+ *Syp* Thph |
| | ימים | ἡμερῶν |
| | | τριῶν ]]] > |
| Jo 3:4 | ל/בוא | τοῦ |
| | | εἰσελθεῖν ]]] [πορεύεσθ]αι ∼ AVOLCQ+ verss |
| Jo 3:8 | ו/ישבו | καὶ ] κα̣ὶ̣ |
| | | ἀπέστρεψαν ]] ἐ̣π̣έστ̣[ρεψ]ε̣ν̣ 130' Cyr |
| Jo 3:8 | מ/דרכ/ו | ἀπὸ ]] ἐκ 407 |
| | | τῆς ] |
| | | ὁδοῦ ] ὁδο[ῦ] |
| | | αὐτοῦ ] [α]ὐ̣[τοῦ] |

| | | |
|---|---|---|
| Jo 3:9 | ישוב | --- ]] ἐπι[σ]τ[ρέψει] C+ Tht Hi |
| | ו/נחם | εἰ ]]] [καὶ] |
| | | μετανοήσει ]] παρ[ακληθήσετα]ι ~L'+ α' |
| Jo 3:9 | מ/חרון | ἐξ ]] ἀπὸ L'+ Chr Th Tht |
| | | ὀργῆς ]]] [θυμοῦ] |
| Jo 3:10 | מ/דרכ/ם | ἀπὸ ] |
| | | τῶν ]] τῆς 130' *Bo* Chr Luc |
| | | ὁδῶν ]] [ὁδο]ῦ 130' *Bo* Chr Luc |
| | | αὐτῶν ] αὐτ[ῶν] |
| | ה/רעה | τῶν ]] [τ]ῆς 130' *Bo* Chr Luc |
| | ו/ינחם | πονηρῶν ]] πονηρ[ᾶς] 130' *Bo* Chr Luc |
| | | καὶ |
| | | μετενόησεν ]] [παρ]εκλήθη<ι> α' |
| Jo 4:1 | ו/יחר ל/ו | καὶ ] |
| | | συνεχύθη ]] ἠθ[ύμησεν] W(c) *Sa* σ' |
| Jo 4:2 | ו/יתפלל | καὶ ] |
| | | προσηύξατο ]] π[ροσ]εύξατο WB*VL+ |
| Mi 1:1 | {אשר~} | καὶ ]] > ~C *Syh E* Thph Hi |
| | {היה~} | ἐγένετο ]] > ~C *Syh E* Thph Hi |
| | ~ אשר | --- ]] [ὃς] C *Syh E* Thph Hi |
| | ~ היה | --- ]] [ἐγένετο] C *Syh E* Thph Hi |
| Mi 1:1 | מלכי | βασιλέων ]] βασιλέως A+ *Ar* |
| Mi 1:3 | ו/ירד | καὶ |
| | | καταβήσεται ] καταβήσεται W'BVQOL'C'+ verss |
| | ו/דרך | καὶ ] κα[ὶ] ASVLWQOC+ verss |
| | | ἐπιβήσεται |
| Mi 1:4 | ו/נמסו | καὶ |
| | | σαλευθήσεται ]]] [τακή]σον[ται] α' ~θ' |
| Mi 2:7 | ייטיבו | εἰσι καλοὶ ]] [ἠγ]άθυναν ~α' |
| Mi 2:7 | הולך | πεπόρευνται ]] [πορευομ]ένου α'θ'? |
| Mi 2:8 | תפשטון | ἐξέδειραν ]] ἐξεδύσ[ατε] σ' |
| Mi 4:3 | ו/כתתו | καὶ ] |
| | | κατακόψουσι ]] συνκόψου[σιν] Just Eus |
| Mi 4:3 | חרבת/יהם | τὰς |
| | | ῥομφαίας ]] μαχα[ίρας] VOL'C'+ Just Or Eus Th Tht Thph |
| | | αὐτῶν ] [αὐτῶ]ν |
| Mi 4:3 | ו/חניתת/יהם | καὶ ] |
| | | τὰ ]] τὰς W'A'Q+ Just Or Eus Cyr BasN |
| | | δόρατα ]] σιβύ[νας] W'A'Q+ Just Or Eus Cyr BasN (ζιβύνας) |
| | | αὐτῶν ] [α]ὐτῶν |
| Mi 4:3 | {עוד...} לא | καὶ ] |
| | | οὐκέτι μὴ ]] οὐ μὴ *Bo* Just |
| Mi 4:3 | {עוד...} ו/לא | καὶ |
| | | οὐκέτι μὴ ]] οὐ μὴ VA'Q*+ *Syp E Ar* Just Eus Cyr BasN |
| Mi 4:4 | איש | ἕκαστος ]] ἀνὴρ Just |
| Mi 4:4 | כי | διότι ]] ὅτ[ι] C'V+ Just Eus Thph |
| Mi 4:4 | צבאות | παντοκράτορος ]] [τῶ]ν δ[υνά]μ[εων] Just |
| Mi 4:5 | ב/שם אלה/יו | τὴν ]]] [ἐν ὀνόματι] |
| | | ὁδὸν ]] [θε]οῦ anon ~Just |
| | | αὐτοῦ ]] αὐτῶν Just |
| Mi 4:6 | ו/אשר | καὶ |
| | הרעתי | οὓς ]] ἣν Just *Sa Ach* (Barth.) |
| | | ἀπωσάμην ]] ἐκά[κωσα] Just *Sa Ach* (Barth.) |
| Mi 4:7 | ו/שמתי | καὶ |
| | | θήσομαι ]] θήσω 147–26 Just |
| Mi 4:7 | על/יהם | ἐπ' αὐτοὺς ]] ἐπ' αὐτῶν Just |
| | ב/הר | ἐν ] |
| | | --- ]] τῷ Just |
| | | ὄρει ] |
| Mi 4:7 | ו/עד | εἰς ]] > Just |
| | עולם | τὸν ]] τοῦ 198 239 Just |
| | | αἰῶνα ]] αἰῶνος 198–239 Just |
| Mi 5:1 | בית לחם | *Βηθλεεμ οἶκος* (2) ]] οἶκο[ς '''''] W *Ach Sa* |

| | | |
|---|---|---|
| Mi 5:1 | מ/ימי | ἐξ ]] ἀφ' V |
| | | ἡμερῶν ] ἡμ[ερῶν] |
| Mi 5:2 | אח/יו | τῶν (3) |
| | | ἀδελφῶν |
| | | αὐτῶν ]] αὐτοῦ L+ *La Ach Sa A* Th Tht Hi α'σ'θ' |
| Mi 5:3 | ו/רעה | καὶ (4) ]]> C Hi |
| | | ὄψεται ]] > C Hi |
| Mi 5:3 | + + + | τὸ ]] > C Hi |
| | + + + | ποίμνιον ]] > C Hi |
| | + + + | αὐτοῦ ]] > C Hi |
| Mi 5:3 | יגדל | μεγαλυνθήσεται (4) ]] μεγαλ[υνθή]σονται SVAQOC verss patres |
| Mi 5:3 | אפסי | ἄκρων (4) ]] περάτων σ' |
| Mi 5:4 | אשור | Ασσουρ (5) ] B+ *Ach* (most MSS: ἀσσύριος) |
| Mi 5:4 | נסיכי | δήγματα (5) ]] ἄρχοντας *A* ~θ' |
| Mi 5:5 | נמרד | τοῦ (6) ]] > 86* Tht |
| | | Νεβρωδ ] |
| Mi 5:5 | ב/פתח/יה | ἐν (6) ] |
| | | τῇ ]] > |
| | | τάφρῳ ]] παραξ[ιφι'''] *Sa* (Grossouw) |
| | | αὐτῆς ]]] |
| Mi 5:5 | יבוא | ἐπέλθῃ (6) ]] ἔλθῃ C+ Thph |
| Mi 5:6 | עשׂב | ἄγρωστιν (7) ]] χό[ρτον] σ'θ' *Ach* |
| Na 2:6 | יזכר | καὶ ]] > *Ach* |
| | | μνησθήσονται ]] μνησθήσεται |
| Na 2:6 | + + + | καὶ ]] > C *Syh* — |
| | | φεύξονται ]] > C *Syh* — |
| | | ἡμέρας ]] > C *Syh* — |
| Na 2:6 | ב/הליכת/ם (K) ב/הלכות/ם (Q) | ἐν ] |
| | | τῇ ]] ταῖς A' *Bo* |
| | | πορείᾳ ]] πορεία[ι]ς A' *Bo* |
| | | αὐτῶν ] αὐτῶν |
| Na 2:7 | ה/נהרות | τῶν ] |
| | | ποταμῶν ] S* (other MSS: πόλεων) |
| Na 2:8 | מתפפת | φθεγγόμεναι ]] ἀποφθεγγ[ο]μέν[ων] ~36–49 |
| Na 3:7 | ידוד | καταβήσεται ]] ἀποπ[ηδήσεται] W *Ach* BasN Thph σ' |
| Na 3:7 | שׁדדה | δειλαία ]] [τεταλαι]πώρηκε[ν] ~*Bo* |
| Na 3:8 | ה/תיטבי | ἅρμοσαι ]] > |
| | מ/נא | χορδήν, ]] μὴ ~α'σ' |
| | אמון | ἑτοίμασαι ]] ἀγαθύνεις α' |
| | | μερίδα ]] ὑπ[ὲρ νω] ~α'θ' |
| | | Αμων |
| Na 3:9 | פוט | τῆς ]]] > |
| | | φυγῆς ]] φουδ ~L'+ 68 Th Hi Tht Thph A |
| Na 3:11 | גם | καὶ ]] [κ]αί γε A'Q+ BasN |
| | את[1] | σὺ ]] > 130' |
| Na 3:14 | מלבן | ὑπὲρ πλίνθον ]] [π]λινθε[ί]ου α'σ' |
| Na 3:15 | התכבד | --- ]] καταβαρύνθητι |
| | כ/ילק | --- ]] ὡ[ς βροῦχος] ~VC+ *Syh* Thph Hi |
| Na 3:16 | מ/כוכבי | ὑπὲρ ]] ὡς ~VSC *Bo A* Spec Hi |
| | | τὰ ]] τοὺς |
| | | ἄστρα ]] ἀστέρας |
| Ha 1:5 | + + + | καὶ ]] > C *Syh* — |
| | | ἀφανίσθητε ]] > C *Syh* — |
| | כי | διότι ]] ὅτι Act |
| Ha 1:6 | כי | διότι ]] ὅτι A |
| Ha 1:6 | ה/מר | τὸ πικρὸν ] (sequence) WBSVOLC+ |
| Ha 1:8 | ערב | τῆς ]]] > |
| | | 'Αραβίας ]] [ἑσπέ]ρας α' |
| | ו/פשׁו | καὶ ] |
| | | ἐξιππάσονται ]] ὁρμή[σουσιν] ~σ' |
| Ha 1:9 | כלה | συντέλεια ]] [π]άντα σ' |

| | | |
|---|---|---|
| Ha 1:9 | פנ/יהם | --- ]] τοῦ σ' |
| | | προσώποις ]] προσώπου σ' |
| | | αὐτῶν ] |
| | קדימ/ה | ἐξ ἐναντίας ]] καύσων σ' *Ach* |
| Ha 1:10 | יתקלס | ἐντρυφήσει ]] [ἐν]παίξει ~σ' |
| Ha 1:10 | משחק | παίγνια ]] γ[έλως] σ' ~α' |
| Ha 1:15 | ב/חרמ/ו | ἐν |
| | | --- ]]] [τῷ] |
| | | ἀμφιβλήστρῳ ] [ἀμ]φιβλήστρῳ |
| | | --- ]] αὐτοῦ L'+ *La Co E A* Th Tht Hi |
| Ha 1:15 | ו/יגיל | καὶ (16) |
| | | χαρήσεται ]] χαρεῖται W |
| Ha 1:15 | + + + | ἡ (16) ]] > σ'(c)VC *Ach Syh* Th Hi |
| | | καρδία ]] > σ'(c)VC *Ach Syh* Th Hi |
| | | αὐτοῦ ]] > σ'(c)VC *Ach Syh* Th Hi |
| Ha 1:16 | ל/חרמ/ו | τῇ ]] [τῷ] |
| | | σαγήνῃ ]] [ἀμφιβλή]στρῳ W'VA'Q'+ *Co Ar* Cyr BasN |
| | | αὐτοῦ ] |
| Ha 1:16 | ל/מכמרת/ו | τῷ ]] τῇ W'VA'Q'+ *Co Ar* Cyr BasN |
| | | ἀμφιβλήστρῳ ]] σα[γήνῃ] W'VA'Q'+ *Co Ar* Cyr BasN |
| | | αὐτοῦ ] [αὐτ]οῦ |
| Ha 1:16 | שמן | ἐλίπανε ]] ἐλιπάνθη W(c)~OC |
| Ha 1:17 | חרמ/ו | τὸ ]] > VC'+ Thph |
| | | ἀμφίβληστρον ]] μάχαιραν 86marg *Bo* |
| | | αὐτοῦ ] 86marg *Bo* |
| Ha 2:1 | ו/אתיצבה | καὶ ] |
| | | ἐπιβήσομαι ]] στη[λώσομαι] *Ach* (Barth.) |
| Ha 2:1 | ל/ראות | τοῦ ]] > C |
| | | ἰδεῖν ] ἰδ[εῖν] |
| Ha 2:3 | ו/יפח | καὶ |
| | | ἀνατελεῖ ]] ἐνφανήσετ[αι] *Ach* (Barth.) |
| Ha 2:3 | יכזב | εἰς κενόν ]] [δ]ιαψεύσεται α'σ' *Ach* (Barth.) |
| Ha 2:3 | יתמהמה | ὑστερήσῃ ]] στραγ[γεύσηται] σ' |
| Ha 2:4 | ב/אמונת/ו | ἐκ ]] ἐν α' |
| | | πίστεώς ]] πίστει α' |
| | | μου ]] αὐτοῦ α' |
| Ha 2:5 | ו/לא | οὐδὲν μὴ ]] καὶ οὐ Thph |
| Ha 2:6 | ישאו | λήμψονται ]] λήψε[ται] S* 239 |
| Ha 2:6 | ל/ו | ὄντα ]] > |
| | | αὐτοῦ[3] ]] αὐτῷ 26 239 544 |
| Ha 2:7 | נשכ/יך | δάκνοντες ] |
| | | αὐτόν ]] σε W(c) |
| Ha 2:8 | אתה | σὺ ]] > BS*V+ |
| | שלות | ἐσκύλευσας ] ἐσ[κ]ύλευσας |
| Ha 2:14 | על ים | αὐτούς ]] [ἐπὶ] θαλάσσ[ης] ~L'CV+ *A* Chr Cyr Th Tht Thph Hi *Ach Syh* |
| Ha 2:15 | משקה | ὁ ]] τ[ῷ] anon |
| | | ποτίζων ]] [ποτίζοντ]ι ~anon |
| Ha 2:15 | מעור/יהם | τὰ ]]] [τὴν] |
| | | σπήλαια ]] [ἀσχημοσ]ύνην *Ach* σ' |
| | | αὐτῶν ] αὐ[τῶ]ν |
| Ha 2:16 | שבעת | πλησμονὴν ]] ἐνεπλήσ[θης] *Ach* |
| Ha 2:17 | חמס | ἀσέβεια ]] ἀδικία α' |
| Ha 2:17 | מ/דמי | διὰ ]] δι' VOLC+ patres |
| | | αἵματα ] |
| Ha 2:17 | קריה | --- ] Q+ (other sources: καὶ) |
| | | πόλεως ] |
| Ha 2:17 | ב/ה | αὐτήν ]] ἐν [αὐτ]ῇ VC+ *Syh* Thph Hi |
| Ha 2:18 | יצר/ו | ἔπλασεν ]] ὁ πλάσας ~θ' |
| | | αὐτὸ |
| Ha 2:19 | הוא[1] | καὶ ]] > |
| | | αὐτό ]] αὐτὸς W+ |
| Ha 2:19 | ב/קרב/ו | ἐν αὐτῷ ]] ἐν μέσῳ αὐτοῦ α' |
| Ha 3:10 | הרים | λαοί ]] ὄρη α'σ'θ' |

| | | |
|---|---|---|
| Ha 3:10 | זרם | σκορπίζων ]] ἐντίνα[γ]μα α′σ′θ′ |
| Ha 3:10 | תהום | ἡ ]] > 26–239 |
| | | ἄβυσσος ] ἄβυσσọ[ς] |
| Ha 3:13 | ראש | κεφαλὰς ]] [κεφαλὴ]ν *Ach* (Barth.) |
| | מ/בית | ἀνόμων ]] ἐξ οἴκου *Ach* (Barth.) |
| | ~ (רשע) | θάνατον ]] [ἀσ]ẹβ[οῦς] *Ach* (Barth.) |
| | ~ רשע (מ/בית) | |
| Ha 3:13 | ערות | ἐξήγειρας ]] [ἐξε]κ̣ένωσα[ς] ε′ *Bo* (Barth.) |
| | יסוד | δεσμοὺς ]] θ̣εμελίους ~θ′ε′ |
| Ha 3:13 | סלה | διάψαλμα ]] σελε ε′ |
| Ha 3:14 | ל/הפיצ/ני | --- ]] τοῦ |
| | | διανοίξουσι ]] σκο[ρπίσ]αι σ′ ~ α′ |
| | | --- ]] ἡμᾶς |
| | עליצת/ם | --- ]] τὸ |
| | | χαλινοὺς ]] γαυρίαμα α′ ~ σ′ |
| | | αὐτῶν ] |
| Ha 3:14 | ל/אכל | ἔσθων ]] [ἐσ]θίων VOLC+ patres |
| Ha 3:14 | ב/מסתר | λάθρᾳ ]] κρυφῇ ~α′σ′ |
| Ha 3:15 | דרכת | καὶ ]] > 711 *Ach A* Ambr |
| | | ἐπεβίβασας ]] ἐνέτει[νες] |
| Zp 1:4 | ירושלם | Ιερουσαλημ ]] ἐν ιερ[ουσαλημ] L+ *La* Cyr |
| Zp 1:4 | ה/כמרים | --- ]] τῶ[ν] |
| | | --- ]] [χωμα]ρειμ ~θ′ |
| Zp 1:5 | ו/את | καὶ ]] > 407 Cyr |
| | | τοὺς ] τ[ο]ὺς |
| Zp 1:5 | ו/את ה/משתחוים[2] | --- ]] κ[α]ὶ [τοὺς προσκυνοῦντας] (calc. of space) BSC+ *Syh* |
| Zp 1:13 | + + + | --- ] --- W Cypr (other MSS add: ἐν αὐταῖς) |
| Zp 1:14 | + + + | ὅτι ]] > C |
| Zp 2:10 | עם | --- ]] λαὸν L′+ *Ach* Th Tht |
| | יהוה | τὸν ]] > C+ |
| | | κύριον ]] 𐤉𐤄[𐤅𐤄] |
| Za 1:1 | עדו | Αδδω ]] εδδω V+ Th |
| Za 1:3 | צבאות | παντοκράτωρ ]] [τῶν δ]υνάμεων BA′LC+ *La Syh A* Th Tht Hi |
| Za 1:4 | אל | καὶ ]] > 449′ *E* Cyr |
| | | μὴ |
| Za 1:4 | צבאות | παντοκράτωρ ]] τῶν δυνάμεων Hi |
| Za 2:2 | ו/ירושלם | --- (1:19) ]]] [καὶ] |
| | | --- ]]] [τὴν] |
| | | --- ]] ιερου[σαλημ] BSVCL+ Th Tht |
| Za 2:3 | ארבעה | τέσσαρας (1:20) ]] [τέσσα]ρες S Q* |
| Za 2:16 | ו/בחר | καὶ (12) |
| | | αἱρετιεῖ ]] [ἐκλέ]ξεται Just |
| Za 3:4 | מ/על/יך | --- ]] ἀπὸ L′C+ *E A* Th Tht Hi |
| | | --- ]] σοῦ L′C+ *E A* Th Tht Hi |
| Za 3:4 | את/ך | αὐτὸν ]] σε *E* |
| Za 3:5 | ו/ישימו | καὶ ]] |
| | | ἐπέθηκαν ]] ἐπέθηκ[αν] BSVOC+ (sequence) |
| | ה/צניף | --- ]] τὴν 407 |
| | | κίδαριν ] κίδ[αριν] |
| Za 3:7 | ו/גם | καὶ ]] καί γε W*A′Q+ Cyr BasN |
| | תשמר | διαφυλάξῃς ]] φ[υλ]άξεις ~A+ Cyr |
| Za 8:20 | + + + [רבים] | πολλοὶ ]] > 490 *E* Cyr |
| Za 8:23 | אלהים | ὁ ]] > BA+ BasN |
| | | θεὸς ] |
| Za 9:1 | מנחת/ו | θυσία ]] κατάπαụ[σις] ~147 198 534 Cyr α′ |
| | | αὐτοῦ |
| | כי | διότι ]] ὅτι Q′ Tht |
| Za 9:2 | ו/גם | καὶ ]] καί γε α′ |
| Za 9:2 | חכמה | ἐφρόνησαν ]] [ἐ]φρόνησεν VC+ Tht |
| Za 9:4 | יורש/נה | κληρονομήσει ] [κληρονο]μήσει |
| | | αὐτὴν ] WAQO |
| Za 9:5 | תרא | --- ]] κ[α]ị L+ *E* |
| | | ὄψεται ] ὄ̣[ψεται] |

### 16.2 *Conclusions*

The full analysis of these data is somewhat complicated since much relevant evidence is excluded, in particular *disagreements* between R and the aforementioned sources. Furthermore, some of the agreements between R and the other sources, while appearing to be significant, when viewed together with the disagreements, are less important. Most of the agreements mentioned above have also been discussed by Barth., but the disagreements there are not covered by his monograph. In spite of this it is clear that R agrees especially with Sym, Aq, the so-called 'Th' and the so-called Quinta, as well as with codex W of the LXX, the biblical text quoted by Just (with reference to the quotation from Mi 4:3–7) and the Coptic translations. The text of the biblical quotations of Just also reflects a very literal translation (beyond the aforementioned citation from Mi) so that it is quite certain that these quotations reflect R. (At the same time, the running commentary of Just reflects the LXX text rather than a literal rendering of the type of R. This mixture of text types belongs to the textual transmission of Just and reminds one of that of the writings of Philo.)

For more full data on the relation between R and these sources, see Barth. 205–70. Mere statistics about the agreements between R and the mentioned sources are of limited value because of the fragmentary state of preservation of these sources, and they do not distinguish between different types of agreements: C (39), V (28), Aq (23), Sym (23), L (22), W (21), *Ach* (18), A (18), Just (15), O (15), Q (15), Cyr (14), Tht (14), Hi (14), Thph (14), B (12), θ′ (12), Th (11), *Syh* (9), *Arm* (9), BasN (8), *Eth* (8), S (7), *Bo* (7), *Sa* (6), *La* (5), *Ar* (4), Quinta (3).

# INDEX

The index contains all words of which at least one letter has been preserved. For words (especially verbal forms) whose base form would have occurred at a *different place in the alphabet* the base form (the first person of the present) is provided in the appropriate place. Unusual spellings (such as *εἱμάτια*) are listed according to the standard spelling. All words are listed exactly as they occur in the reconstructed text, including accents, diacritical marks and hyphens.

# PLATES

The plates are composed of photographs (see note in Section D on col. 2–4) of the fragments, rearranged according to the columns. The numbers accompanying the plates are those of the photographs, almost all prepared by the Palestine Archaeological Museum (PAM) in the fifties, except for the ones indicated as IDAM (Israel Department of Archaeology and Museums) dated 1986. The numbers in parenthesis refer to the present inventory number of the PAM.

The scale of all plates is 1:1 except when indicated otherwise.

References to "Lif." refer to the publication of nine fragments by B. Lifshitz mentioned on the first page of Introduction.

Col. 2–4

IDAM 204.601 (539) — see note in Section D

Col. 2

(23 lines)

**a.** 40.564 (539)
**b.** 40.565 (539)
**c.** 40.565 (539)
**d.** 40.562 (539)

**a.** IDAM 200.296 (539A [Lif. 4])
**b.** IDAM 200.297 (539A [Lif. 6])
**c.** IDAM 200.296 (539A [Lif. 4])
**d.** IDAM 200.297 (539A [Lif. 2])
**e.** 40.565 (539)
**f.** 40.565 (539)
**g.** 40.565 (539)
**h.** 40.559 (539)
**i.** 40.565 (539)
**j.** 40.563 (539)
**k.** 40.562 (539)

Col. 4

(20 lines)

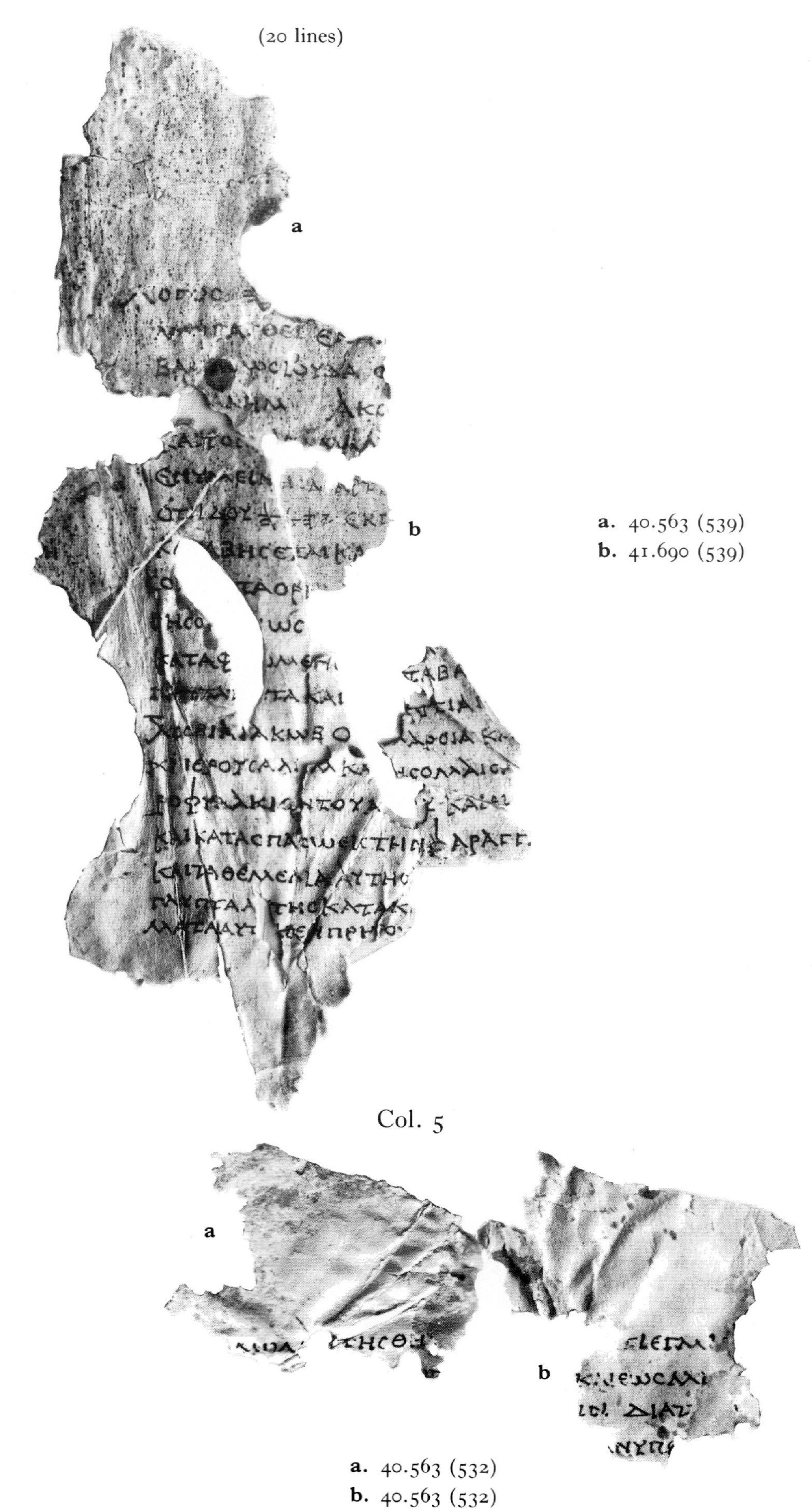

**a.** 40.563 (539)
**b.** 41.690 (539)

Col. 5

**a.** 40.563 (532)
**b.** 40.563 (532)

Col. 6

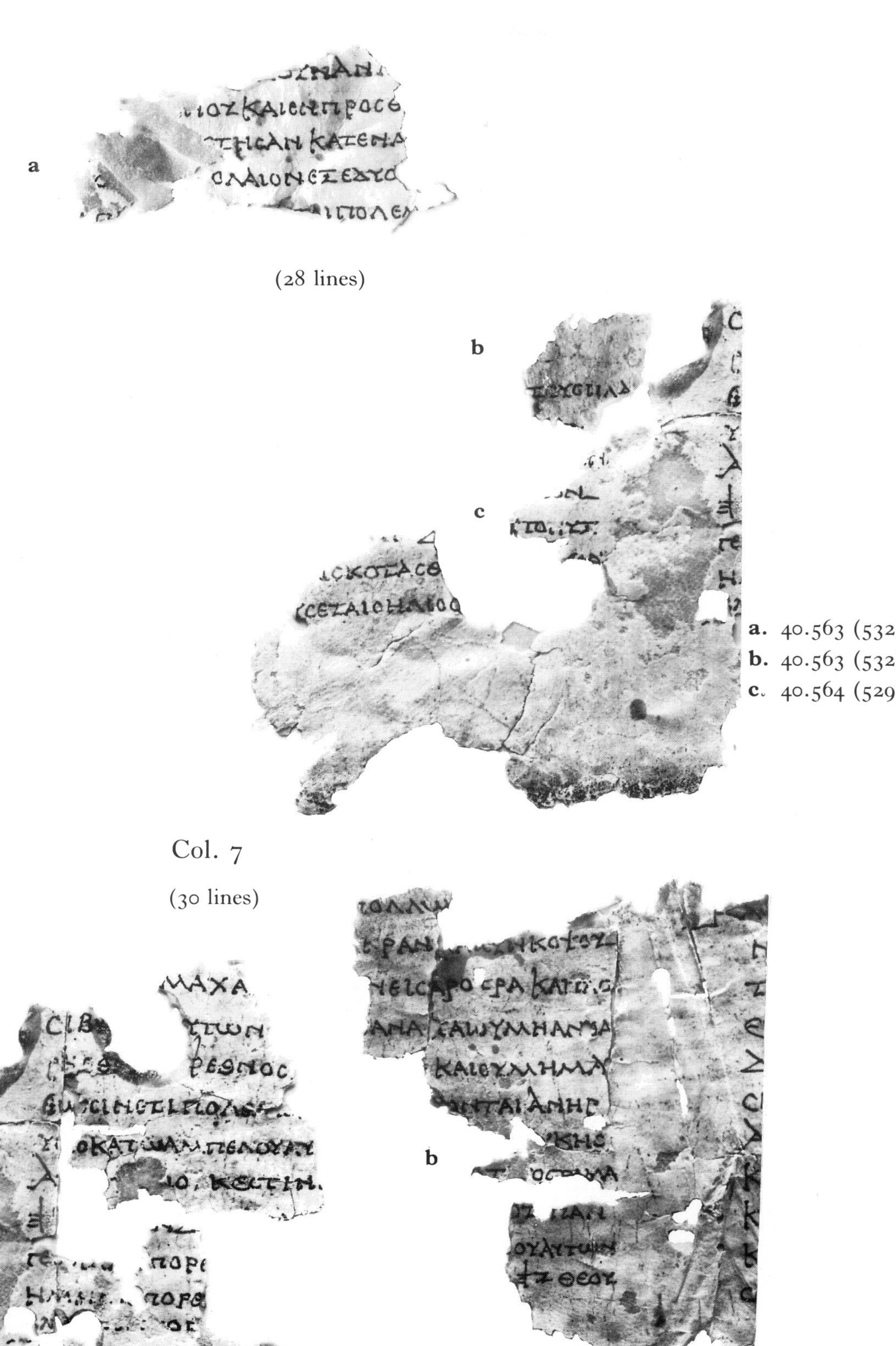

a

(28 lines)

b

c

**a.** 40.563 (532)
**b.** 40.563 (532)
**c.** 40.564 (529)

Col. 7

(30 lines)

a

b

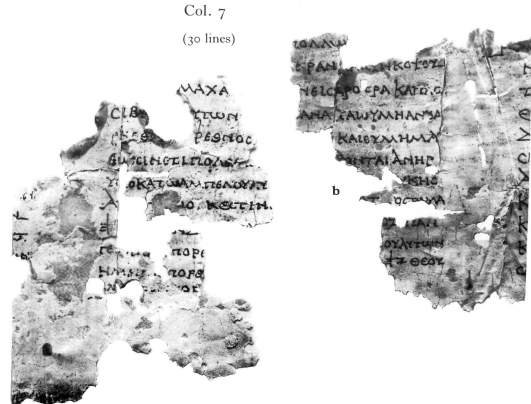

**a.** 40.564 (529)
**b.** 40.560 (531)

Col. 8

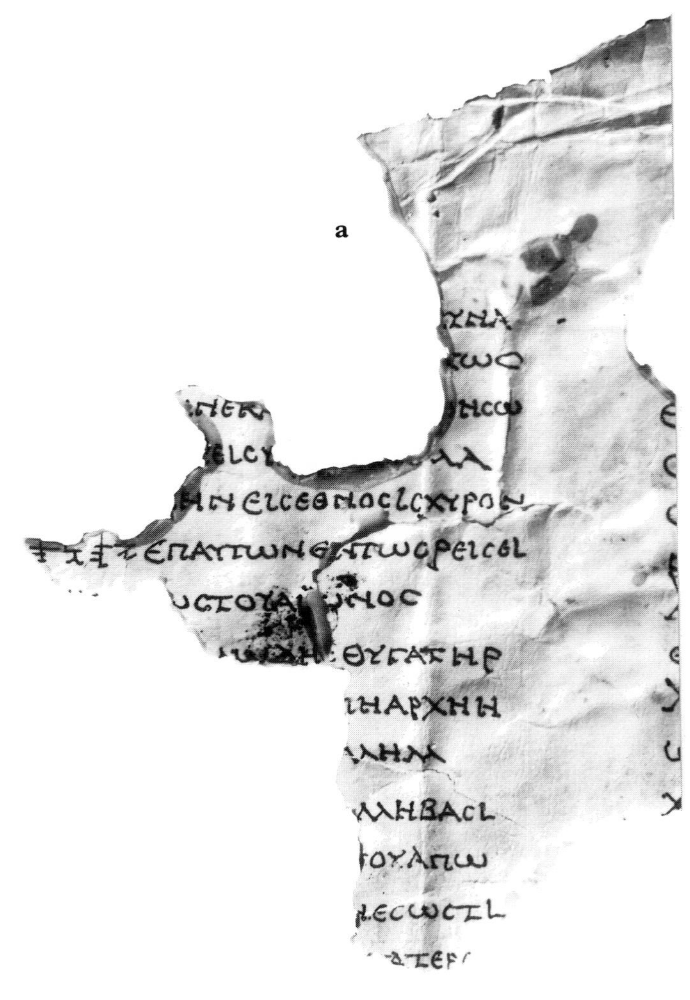

(16 lines)

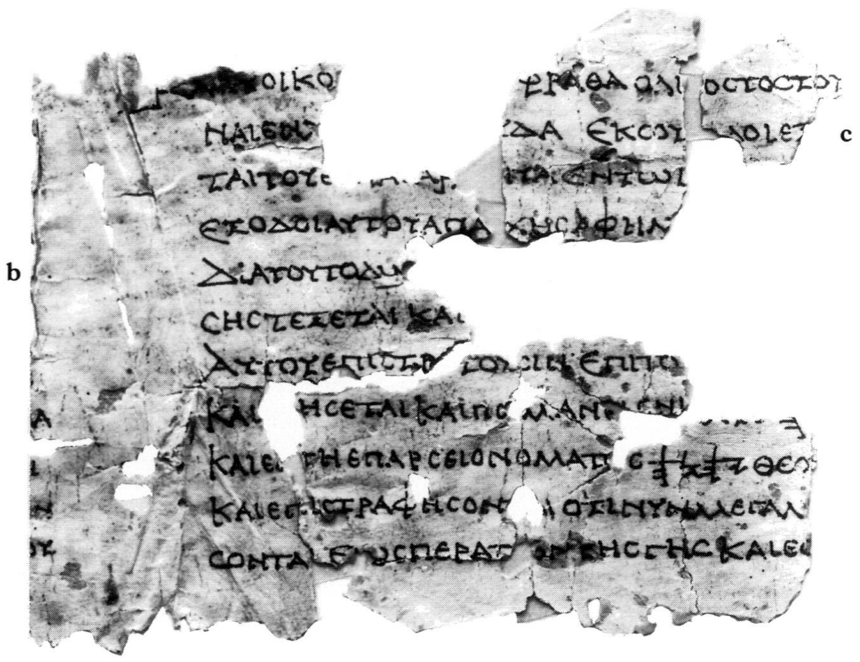

**a.** 40.566 (530)
**b.** 40.560 (531)
**c.** 40.560 (531)

Col. 9

40.566 (530)

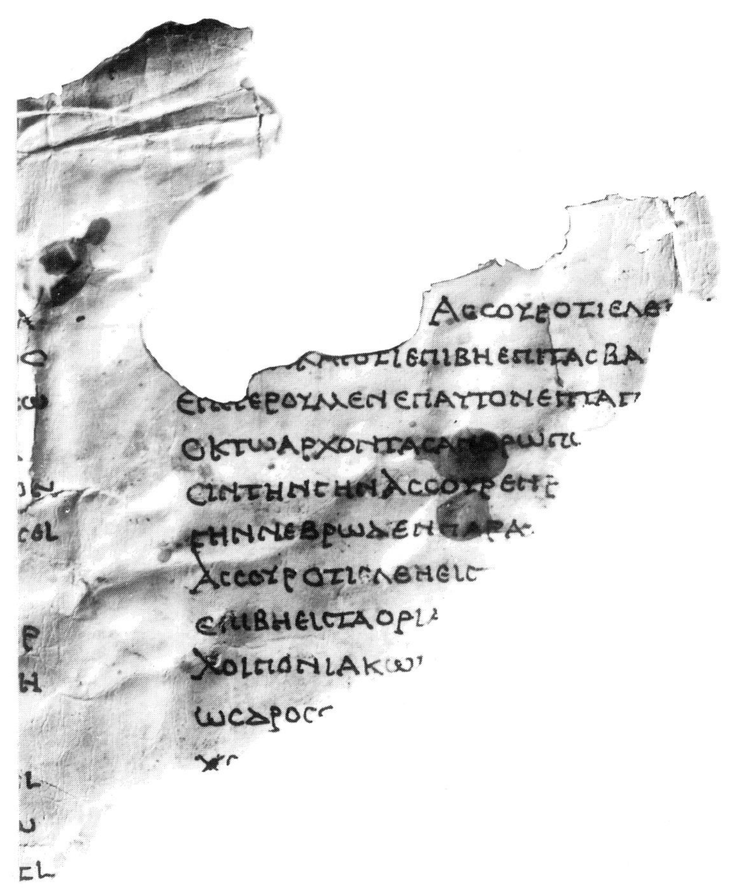

(31 lines)

Col. 13

a b

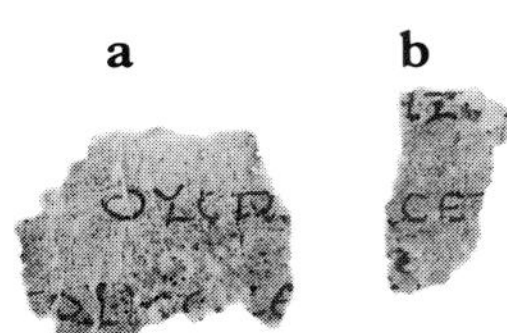

**a.** IDAM 200.296 (539A [Lif. 5])
**b.** 200.296 (539A [Lif. 3])

Col. 14

a

b

c

(8 lines)

d

(6 lines)

e

(4 lines)

**a.** 40.567 (535)
**b.** 40.566 (535)
**c.** 40.562 (535)
**d.** 40.567 (535)
**e.** IDAM 200.296 (539A [Lif. 8])

Col. 15

(6 lines)

(5 lines)

**a.** 40.562 and 40.239 (535)
**b.** 40.566 (535)
**c.** IDAM 200.296 (539A [Lif. 1])
**d.** 40.566 (535)

Col. 16

(21 lines)

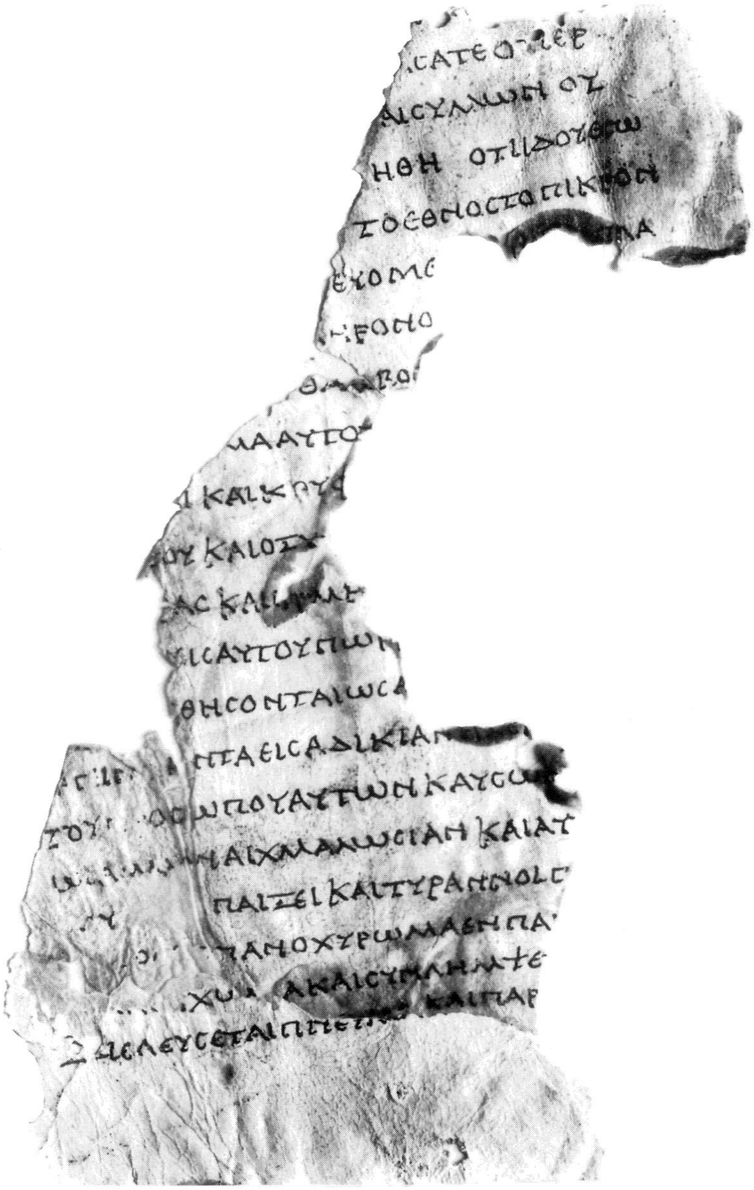

40.559 (528)

Col. 17

(8 lines)

b

a

c

**a.** 40.572, 40.573 (63)
**b.** 40.567 (63)
**c.** 40.564 (530)

Col. 18

(11 lines)

**a.** 40.564 (63)
**b.** 40.561 (63)
**c.** 40.574 (63)

Col. 19

(23 lines)

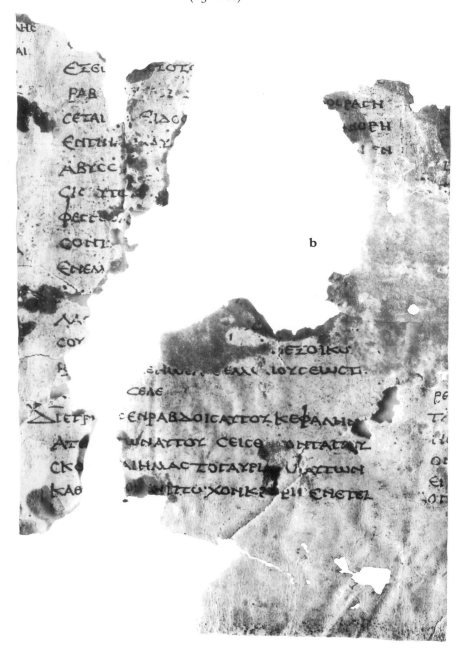

**a.** 40.574 (63)
**b.** 40.568 (63)

Col. 20

(24 lines)

**a.** 40.569 (63)
**b.** 40.570 (63)

Col. 21

(24 lines)

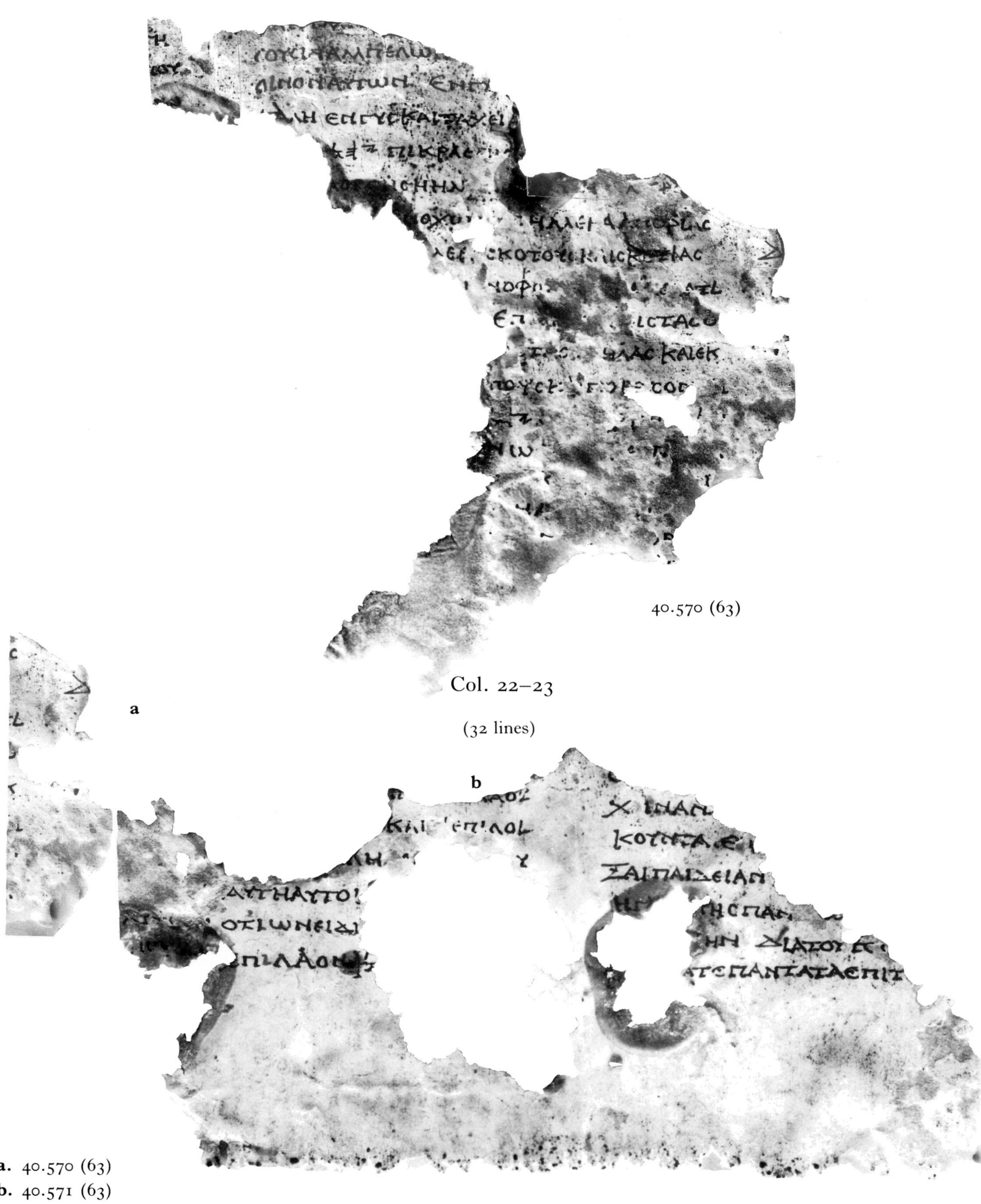

40.570 (63)

Col. 22–23

(32 lines)

a

b

**a.** 40.570 (63)
**b.** 40.571 (63)

Col. 28–29

(32–34) lines

a

b

**a.** 40.559 (530)
**b.** 40.561 (530)

Col. 30–31

(12 lines)

a

b

(4–8 lines)

c

d

**a.** 40.560 (530)
**b.** IDAM 200.296–7 (539A [Lif. 7])
**c.** 40.561 (530)
**d.** IDAM 200.297 (539A [Lif. 9])

Col. 17–23

0 1 2 3 4 5 cm

IDAM 204.602 — see note in Section D

Col. B1–2

a

(10 lines)

b

(2 lines)

**a–b.** IDAM 204.602 (538)

Additional fragments (unidentified)

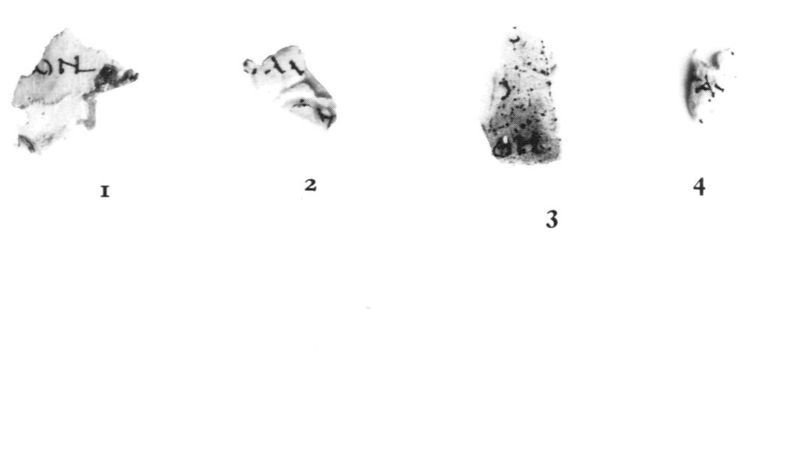

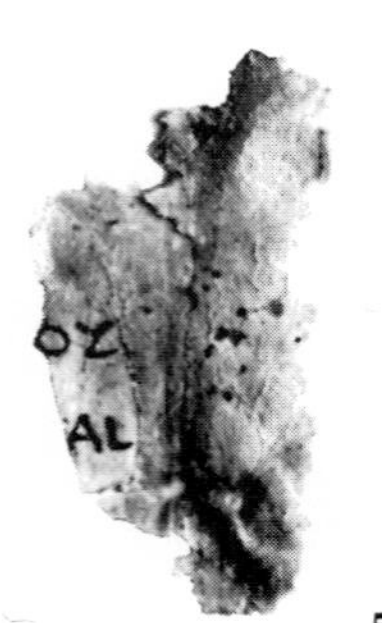

**1.** 40.566 (537)
**2.** 40.566 (537)
**3.** 40.566 (537)
**4.** 40.559 (?)
**5.** 40.566 (539)
**6.** 40.559 (538)